THE ORDINARY CHAOS OF BEING HUMAN

THE ORDINARY CHAOS OF BEING HUMAN

TRUE STORIES. SOUL-BARING MOMENTS. NO APOLOGIES.

EDITED BY

MARGUERITE RICHARDS

First edition published by Penguin Random House SEA 2019
Second edition published by Leave It Better Books 2024

ISBN 979-8-9892984-0-2

leaveitbetterbooks.com

For my sons,
Kavi Jack & Leo Daham

Go.
Meet the world
through as many different stories you can find.
Always listen with your mind,
but remember to hear with your heart.
Come home to report.
Often, please.

Tat tvam asi

TABLE OF CONTENTS

continued on the following page

TABLE OF CONTENTS

continued

FOREWORD

In today's post-9/11 world, the word "Islam" can sometimes feel like a winter coat being forced on you at the height of summer. And when the stereotypes of Muslims bombard you every day from newspaper headlines and social media posts, that coat can start to feel like a straitjacket. Little surprise that each writer who contributed to this anthology wanted to dodge the associations and accusations that have been imposed by an unrelenting world. In writing lies freedom: to be exactly who you are, not as the world sees you. Each writer here has taken that as her personal brief and produced a gem uniquely evolved through the lens of human, and perhaps Muslim, experience.

The difficulty of trying to define an anthology by a religious or cultural background is that it doesn't sit well with everyone. Some are ensconced comfortably in their Muslim worlds, others feel stifled by them; yet others are still trying to define their relationship to them—or against them. Each writer with a connection to the Muslim ethos, as it were, struggles against the collective understanding of Islam, and spends her life trying to draw a map of where Islam lies in relation to her own psychic territory. In a way, we are continuously drawing and redrawing the borders of that amorphous country we call "Muslim" in our own heads.

Anyone who has grown up in a Muslim way—birth, country, parentage, association—is familiar with the Hadith, the texts that record the sayings and daily practices of the Prophet Muhammed, peace be upon him. After the Quran, they are the major source of understanding and guidance for practicing Muslims. For example, the Quran instructs Muslims to pray but the Hadith elucidate the details and mechanics of how Muslims are to pray: frequency, method, manner. The Prophet's Companions memorized and wrote down these sayings and practices, which were then transmitted to their students, and their students after that.

The famous Muslim mystic and philosopher Ibn Arabi famously wrote about a supposed Hadith Qudsi—a "sacred report" of the Prophet's words and phrasing, whose origin and meaning come directly from God—that goes something like this:

When asked about the purpose of creation, God said, "I was a Hidden Treasure, and I wished/loved to be known, so I created the creatures and made Myself known to them, so they knew Me."

The Sufis, who concern themselves with the mystical and metaphysical aspects of Islam, believe this saying revealed one of the driving forces of the universe's existence: the manifestation of God and humanity's recognition of that manifestation. As such, this saying has such a prominent place in Sufi teachings that an entire scholastic-spiritual tradition based on the "Hidden Treasure" concept emerged. Scores, if not hundreds of Sufi texts and commentaries expound upon the subject of the Hidden Treasure: the journey from non-existence to existence, creation and its relation to divine self-disclosure, love and gnosis, and man's relationship with God being one of love, not fear.

On the other hand, Islamic scholars of the more orthodox schools of thought and jurisprudence doubt the authenticity of this Hadith because its chain of transmission cannot be substantiated. They doubt that the Prophet ever relayed such a concept, and say that the narration is in fact a fabrication.

Perhaps they feared that the desire to be known is a weakness, and that God is a Supreme Being without said need or dependence.

Yet, even this point of controversy is fascinating: it proves that contrary to popular belief, Islam is not a monolith, and its believers are far from unified or homogenous. In fact, the argument over this Hadith demonstrates diversity in thought, belief and action among Muslims. Factoring in the vast differences—in culture, nationality, origin, education, class, gender, and all the multitudinous elements of identity and experience—it is a wonder that Muslims can agree on anything at all! And that is even before we consider that not everyone who lives in Muslim lands, or claims Muslim heritage, is a Muslim.

In the words of the Quran, not only have people been made diverse, but they are instructed to learn about one another. In verse 13, chapter 49 (The Dwellings), God instructs the Prophet: "People, we have created you all male and female and have made you nations and tribes so that you would know (recognize) one another." (Translation by Muhammed Sarwar). This diversity is Islam's greatest strength, the source of its people's formidable beauty. It is, in a word, humanity. And while Muslims have been charged to worship their Creator and not confuse Him with the Creation, there is no argument that Islam's foremost teaching is to respect and serve the humanity that He created.

What we see in this collection of stories are people, in an echo of the Hidden Treasure concept, considering their own lives and experiences as hidden treasures that they love and long to make known. The writing in this anthology, then, is deeply spiritual even without an overt claim to religion, because it fulfils one of the strongest precepts of humanity: knowing and recognition. Each story is a glimpse into a constructed or reconstructed world that is completely authentic and true; it offers the opportunity for a kind of witnessing into the life of an individual and the circumstances of that human's ecosystem. And in turn, to set off the recognition of universal human experience.

Just like humans, no story is quite like any other. These tales purport to reveal something about the Muslim world or worlds; take away the word "Muslim" though, and couldn't these stories come from anywhere? Couldn't these people be any people, in any land or time? Or is it that these people, these stories, can only be produced by these particular times, in these particular circumstances? Picking up this collection is like lifting a gem to the light and examining it this way and that so the light reflects its different facets, to shine on a universal truth: that no matter what the condition or circumstances, every person is a human treasure longing to be known.

Still, there are some recurring themes in this collection. There are stories of lives scarred by war and violence: the civil war in Lebanon, the war between Iran and Iraq, the Iranian Revolution, the invasion of Kuwait. In these stories, we encounter death and destruction as witnessed by their protagonists, but we also see love, resilience and courage. There are stories that examine the internal wars fought by many people: to cope with emerging sexuality, straight and queer; to gain the acceptance of a community into which one has migrated or fled or sought asylum; to be seen as normal by a world unused to different faces, languages, appearances, customs. There are the pains of growing up, the riotous adventures of childhood, the safe and loving arms of mothers, fathers, uncles and aunts, and always, the question: what and where is home?

But this is a collection of more than just heartwarming tales. This is a collection with bite, with an edge, cooked al dente, as it were, not pabulum that is easily digested. Because in the early 21st century, nobody with any connection to a Muslim life can truly escape the burden of representation. Muslims are forced to account for every act of violence, every absurdity and anomaly, that takes place in a Muslim land or that involves Muslims. And while the accusers may even admit to stereotypes and lazy thinking, they still blame Muslims for the very existence of those stereotypes, as if saying, "It is your fault we think of you this way. It is up to you to change our minds about you and your kind."

The writers in this collection of short stories do not challenge the stereotypes. Instead, they challenge the assumption of responsibility for those stereotypes. That is to say that they do not contest the stereotype that Muslims are violent or that Muslims are terrorists. What they challenge is the idea that they are responsible for the existence of those stereotypes: that they aren't doing enough to erase them in the eyes of an accusatory West. They are outright refusing the stigma of being Muslim, of guilt by association. Instead of fighting the stereotypes, they are doing something else, something elegant and literary: they are offering up their humanity, honesty and vulnerability by way of these stories.

By writing these stories, they are sending back a challenge to the challengers, with energy and vigour. "Here I am. Not a Muslim, but a human. Not a mindless robot, or an oppressed woman, or a violent terrorist, but a person, with feelings, emotions, dignity, and soul. Do you dare look at me as I am?

Do you dare know me? *Do you have the strength in your eyes to look at me?"*

Well, do you?

BINA SHAH
KARACHI, PAKISTAN

INTRODUCTION

I could lie. I could fudge a polite, digestible story about my clear-eyed, cloud-free path to celebrating the symphony of voices in this collection. But here's the truth. It has been one of the hardest things I've ever done. I have been afraid to reveal how vulnerable my learning process has been, yet I've realized that I must. After all, I have asked the writers in this book to be that vulnerable: to share their most fragile moments—the blind corners, the velvety revelations, the mud-spattered terrain of their lives' most pivotal moments. I should show them the same respect they've given me.

But first, some context. When I started this project in 2015, I was consumed by the fact that so many Westerners are entirely unaware of the breadth of cultural differences coming from Muslim worlds. That so many people are clueless about the tapestry of centuries-old cultures existing under the shroud of stereotypes perpetuated by the media post-9/11. The way that the media operates to disseminate these limiting ideas, whether intentional or not, is just one brick in the wall of racist systems operating to keep power, privilege and attention for those who already have it—and to keep it away from those who don't. In the simplest terms, not enough people from enough different backgrounds get the space to speak. And that needs to change.

In this book, I'm focusing on just a small piece (well, 1.8 billion people small) of an incredibly intricate global problem—one that I'm still working to understand myself. Without having perfect clarity about the systems maintaining an imbalance on the global stage, I am certain of one thing. People's lack of awareness about (and I mean truly seeing and acknowledging) people different from themselves is a contributing factor to major societal and geopolitical problems—at minimum, it comes to poor distribution of wealth and power, at maximum, it comes to the killing of perceived enemies in the quest for that wealth and power.

What I'm probably most afraid to admit, however, is that the underlying impetus for this book is a blind faith that most people desire connection with each other, above all else. The path is undeniably complicated, but the ground rules are simple. If we want to quit hurting each other, we have to start by getting to know each other better. Does that sound patronizing? Finger wagging? Frankly, it sounds like the kind of thing I tell my two small boys on a daily basis. But when I see the hate repeatedly playing out in the papers in the same patterns, I really can't help but feel like it's the adults that are acting like children. I do understand it is a stretch to believe connection is possible when people are under fire. Hope and faith can feel like a luxury when you witness people (or even feel, yourself) becoming violent because your family is suffering and your home is threatened. I think that's why some of the people closest to me say my view is oversimplified, naïve even. But is it? Are we not the most evolved species? Have we not figured out how to get to the moon and back? I think we can do this.

For me, one of the best ways to get to know a culture different from my own is by reading personal stories. Reading, imagining, marinating in the experiences of another is one way to lift the fog. So, for this book, I imagined indiscriminate points of light shining around the planet, like stars dazzling the night sky. The collection would be bound by universal experiences that would simultaneously reflect the nuance and wealth of world cultures—its diverse beauty set beside its diverse madness, all mixed up together in one book: *The Ordinary Chaos of Being Human.* Still, the project has been full of nail-biting, tail-chasing pitfalls.

One of the biggest conundrums in making this book came with the need to use the label "Muslim." Do a Google search for books with the word "Muslim" in the title and you'll get a similar list as you do when you search with the word "Christian." They are all books focusing on faith. But this book is not about religion, and I did not require writers to identify with Islam or to write about their faith.

It was also impossible to say this book was by Muslim writers because people from the Muslim worlds featured in this book are a mosaic. They are atheists, agnostics, pagans, Muslims of all sects and, sometimes, all of the above at different times in their lives. Some, in fact, follow other faiths altogether even though they were born in predominantly Muslim countries. I found myself asking how I could possibly celebrate the multiplicity of Muslim experiences with a one-word label that would simultaneously diminish their diversity. Also, many writers from Muslim worlds were wary of the label, of having to defend themselves under it, and prefer largely to portray themselves as they are, period. So it became a collection of intimate stories written in the context of many Muslim worlds, the plurality of "worlds" being imperative to the conversation.

It became clear that the fundamental goal was to celebrate voices around the world just as they are, without further stifling them with labels that they may or may not want to use themselves. Like a person's sexual identity, or any other imperceptible layer of identity, one's religious or spiritual path is a personal matter. We should all have the choice: to keep that layer quietly in our hearts, or to wear it proudly on our sleeves.

Through these stories, you get to know the writers as if you're meeting them for the first time in person. Some will share their religion, and some will not.

As the submissions rolled in for the book, I also feared inappropriately treating certain key subjects because of my limited knowledge about the countries and cultures appearing in the book. I haven't been to many of the places featured, and I really should take a class to properly appreciate the Quran. But I did know that it wasn't my place to choose or reject stories for the writers' opinions, for the way they represented their country, or for their interpretation of Islam. In the end, I saw that the selection process was simple: I chose writers for their ability to convey their own personal truth, whatever that may be. These are stories of the heart, written to be shared, heart to heart.

From extraordinary situations to quite ordinary ones, each story in this collection illuminates a very particular world, which may have nothing to do with being Muslim at all. Because this is also a book about being the feminist, devout, queer, rebellious, loving, winning and losing heroes in the stories of our lives. The result reveals identities that are immeasurable, limitless, undefinable, and an incredible opportunity for readers everywhere to empathize with staggeringly diverse perspectives from around the world.

I chose stories about uncomfortable situations, like prickly moments with neighbors which reveal something about ourselves or the surrounding community, as in "Summer's Ruin" and "Those Eyes of Hers." I chose "The Unfinished Report," not because of the backdrop of the Iranian revolution, but because the writer revealed a moment of naïve bravery in her childhood so vividly, I felt like I was right there with her when she was lost in the rain. I included "From Sulu, a Farewell to Dad" for the author's plight to know her father before his death. I chose "Khaleh Mina" for the meaningful portrayal of the safe, warm feeling of being mothered by an aunt. My appreciation for "Islam and the End of the World" had little to do with its Cairo setting or 9/11 subtext, and everything to do with a man struggling to find himself. And I had to include "Pink," not only for the brutal account of something so many women won't dare speak of, but also for the testimony of friendships women are capable of. I chose writers who conveyed their emotions so clearly, it was like reading their hearts. I also included writers whose points of view I didn't necessarily agree with, because they were so unapologetically sincere. I found the honesty disarming, and for me, that commanded respect.

The writers in this book are people you might not ordinarily get to meet, and while their backgrounds and perspectives may vary greatly from yours, there is a touch point. It's the human emotion we all experience in our lives' most pivotal moments. I believe that getting to know the wealth of other worlds through its storytellers is instrumental in breaking down centuries-old walls between people. Personal stories like these have the power to make up our collective world history, with its glorious cast of very different characters striving to know and understand each other—as long as we keep writing and reading from the heart.

MARGUERITE RICHARDS
COLOMBO, SRI LANKA

LOVE AND RUIN IN AIDA

Noreen Moustafa revisits the memory of a young summer love in Montazah, a heritage landscape now under deconstruction in her ancestral Egypt. Here, she recognizes the value of personal storytelling as a way of building our collective history.

NOREEN MOUSTAFA

NOREEN MOUSTAFA was born in Los Angeles, California to Egyptian parents. She is a writer and a news/documentary producer who seeks to inform and inspire with integrity. She began her career at Vice President Al Gore's *Current TV*, working on the Emmy-nominated and Peabody award-winning international documentary series, *Vanguard*. Next, she joined *The Young Turks* as a producer, helping bring "the world's biggest online news show" to television. Later, she worked as a producer for both *Al Jazeera Americ*a in Los Angeles and at *Al Jazeera English* headquarters in Doha, Qatar. She is currently living in Florence, Italy with her husband and two children, and working on a memoir.

From my most beloved cove, I try to get my bearings. I imagine myself as a pin on the map, where the Mediterranean edges the tip of Alexandria in Egypt. Buoys and boats bob in the distance as if to tell me my desire for stability is futile. It has been years since my teenage love ended, but today I struggle to accept its erasure. Although I grew up in Los Angeles, I spent my childhood summers in Alexandria. And strangely, it was there on Aida Beach in Montazah that I felt the freest. It is where I felt the whole sun shine on my face, let the sea carry me, and where I had my first summer romance. It was not the profound love I'd know later in life, but because summer love is fleeting, every moment burned like a dying star, and loaded encounters densely strung over three months left their mark. And when the season was over, it was okay. I was okay. I didn't need it to last. But standing here today, I realize I thought Aida always would.

Montazah, built in 1892, was once a royal complex and spans 360 acres. On the grounds are two palaces and five beaches. Aida is one of them. After the revolution of 1952, the Egyptian government acquired the complex. The largest palace became a museum, and the massive gardens were opened to the public for a fee. And lining this gulf, where palm and pine forests meet the sea, 896 small beach cabins were built. Wealthier Egyptians, acting in class solidarity, scooped them up quickly. Seeking refuge from the heaving public beaches on the corniche, these families kicked off decades of treasured summer memories beyond the palace gates. And of all the private beaches there, Aida became the place to be as a teenager in the nineties.

Long before we dreamed of revolution and the Arab Spring, Aida was the setting for our small rebellion. It's where we blurred the line between the public and private self to find ourselves. For a long time, I couldn't talk about what Aida meant to me. But now that it's become a place that can only be visited in words and in memory, I am compelled. Aida is in ruins.

This summer, I am in Alexandria visiting family—this time with my husband and two children. Egypt, in general, has taken on more Western characteristics, and today's teens have long since moved on from that beach. But for me, the pull of Aida remains. And so, upon arriving, I arranged a visit, despite the warning that Montazah "is being worked on."

The main gate looks the same as we drive in, but the unpaved roads create disorienting dust clouds around the car. I ask the driver to drop me off at what I think is the entrance to Aida. "Wasn't this where the mini mart was?" I wonder. On foot, amidst all the construction, I recognize where the security post had been and recall the day my older cousin Mandy forgot her membership card.

"Noreen, listen." Mandy linked her arm with mine, pulled me close to her side, and whispered, "When we walk past the guard, talk to me in English and don't meet his eye."

"Wait, why?" I laughed, always a little nervous about breaking the rules.

"Trust me," she said. And I did. Completely. Mandy was my cultural attaché, the sister I never had, and long the key to my Egyptian heritage.

As we approached the checkpoint, she hoped that my American accent would be enough of an indicator to the guard that we belonged.

"And then I was all like, no way," I said in my best valley girl impersonation.

Once past his station—nothing more than a white plastic chair under a faded orange beach umbrella—we exhaled in relief. We were now in Aida. A different world. We'd usually get there around 4 pm, when the sun began its long, western slouch. Warm, but not scorching. The sparkling sea's surface shined like liquid silver and weak waves curled on the sand. The smell of tanning oil combined with barbecued kofta hung in the air. And under the shade of arching pine trees, the elderly sat in a circle, their unsteady hands cradling tiny cups of hot tea. Under their feet lay a carpet of brittle pine needles. Comically oblivious to all the sticks stuck in their sandals, they chatted about their good old days: the brilliance of Abdel Halim-Hafez, the easy elegance of Souad Hosni. Unaware that we would eventually join their nostalgic ranks, we breezed past them. Our generation's slice of Aida was beyond the grass lawn.

The epicenter of our social activity was the winding sidewalk parallel to the shore. Different cliques dotted the path, sitting or standing in clusters. The kids showed off their private educations—chatting in English, flirting in French, and comparing fashion statements acquired abroad. Mandy flitted down the path, pausing every five feet to greet friends with a double-cheek kiss as if we were on the French Riviera. I trailed behind her, rolling my eyes at their accents, the speedos, the designer handbags. I was American and that was enough to make me feel superior. Globalization was already on the march but my musical taste, shoes, hairstyle, you name it, was at least a year ahead of their trends. But despite all that, I still wanted to fit in. On this day, Mandy found her friends in their usual spot on the sidewalk. After five rounds of bisous, I removed my sandals and shoved my feet into the sand—past the hottest layer, down to where it was cool. I was ready for my guava juice and wondered how long it would be until we were in the water. The chit-chat began as it usually did, with gossip.

"How about Dina?" Eman said.

"She's fine. But did you hear about Khaled?" Mandy asked.

"He went to rehab," Mona jumped in. "You didn't know that?"

"Amira's brother?" I gasped. The better the gossip, the more we'd fidget with our juice box straws.

"Yeah, both of them don't come to Aida anymore. He was addicted to this cough syrup that's illegal now," Mandy said.

"Cough syrup? Illegal?" I couldn't help but laugh, unaware that abusing codeine cough syrup was rampant among Egyptian teens. It was an over-the-counter solution for those desperate to escape their realities and had recently been banned. I dismissed it as another nebulous restriction in Egyptian society, another ridiculous rule. Like when Mandy told me not to snap my fingers a certain way in public because that was a "belly dancer move." Or how she laughed at me when I tried to sit next to the taxi driver when the back seat was full. "Only boys sit there. Come here, sit on my lap." Okay, noted—no snapping, no front seat, and no cough syrup allowed. In Aida, I didn't have to worry as much about these constant corrections to my behavior, these invisible rails that kept me in line. It felt like beyond that orange umbrella, we were outside of jurisdiction.

When the sweat began to collect on our brows, we headed for the shore. We made a pile of our clothes and rushed into the glistening water in our suits. While Mandy and her friends resumed their chatter treading water, I floated on my back, listening to the underwater crackle instead. Once out, the girls would put on their sheer cache maillots and parade on the 200-meter sidewalk until their swimsuits dried. It was hard to understand why the conservative customs of dress didn't apply here. How could we be so free?

"Like, why do you guys even bother wearing these coverups?" I asked.

"Because bikinis are haram," Mona giggled.

Just then, a group of muscular boys with blown-up arms walked by. The girls looked at each other instead of at their inflated biceps, and then to the floor. Gyms had started to pop up around town and many guys had taken to weightlifting. Pumping iron apparently helps alleviate the malaise of growing up amidst diminishing job and marriage prospects.

We'd spend the afternoon feeling each other's eyes on our backs but never making contact. But eventually, when families with young kids and the elderly would go home, the mood on the beach would change. We'd form desegregated huddles when the sun was low and the tide began to come out again. We had safety in numbers as passersby couldn't identify the couples amongst us. Someone started playing music from an iPod plugged into a boombox and jokes gave way to playful shoves or any other excuse to touch. We moved to the music, never really dancing but swaying—anything to relieve the tension. At the purple arrival of dusk, there didn't seem to be an adult in sight. Every night, Aida was ours.

When I noticed two people surreptitiously holding hands under a towel, I felt the electric exchange as if my own hand was being held. Every glance was charged, and this bit of spark gave an edge to our banter. We had many things to work out, from the frivolous to the existential, and talked for hours. Then Mandy's boyfriend appeared, a silhouette on the sidewalk. Their smiles beamed across the distance, their connection unmissable even though they never touched. I smiled too, caught in their radiance. Love is so great it doesn't have to be your own to be moving.

That summer, I served as an alibi for Mandy who, like many of her friends, would meet her secret boyfriend at Aida. Like vines seeking light, they weaved and coiled their way through repression. Dating doesn't exist in Egyptian society. The expectation is a formal engagement sanctioned by your parents, should you wish to get to know a potential spouse. These evening encounters didn't come easily though, and I marveled at how Mandy set up her dates.

She could speak so softly on the phone that she was inaudible to anyone in the room—and yet, entirely understood by the person on the line. It was amazing. Concealing her mouth using the receiver, she could also prevent any lip-reading by her older brother. There was a rush of excitement at the end of each clandestine call, a sense of accomplishment. Egyptian boys had their tricks too. In the age before caller ID, the number of times you let the phone ring served as a code. When Mandy's boyfriend wanted him to call her, he would call the landline and let it ring just once. If it was urgent, he would wait until someone answered and then hang up. What a thrill it was when my uncle would shout in frustration, "Who keeps calling and hanging up?" I knew it meant we would be going back to Aida soon. Back to our seaside paradise. My uncle would joke, "Every night, Auntie Aida, Auntie Aida. Why don't you go visit your real aunts?" I loved those aunts, of course, but nothing compared to the beach. The more freedom and flirtation I experienced there, the more stifling every other experience in Alexandria felt. In Aida, I didn't have to carry the burden of representing my parents and wasn't subject to constant public scrutiny. After all these summers here, I had finally found my own foothold.

And when I met Gogo, I had to be there every day. His actual name was Mohammed because...of course, it was. His nickname suited him because of his fixed smile and buoyant energy. His eyes seemed to rest on me a little too long in a way I liked. His smile automatically drew one out of me. Every time. And when our eyes did meet, a darting energy set off in my body like a pinball machine lighting up. Just knowing an Egyptian boy with features like mine had a crush on me instantly healed years of insecurity. I delighted in his curly-haired attention and brown-skinned humor. No longer self-conscious about the fullness of my lips, I smiled broadly.

"Oh Noreen, he's very cool. He has been going to English school his whole life. You guys match very well, wallahy." Mandy's endorsement was clear, and then her girlfriends chimed in.

"Yes, go for it. He's not judgmental at all. And he has an energy, mesh keda?" Mona looked to Eman for confirmation.

"Yeah, it's his personality. He's attractive for sure," she said, applying her lip gloss while talking.

There was much talk about how lucky I was that he was so open-minded. I was meant to feel lucky that Gogo would look past my frequent cultural errors. I see now that part of Mandy's enthusiasm was also her growing desire to be alone with her boyfriend. And eventually, the night came when we'd separate, each with our respective companions.

"I'll meet you guys at the mini mart at 9 pm," Mandy said. "Gogo, take care of her, okay?"

"Min aynaya leh tneen," he responded, shorthand for "she is dearer to me than both my eyes."

Was it he who was so romantic or the language? I couldn't be sure, but I was enthralled. I felt so looked after but also nervous. Alone with my first Egyptian boyfriend, I leaned into a more feminine energy than I was used to. After observing Mandy and her friends for weeks, I had taken on some of their affects—more hair twirling, giggling, and playful eyebrow-raising. I'd also become very good at applying kohl eyeliner which felt transformational.

Gogo was 17 years old and about to join the Faculty of Engineering next year at my father's alma mater. In Egypt, the title of "bash mohandas"—sir engineer—was as esteemed as "doctor", and Gogo exuded a confidence that seemed to justify the misogyny I observed around me. He walked chest first and I'd never seen someone wear a t-shirt so well. Sitting on the sand, I badly wanted to rest my head on his shoulder. "Maybe men were meant to take care of women?" I thought, instantly abandoning any early feminist ideals I may have had for his affection. Just for a chance at belonging.

"You know what 'thanaweya amma' is, right?" he asked, spinning his zippo like a wheel on his index finger.

"No." Here I was again, clueless.

"You see, that's why I like hanging out with you!" His laughter seemed exaggerated, especially since I had no idea what he was talking about. "It's the only thing people talk about here. My family has been pressuring me about this test since I learned how to walk." He struggled to swallow the bitterness on his tongue.

"Oh, so it's a test? Like a school test?" I could tell this was important to him and so I leaned in.

"Yeah, so at the end of high school, you take this state test to see what you can study. It's not like you can study whatever you want." I must have looked confused so he continued. "There are only 22 public universities in all of Egypt. They have to make it as hard as possible. They have to block us."

"Block you? You think they don't want people to go to college?" I was still naïve enough, and programmed as an American, to believe that anyone in the world could become anything they wanted to be.

"Noreen, there are over 60 million people in Egypt. Not everyone can be a lawyer or doctor. Basically, this test determines your life."

I felt so stupid. There was so much I didn't understand. He must've sensed my embarrassment when he pivoted.

"Anyway, have you ever been to a concert?" he asked. "They keep saying Metallica will play here but I doubt it." Instead of *Waiting for Godot*, in Egypt, year after year, they waited for Metallica. We both knew they weren't coming.

His dimples returned when we chatted about music. We were mutually fascinated and small exchanges like this turned us into bridges. Then there were the nonverbal exchanges. We'd often go swimming as a group but once we were far enough out, Gogo and I would find each other. We were still kids, choking on salt water as we tried to dunk each other down. Our bodies slipped past one another like shiny fish in a bucket. Taking turns diving down, we'd time who could hold their breath the longest, bringing up handfuls of sand as proof we'd touched the floor. From there, Alexandria's skyline stretched infinitely to the right of us. And at sunset, when the city lights would turn on, I'd often think that no one but us has this view right now.

One night after a swim, Gogo and I decided to venture out into the dark, away from the brightly-lit sidewalk of Aida. Past the green lawn where the elders sat and through the part of the pine forest that served as a parking lot. Our exploring brought us to a cluster of cabins that appeared to have been unoccupied this season and to another smaller beach. It was so dark that the sea was barely decipherable from the sand, except where the moon glistened.

Perpendicular to the sea was a very tall wall, creating a cul-de-sac. I leaned against the wall as Gogo pulled a pack of cigarettes from his back pocket. Since we were alone, I asked if I could have one, then watched his fingers fumble to open the lid and slide two out. He put one behind his ear and then, instead of handing me the second, moved his hand toward my mouth. He traced the outline of my lips with his finger. I smelled tobacco and tasted salt. My whole body tingled, yearning to respond, but I had to hold back. I had been holding back for weeks. He smiled and it was automatic, I smiled back. My hair was still wet from our sunset swim and I felt myself tremble, but not because I was cold. Restraining myself was more than a mental effort. My body was fighting itself. As the tension and desire became too much to bear, he parted my lips with his finger and kissed me. I feigned protest, as a good Egyptian girl should. Then, as a floodgate collapses, I gave in.

We slid down the wall to the sand and kissed for who knows how long. Lost in our own world, in Gogo's embrace, I barely heard the muffled thump that made him pull away. It took me a few seconds to figure out what was going on. Sitting on the sand in the darkness, I could just make out the contrast of four laced-up, black leather boots. Lifting my eyes, I saw their uniforms next. Two army officers had jumped over the wall against which we were sitting.

"What are you doing here? Get up!" One officer barked, grabbing my arm with such violent force that, in one move, I was on my feet. I felt dizzy as the officer twisted my arms behind my back, the Arabic stinging my ears.

"Let go of her!" Gogo yelled, at which the officer tightened his grip.

In my charmed life until then I had never been in danger, but I recognized the moment when it came. The second officer grabbed Gogo, bent his arms back, and painfully forced them toward his neck. I saw my fear mirrored on his face. Bursting into tears, I bucked and twisted, trying to free myself of the officer's painful grip. He snapped me back upright, repositioning himself so that he could bind my two wrists with just one of his hands. Then, with his second hand, he reached down my shirt. I was wearing my swimsuit beneath the shirt. He cupped my breast and pulled me closer, his damp breath on my neck. I froze in terror.

"Stop struggling, prostitute," he whispered in Arabic. "You didn't mind this from your boyfriend."

My body exploded in rage. I flailed even more desperately. I cringe now recalling my words, indicative of what I imagined to be my only source of power.

"Get your hands off me! I'm American!" I howled in Arabic. "Amrekanaya! You better let me go!"

Disturbed by all the noise, a middle-aged man rounded the corner to see what was happening. He began shouting at the officers, who disappeared as quickly as they had materialized. The officer who had been holding Gogo had stolen the cash in his pocket. Was that what this was all about? Money? Did they want to pleasure themselves? Or to punish me? Perhaps there was no difference between the two. Gogo thanked the man;

together they cursed the crooked officers. I wondered how he managed to get words out as I felt my throat close in shame. They were two men at ease in a world they understood—and I did not. I stood there rooted to the spot, unable to look the older man in the eye. I felt foolish for ever having felt free. For believing this beach was mine as the waves rolled on indifferently. I didn't even feel like my body was mine anymore. The way the officers had appeared out of nowhere filled me with a terror that authority was, in fact, everywhere. Years later, I realized how that fear changed me. It had made me more Egyptian.

In stunned silence, Gogo and I made our way out of the dark and back to the sidewalk, towards the mini mart. Gogo, wracked with guilt, vacillated from extreme anger to disappointment that he couldn't protect me. He sat me on the steps of the mini mart, trying to console me but did not touch me. I could not be touched. He went inside to get us something to drink. How was that going to help? I didn't want juice and he could do nothing for me. I wanted to go home—my real home. I squinted as my eyes, welling with tears, adjusted to the store's fluorescent sign that buzzed above me. I could never tell anyone, apart from Mandy, what had happened. And I never did.

Adrift amongst the current destruction, I retreat again into memory, recalling how I told the story to Mandy that night. Huddled on the steps, we cried as customers stepped over us to get to the shop. Gogo kicked rocks in the distance, smoking and pacing, consumed by an anger that had nowhere to go. I laugh now thinking of how we told the story to each other thereafter. With each recounting, we were braver and tougher than we'd been. We had avoided detention and injury, after all.

Just by continuing our romance there, we were rebels. Still, we didn't push our luck and stuck to the sidewalk, along with our comrades in love, for the rest of the summer.

I didn't know then that the next time the Army would try to take Aida from me, they'd win. Coming here today, I expected to find my summertime playground a bit more run-down than last time. Instead, I'm scanning the beach for any orienting landmark at all. The acres of rare pines and palm trees that once surrounded the mini mart are razed. The shop itself, gone. I make my way toward the shore in a stupor. I recognize the remains of the sidewalk amongst various piles of broken rock because of its zig-zag pattern I used to trace with my fingers. I read the other piles like grave markers, and they tell me what has come of the beachside cabins. All leveled in the name of development. Progress.

Some green shutters, hanging crookedly off their hinges, remain amid the rubble. Tattered awnings violently snap in the wind as if to warn me not to take another step. The government had forced the evacuation of the cabins despite over 200 lawsuits brought against them. Legal contracts simply dissolved. Landmarks of my personal history, in turn, demolished. Diggers and cranes parked in the wings promise more destruction. My mind begins repopulating the shore just as it was when I was 15. Like a movie director creating a scene, I put everything in its proper place. The responsibility to recall every detail is overwhelming but a clear picture comes into focus. I see children running out of the water, their tan skin glistening and feet gathering more and more sand. I hear their parents calling them in for lunch. My stomach cramps as I remember the hunger that comes after a full day of swimming. Or maybe it's the gutting loss leaving me sick and empty.

There may be something about being Egyptian that always has us looking back. A wistful longing for the past hangs heavy in the air—a deep-rooted nostalgia stemming from pride in our history. But our cultural inheritance also weighs heavily. Does our greatness exist only in the past? Must it? A new museum in the capital has been built to showcase Egypt's ancient artifacts yet no structure exists to honor our desire to be free. If the recent past is to have its place in the grander story of Egypt, we need to share and record the truth of our lives. And assign agreed-upon meaning and value to the experiences and places that shaped us before they vanish. We are walking monuments, crumbling in our own ways, holding on to the unspoken. I want to leave a trace, my mark on Aida, to honor young love that wasn't given public space to thrive. There isn't even a tree left here at this beach on which to carve my name. So instead, facing the water, I write my name in the sand and step back, welcoming its erasure by the waves. For as indifferent as it is, the sea is at least a steady witness to love and ruin in Alexandria.

Back at Mandy's house, where I am staying on this visit, I tell her what I've seen.

"At least they didn't take the sea away," I say, trying to laugh.

"Well, they've taken away our view of it on the corniche," she sighs.

She means the dozens of coffee shops, mini malls, and an actual circus that have disfigured the city's famed seaside road. On the way home, the driver told me blankly that there is no return. "Alexandria has been bought and sold." The Army's Engineering Authority promises that the new commercial structures in Montazah will be a boon for tourism and expects locals to applaud. A yacht dock, shopping center, and luxury resort are coming soon.

CAGED ANGEL

Here, Threa Almontaser plays hooky with her classmate and adventures through the Yemeni countryside, depicting a connection between innocent souls, the restlessness of youth and a curiosity without bias.

THREA ALMONTASER

THREA ALMONTASER is an Arab-American writer and translator. Her childhood spent in a small tribal village in southern Yemen has greatly influenced her writing. A first-generation college student, she is an MFA graduate from North Carolina State University and the recipient of scholarships from the *Tin House* Writers' Workshop and The Kerouac House in Orlando, among others. Her work is forthcoming or published in *Sundress Publications*, *Oxford Review*, *Nimrod International Journal*, *Tinderbox Poetry Journal*, and elsewhere. She teaches English to immigrants and refugees in Raleigh and enjoys traveling to places not easily found on a map. threawrites.com

We flatten our hands on wooden desks. Ustadha Ratha walks around during homeroom to inspect our nails. She taps her thick stick on the ground as she circles us like she's searching for water. If they're too long, too short, caked with grime or covered with polish, she has us line up in front of her with our palms outstretched. The girls take the punishment impassively for the most part. I heard the boys in the classroom next door press their hands in their armpits afterwards and cry.

"Why were you late this morning?" Lena asks, peeling bright pink polish she stole from her sister off her nails.

"Loza has a thing for the falcon trainer's third son, Yahya, even though she's already engaged to her cousin. Anyway, Loza and Yahya are making me pass secret messages between them for a whole riyal!" I sniff the money in my hand. "Ah, love never smelled so good... Let's buy gum with it later."

Lena isn't paying attention. She's peeling pink as quickly as possible, but there's no time. Ustadha Ratha taps her stick closer to where we sit. In a fit of hysteria, Lena jumps out of her seat screaming for the bathroom. I rush after her, Ustadha Ratha threatening extra classroom chores, everyone's laughter trailing behind us.

Outside, juniper trees spiral into the sky, squeezed by a giant's hands. The edges of everything caked with tufts of dried weeds, sun strong enough to break the baked air with waves. Boys skipping class have 10-cent hard candies lumping their cheeks to look like the chewing tobacco their fathers' mouths constantly consume. My brother is among them. He spits sunflower seeds as he talks, telling his friends about our time in Aden last week, how he saw a girl get snatched in a whirlpool right in front of him in the Red Sea. Another boy cuts in about his neighbor doing laundry on the roof, how she turned around for two seconds, clothespin between her teeth, before the red kite seized her newborn with its talons, mass of raw flesh, loose pinky left for her like a parting gift. The only other kid in the small farming village with a TV besides us butts in, says Michael Jackson dangled a baby off a hotel balcony, and we all know he wins. Some of the boys start moonwalking into each other, then fight in the dirt they fall on.

We cover our faces with our scarves and rush past before they recognize us. We race outside of school grounds, down sand dunes, up rock ledges. We hide behind a parked donkey cart and a pair of goats munching on a bowl of leftover rice. The owner spits qat onto the ground, staining his teeth a cutthroat red, a confetti of discarded branches and leaves behind him. The street is sprinkled with wads of phlegm that glisten like freshly shucked oysters. The bags under his eyes bulge like a second pair that have yet to open.

When he spots us hiding, he laughs, then rummages in his basket of freshly glopped hive-honey. He places a glittery birthday hat on each of our heads—a little crumpled, American cartoons on the front—before praying over us and moving on. We touch our new hats and shrug before trekking into a nearby neighborhood where we duck in and out of people's houses, giggling when they try to invite us to tea. Lena uses someone's outdoor squat toilet and accidentally drops her Hello Kitty whistle in the shit-filled hole. We walk and walk, past women planting in mud paddies. Salty water strokes their ankles, hair smelling of henna, skin a burnt umber. Children hang from their backs like baby monkeys, or catch large desert locusts in mid-air when they hop from the tall grass, biting off the locusts' head as a juicy snack. An old lady twists and stretches dyed rags in the field. Rusty buckets slop with orange stains, holding what can take strain without tearing, then becoming something beautiful to wrap herself in. Deep in the crops, the air is bone-dry as ripe coffee fruit. We love breaking the berry's husk, bitter mocha up our noses, lining them into flowers and shapes. We find someone's hen and rooster to chase, make their beaks touch and kiss. As we discuss stealing an egg to raise as our own little chicken daughter, an auntie finds us and shoos us away with her slipper.

We walk hand-in-hand under the unforgiving sun, the one that raised us dark and spotted. At the well, we cup water into our palms, slurp slowly, noon sun a golden disk. Everything is quiet except for the dusty hawks circling above. The village lies on her stomach, snoring. A smooth virgin cover blankets the village after last night's sandstorm. The heat reaches over a hundred, flows in our veins, throbs in our temples and wrists. My necklace burns my skin. I tell Lena about last night as we take small, cool sips. How I tried to bathe in our ceramic bathtub but found a giant king lizard resting in the middle, so I had to bathe with a bucket of cold well-water beside it.

"Mama says there's a jinn living inside my Baba," Lena interrupts. I stop drinking. "He won't talk to anyone and I hear him crying at night when the crickets are loudest." She goes on, "But Mama says he'll get better once we ask the sheikh to read Qur'an over him. That'll take the evil out."

"He just sounds plain sad to me," I say, knowing people blame black magic on any sort of mental sickness.

Lena shrugs at her sand-encrusted toes. "Maybe it's a sad jinn."

"Yeah. Maybe."

"I don't want to go home," Lena sighs. "I'm already on my final strike this week."

"We will surely die if we do," I nod.

"If my mama finds out I skipped class, she'll marry me off to some old blimp."

"That won't happen," I say, not really sure, but wanting to make Lena feel better. "Where should we play next?" I ask instead.

Lena rips the tail off a tiny lizard as she thinks, like plucking off a flower petal. The limb wriggles in her fingers, the lizard scurrying into a crevice to regrow its missing part. "We could sit in front of someone's cooler and drink glasses of orange Fanta? Or watch Indian films at Gede Genya's house. She won't rat us out. She'll just give us a bowl of sweet grapes and braid our hair."

We crouch near acacia, thyme, drooping sedges, bored and waiting for any inspiration to hit. A baby frankincense tree saturates the air around us. Lena dots the musk on my hot pulse, the strong atr sticking immediately to my skin. "What's that bulky thing?" Lena unbuttons my school uniform's black robe and gasps. "Who did you steal this from?" She is smiling.

I stand on my toes. Look left, right, up into the sky. "Don't tell a soul. I sneaked it when my uncle was napping. All the boys have one, showing off everywhere they walk. It's not fair!"

"Can I hold it?" I hand the gambia blade over to Lena like it's something holy. It fits perfectly in her little palms. The ritual scimitar gleams with threat, forged iron, the hilt an Eritrean ivory, two jeweled serpents wrapped around the handle. A band of rubies at the thumb, an embossed hawk's head on the lip of the hilt. "Will you ever use it?" Lena asks, and I have no answer.

In the end, my friend and I go for a long jaunt on empty terrain. Kicking up sand with our sandals, we head to the edge of the village where traveling caravans and market stalls are stationed. Halfway there, we catch a ride with migrant workers. They nap with red and white checkered kufiyahs pulled over their eyes. Our seat smells of worn leather and melon rinds, a comforting amalgam.

A boy our age sits beside me as we bump onward, reed-thin, arms the color of chestnuts. His sweat smells of places I cannot enter: salas where men sit, play lute music, smoke shisha, reign supreme and of streets I'm forbidden to walk, mountains I could never climb. He wears a necklace of pebbles that hit each other whenever the cart bobs and dips. The clack, clacking.

"What are you reading?" Lena asks him.

The boy finally looks at us. "About how a sandstorm here can move across the ocean and into the Amazon Basin. We're the perfect fertilizer. We're the dust the rainforest needs to grow." Our Arabic is not complicated enough to understand what he said. At our blank faces, he puts the worn book away and shows us a trick with water and the gap between his teeth. When we clap, he hops off the moving cart and butts heads with the toughest ram. We cheer louder and he glows from it.

He jumps back into the cart and gives me a pebble from around his neck, the slingshot in his pocket. "Try." He points at a skyline of screeching red kites. I try and try and try. He takes it from my tired hands, hits a bird right away, its body falling in the distance like how Iblees must have dropped from heaven. The moment he hits his mark, something irreversible is done. He jumps down again and rushes off to inspect the bloody feathers. I see in his eyes before he leaves an ecstasy that pumps his veins and sparks his brain like qat.

Lena and I stay seated, passing mud-brick homes stacked along the mountainsides. They look like painted gingerbread houses. We move by men wearing long, colorful foutas around their waists, their carts tilted back from the vast amounts of weight—fruit, cloth, cheap toys from America. Children sell decorated tissue boxes to anyone, shout and dance for their attention, and we can't help but admire how creative mothers get when trying to put food into their babies' bellies. We whiz past mosques like thumbtacks stuck on every block. A voice rises from one of the towers. The call for prayer echoes and spreads, reaches cribs, grazing goats, the ears of thieves, repeats, *Creation is striking and full of daybreak, prayer is greater than sleep.*

When we finally arrive at the souk, we find beggars from Somalia flattening their bodies on each corner, their hands open for alms, eyes half-closed with the shame of it. Women in black paperclip themselves to their husband's sides. Their veiled faces make them look like floating reapers. Everyone haggles loudly, as is courtesy. They challenge one another, laughing, engaging each other in barter. A vendor selling stained-glass windows calls me daughter, ground meat where his thigh once was. Orphans go from tent to tent, insisting to sweep with a straw broom or take their trash, salvaging any scraps they can find there.

Outside one of the tents, a dispute between elders takes place, sharp gambias drawn. I hold my breath, clutch the one I have strapped to my side. Someone calls for poets to settle the score, and the chosen two clash in the center, everyone tuning in to their word battle. A man standing beside us from one of the northern cities gives Lena a purple juri flower, says she looks too fair-skinned and full of food to be from the south of Yafaa, and waits to be thanked. Around the corner, a wave of women beat one of the shopkeepers with shoes, sticks, small fists, after he gropes one of their little girls in the crowded stall. No man tries to stop them. On our right, she-camels chew Bermuda like unamused teenagers. Little boys toss pebbles at their humps. The camel spits at them. Ships of the desert, ata Allah, gifts of God. Children race between the camels' lanky legs, clap at flies, line seven in a neat row to jump over. We watch them hug a dromedary's belly and race, trying not to let go.

Bedouin women sift through a tray of lentils for ants or chase after their young girls, some of whom are dressed like wild, desert brides—red henna painted on the soles of their feet, evil-eye trinkets braided into their hair, gold rings on each of their fingers to look like a second set of knuckles. They shine with the blue luminescence that makes me wonder if they've traveled to ethereal worlds and took a little bit of magic back with them. I pick one of the babies up and she smells like the wind when it passes through holes in a mountain.

Gypsies in a clearing amidst a collection of dunes conduct a show for coins. A one-eyed dog the size of a small bear is faced against a tiny monkey. Everyone knows the monkey will be ripped to shreds. Still, the men cheer in a circle around the chained animals and make bets, revving for a good fight. The monkey's eyes are large, black orbs. He pets his tail in an attempt to comfort himself.

Smoke from a hookah pipe swirls inside a particular tent like the trail from a genie's lamp. Lena pulls me inside. It's the only tent dyed a happy yellow, empty except for a single cage, rusted and peeling. Its single elegance is the wide, maroon cloth concealing the mystery within. A piece of cardboard has "Freak of Nature" scribbled in Arabic in front of it. I feel a creeping on my skin like a snake on a hot summer wall.

"Maybe there's magic here, someone who can make your Baba not sad anymore," I tell Lena so she doesn't run out. We want desperately to pull the cloth aside, but we're too afraid to go any closer because we'd heard whispers in school of the hooved jinn who might be in town to steal bad children.

I peek outside the tent flap. Everyone is preoccupied with the fight. The monkey shrieks like he's being burned alive. I spot someone selling salted fish from the city port north of here. An overweight man wields his clumsy spit-wet knife over the clotted scales of a freshly caught mackerel. He flays them blind, all of his attention focused on the match.

Before I can get Lena to go there with me, I hear her gasp and zip to her side. Whatever is in the cage is moaning the kind of moan reserved for weary soldiers. We pull the cloth away. Curled like a fetus in the womb is a young girl. She wears an old dress that might once have been purple and pretty. I've seen children like her lying creased in corners of the city, their mothers making them stretch their bodies out on cardboard, cough, look pitiful to the foreigners with thick pockets. But there is something different about this girl, something our tongues can't name. The light shining through a slit in the tent hits the girl's fish-hook spine. That small touch of heat rouses her.

She freezes when she spots us like maybe she sees wasps on the tips of our noses. Her shaved skull is like the bulb of a scallion attached to clavicle, elbows, and knees, her skin the color of the bottom of a well. We try to get a glimpse of her hooves that jinns have when taking on a human form. She snarls and we see her teeth are all pushed together to look like chickens climbing over one another in a crowded coop.

"Let's leave," Lena says, but we're staked to our spots.

The girl twists around like a stepped-on worm, writhing away on her arms. Her dress pulls forward and we see for the first time her hooves. Where her feet should have been, there are two, short stubs. Baba told me about these children, hit by a rebel-planted landmine disguised as a stuffed animal or another harmless toy, so that after a while, most of the children who lived deep in the city lost parts they can't grow back.

Disappointed we hadn't witnessed a wish-granting mythical creature from the spirit world, we turn to leave. I glance behind my shoulder and find something familiar in the girl's face. "Wait," I motion to Lena. The girl watches the pink on my thumb shimmer, the one finger I didn't have time to scrape off.

"You want some?" Lena digs out her bright nail polish, the bottle warm from being in her pocket. She opens it. Strong formaldehyde stings our nostrils. The brush comes out gooey and melted. We take turns prettying the girl's nails. She doesn't retreat when we pull her fingers through the bars, all of us giggling as we paint her.

She flaps her hands up and down to dry them, the sorriest excuse for wings. She sniffs them and smiles. I tap the knife at my side, wonder how strong the cage lock is. The gambia grows hotter with each passing second I stand there, unmoving, until I imagine it leaves a long burn scar on my skin.

After inspecting her nails, the girl nods like we've given her the payment she needed. She pulls her dress all the way up, exposing her tender underside. Lena and I ogle. Another person sleeps in the space her chest should be. It's misshapen and rubbery, with only half of its head sticking out, along with an arm and some toes. Its eyes are shut, sleeping or dead. It must sense our awe because it wakes up and we see the same inky eyes as its sister. It yawns and shows us black gums. A small frown is knitted into its face as if listening for something, mouth open. But there's nothing.

We wait for answers. For an introduction. Anything. A thought crosses my mind—that I stand in front of a caged angel willing to grant my wishes, those secreted inside the deepest part of me, if only I'm brave enough to speak them out loud. Before I can say a word, the girl lifts her twin's tiny arm. It mewls. Lena steps back. "She wants us to paint its nails, too."

A crash from outside makes us jump like rabbits on a hook. Lena and I run out of the tent in a panic without saying goodbye. Outside, the fight is clearly over. Though I'd hoped the little monkey would be found standing on top of a furry mountain, victorious, I knew that wasn't possible.

I step on something soft. When I look down, I find his tail, long and bloodied. The rest of him is torn open like a guava fruit. Fat flies hum around it, ready to inherit the mound of fresh meat before the birds do. The dog will be tossed back into its cage. And there will be no burial for the monkey. No ceremony or revenge. Scavengers, we are too full of dust, too far south for anything else.

People continue to barter, spit, chew, laugh, oblivious to the scene before them, to what lies beyond the yellow tent. I hear twin heartbeats from inside, feel as if I'm peering through a chink into the lap of the world. I ignore the gambia poking my tummy, still unsheathed, its weight heavier than before. Lena takes my hand and pulls me back the way we came. I almost bump into the chained dog-bear. He stares through me, his one good eye restless and roaming.

KHALEH MINA

Through memories of the freedom-loving, rooftop-climbing glory of her childhood before the Iranian revolution, Kamin Mohammadi writes a moving portrait of a devoted aunt's motherly love.

KAMIN MOHAMMADI

KAMIN MOHAMMADI is an author, journalist, broadcaster and public speaker. Born in Iran, she and her family moved to London after the 1979 Iranian Revolution. For her journalism, she recently won two awards from the LA Press Club, and has been nominated for awards by Amnesty International and the American Society of Magazine Editors. Her books are *The Cypress Tree* and *Bella Figura: How To Live, Love and Eat The Italian Way*, which is currently in development as a TV series. She lives in London and Tuscany, where she farms an olive grove, makes organic remedies, grows her own veggies, hosts yoga and writing retreats and raises Shiba Inu puppies. kamin.co.uk @kaminmohammadi

I thought I would be different today. Today, the 40th anniversary of the revolution that changed my life, that changed my country Iran, that changed the outline of so many lives, has passed unremarked by me. I have not reflected on Facebook or posted on Instagram. I have not spent time digging up images that summed up those times—swarthy young men in wide collars and flared trousers, their hair fanned out around them as they burned flags and chanted Death to America—to share them via Twitter with a few well-chosen words on the day that Iran became the Islamic Republic.

I had been a child living in Iran and I remember every day of those months as clearly as if they had just unfolded. The weeks leading up to that point had been marked by the unthinkable happening. So many unthinkables. The Shah leaving. The Ayatollah arriving. Saying, when asked how it felt to return to Iran having led a revolution that had toppled the monarchy, "Nothing, I feel nothing." The absolute shock of those words, the silence that had fallen in our house, in every house across the land at that moment. This man—the charismatic leader that had so enchanted people that they raised their eyes to the moon and saw his face in it—felt nothing. So normal had become the abnormal that we were powerless but to stay home (there was a curfew so we had little choice) and watch it all unfold on our television set as it took over the country. It was the first such event to be thus screened, unprecedented in world history. They kept us children inside to protect us from the foment on the streets, and it was weeks since we had been to school. The worst of it for me, a tomboy of eight years old, was that the rooftops were now out of bounds.

It was my habit to lead the neighborhood children on expeditions across the flat roofs of the houses that almost touched, making it possible to roam the street at rooftop level while the adults slept after lunch, while we too were meant to be sleeping. Instead, we all sneaked out and met at the back corner of our rooftop, where we huddled and planned out a rough route. To get onto the roof, we had to clamber up a wall that divided the front garden from the back garden and we had become expert at doing this silently. Only once had we been caught, by Khaleh Mina. My Khaleh Mina (Khaleh is the Persian for aunt, specifically, maternal aunt) was the person I loved the most in my large extended family. Out of four aunts and seven uncles (on my mother's side alone), Khaleh Mina was my absolute favorite, which was quite an accolade, as I loved all of my extended family with the whole of my heart. The day she caught us scaling the wall, she too had sneaked out, to smoke a secret cigarette. She looked at us, frozen in terror halfway up the wall, and silently raised an eyebrow, reacting unlike the other adults in our lives who were as liberal with their scolding as with their loving. Then, touching a finger to her lips, she had turned away and smoked her cigarette as if we didn't exist, and we scrambled away.

And today, when as a good journalist I should be reflecting on the revolution that ushered in Islamic law in Iran, which sent ripples across the region and the world, which exiled me from my country and turned me into a refugee, all I can think of instead is Mina. I woke up this morning with my head filled with thoughts of her, my eyes brimming with pictures of the past. Instead of the pale, gray skies of London, I see the intense blue of the sky as it rolled past the window of Khaleh Mina's pink VW Beetle, in which we would ride around on the days she picked me up from school. She would put in a tape of Googoosh's latest hits, and we would open the windows and drive, singing at the top of our voices, the sun beating down on the car as we sped along.

The sun beats down still in Iran, the sky a brilliant shade of turquoise setting off the minarets and domes of the vibrantly tiled mosques. Aby—the Farsi for blue—means, literally, watery. Like the familiar turquoise dome rising out of the desert, offering shade and shelter in the cruel heat of the day. Aby. In a land of vast deserts, it makes sense.

My Khaleh Mina now lives in Shiraz, a town in central-southern Iran, capital of the province of Fars—the cradle of the Persian race. It was in Fars that the lauded Achaemenian kings erected Persepolis for the Persian New Year celebrations in the semi-desert to receive tributes from their subjects from all corners of the known world. Shiraz, where the grape was transmuted into wine, long before being transported to the soils of Australia and California, and before Iran stopped carousing to become the Islamic Republic, teetotal and chaste.

But when she was my Khaleh Mina who drove me around in her pink Beetle, she lived in Abadan. Hot, humid and embraced by the tributaries of the great Euphrates river near the Persian Gulf, Abadan swayed with palm trees and the overwhelming sentimentality of its natives' souls. Khaleh Mina had a house with a courtyard and a flat roof, where we would sit, my mother, a brace of aunts, my sister and myself, at night, under a sky inlaid with stars. My sister and I would stay up late, drifting into a delicious semi-consciousness while the women chatted and gossiped and laughed. First they would drop their voices a little when talking of sex or marriage or mocking the mullahs, but as the night wore on, they forgot our presence and they slapped their thighs, rocking forward with hilarity and cackling. I had my first drag of the hubbly-bubbly pipe up there on that roof, at the age of five.

I remember sobbing with Khaleh Mina in that house. Arriving there with newly-pierced ears, woozy and sore, not allowing my mother to touch them, the studs encrusted solid with goo. Khaleh Mina took me in her arms and cried with me. Then she sat me in the yard edged with jasmine flowers and, under a yellow moon, she gently massaged my ear lobes with cream and slowly, slowly, eased out the throbbing studs, replacing them with little gold pin-points of her own. I snoozed in her arms, exhausted by the force of tears and the relief from pain.

Khaleh Mina. Born to be an aunt. Forever an aunt. If there is a talent to aunting, as opposed to mothering, then she has it in spades. When I returned to Iran after many years away, I found her aunting a whole new generation. And when they grow up they too will deliver up their babies and she will be their Khaleh Mina: loving, sharp-tongued, wickedly witty and dynamic as the devil. Even her sisters and brothers, my mother included, call her Khaleh Mina.

Abadan in the early sixties was swinging. My mother and her multitudinous siblings were treading an uncharted line between traditional and modern life. Black and white pictures show them stylised, made up and grinning from ear-to-ear. You feel the sun beating down, the money in their pockets, the sense of freedom and possibility. The four eldest daughters clicked around town in their stilettos, their skirts short, their hair backcombed high, their eyeliner black and winged. The eldest two had been married off to my grandfather's specifications, while my grandmother, small and strong, her green eyes set wide apart, picked a husband for the bee-hived,

18-year-old Mina. One of her own kinsmen, a kindly, scholarly man with Brylcreemed hair and a pencil mustache. As short as my grandmother and nearer her age than Mina's.

Apparently Mina (as she still was then) cried for days. I've never found out if she was already in love with a young man, but knowing girls of 18, I expect she was. She couldn't cross her mother but she was horrified by the thought of marrying a man more than twice her own age, even in a country where this was common. It was her most passionate wish to have her own family; her elder sisters had already started. No reason why not, my grandmother had pointed out, sitting cross-legged on the floor of their central courtyard as she cleaned a bundle of herbs. Just because the man is mature, that's no obstacle to love, she had said. Mina's silent tears fell into the basket of parsley in front of her, her deft fingers automatically picking off the leaves and tossing them into a basket in the center. My mother had looked up from the fennel seeds she was grounding and ventured to say that he was rather handsome, like Clark Gable. Mina smiled weakly, but in the years to come, it became one of their favorite jokes.

Khaleh Mina's Clark Gable is still a kindly and scholarly man. His hair is still Brylcreemed and his mustache slim as a pencil, now snow-white rather than jet black. Mina's excessive tears may have sprung from an instinct she had about him: they never had children. The reasons why are hidden behind the veil of family history and gossip, but it was always said that the problem lay with him.

Luckily for Khaleh Mina, by the time her mother's youngest child was born, my grandmother was more than glad to help, little Yasmin being her 12th child in as many years. Gradually, seamlessly, Yasmin's visits to Mina became permanent: one day, she simply never left. And Khaleh Mina got to raise her youngest sister as her own and feel the joy of a child running about her house. Despite being sisters, she was called Khaleh by Yasmin: hence the legend was born. Yasmin was married from her house, a day of pride for Khaleh Mina, and the young couple, unable yet to afford their own place, were ensconced, giggling, in Khaleh Mina's spare room.

By then my own family, as many others, had already been wrenched from Iran by the revolution. While travel was still relatively easy, Khaleh Mina came to spend a few months with us, filling my depressed and unmoored mother with her energy, leaving Clark Gable to fend for himself. And this was the last time we saw her in many years. The Iran-Iraq war came and, eventually, went, leaving a nation broken-hearted and bereft of its young. The horrors of a medieval war with modern weapons I leave for other pens, but its repercussions in one respect concern me here.

Abadan, my mother's family home, was one of the towns worst hit by the war. By this time Yasmin had just moved into a flat with her husband and started her own prodigious family. Bombs were falling in rapid succession; my grandmother's house had a direct hit. The inhabitants of Abadan were leaving in droves, pouring out of the city, over-running any form of transport available. Men obliged to stay with their work in the oil company were packing off their families to relations in Tehran, Shiraz, Isfahan, Mashhad, anywhere away from the Western border. Within this chaos, Khaleh Mina provided strength and humor. She kept Yasmin's eldest, Maryam, locked in her arms all night when bombs were falling and the wailing of women filled the night air. She had a strange glow, a calmness, a blooming beauty. Everyone noticed, but in the mayhem, few registered and no one commented.

The day the bomb fell on my grandmother's house, Mina, with the unerring instincts of a seer, had called round in the morning and made grandmother agree to stay a few days at Mina's house. As they were walking away from the house in the early evening, Khaleh Mina dragging my grandmother's bag and urging her to hurry, the bomb fell. Despite being some distance away, the women were badly knocked over with the shock of the blast. Khaleh Mina picked herself up and rushed to her mother, got her to her feet, dusted her down and made sure she was unhurt before she allowed herself to feel the searing pain in her womb. She collapsed, blood snaking out of her.

In the hospital they announced to her dazed family that she had miscarried. Her one and only pregnancy. This was the first anyone had heard about it. Khaleh Mina, in her late thirties and resigned to a childless marriage, had surprised herself and Clark Gable by getting pregnant some two months before. But now any possibility of offspring was sealed with clots of ruby blood.

She eventually went home, where she wandered around dazed, uninterested in getting dressed in the mornings. Her laughter had died, her love was trapped in some remote place, she was a shadow. For two more months she hardly felt a thing, especially not any interest in life. Then one day Yasmin rushed in. "I have found a friend's truck driving to Shiraz and there is room for us, the babies and our husbands. Get Clark Gable. Get packing. They are picking us up in half an hour. Come on Khaleh Mina, there is no time to lose." Khaleh Mina couldn't care, but Clark Gable chucked a few things in a bag (there was not much room for luggage, and they all erroneously believed they would be able to send for their things). When the truck arrived, Yasmin made Khaleh Mina put a coat over her dressing gown and Yasmin's husband shuffled her into the truck, still in her slippers.

A few days later they heard that Khaleh Mina's house had taken a direct hit. Her life had disappeared. In Shiraz, cramped into another sister's spare room with their brood, Khaleh Mina began, slowly, to return to herself. She got dressed. She started to rebuild. She found comfort in the reassuring presence of Clark Gable and joy in the new babies that Yasmin soon started to deliver at regular intervals.

And she is there still now, 40 years after we fled Iran for our lives and her own life changed so absolutely. Living in a tiny flat in a high-rise in Shiraz, with her new, small life gathered tight around her, laughing and cleaning and cooking and scolding her husband. There is no jasmine-scented yard, no flat roof from which to go traveling through the galaxy, but Maryam and Ali, the eldest grandchildren of Yasmin who simply never left her house, don't seem to mind. They still find magic in her presence and adventure in the far-away mountains just visible from the kitchen window. And Khaleh Mina's hips grow ever wider as her love continues to transform young lives and her memory fills my heart.

A SUMMER'S RUIN

A politically charged mind trip rife with dark humor set in Amman, Jordan, Hisham Bustani's story is an uncensored, passionate account of a summer spent simmering in his biases about the Saudis vacationing next door.

HISHAM BUSTANI

HISHAM BUSTANI is an award-winning Jordanian author of five collections of short fiction and poetry. He is acclaimed for his bold style and unique narrative voice, with much of his work revolving around issues related to social and political change, particularly the dystopian experience of post-colonial modernity in the Arab world. His fiction and poetry have been translated into many languages, with English-language translations appearing in prestigious journals and anthologies, including *The Kenyon Review*, *Black Warrior Review*, *The Poetry Review*, *Modern Poetry in Translation*, *World Literature Today*, *The Los Angeles Review of Books*, and *The Best Asian Short Stories*. His book *The Perception of Meaning* (Syracuse University Press, 2015) won the University of Arkansas Arabic Translation Award. He is the recipient of the Rockefeller Foundation's Bellagio Residency for Artists and Writers for 2017, and his most recent book is *The Monotonous Chaos of Existence* (Mason Jar, 2022).

They will not stop talking.

Those bastards.

All night. All day. They go on and on, occasionally interrupted by bursts of shisha bubbles and gray smoke, or an unexpected thunder of laughter: a gunshot that tears the air for a moment and leaves behind stagnant despair in the opposing room. My room.

I can't shut them out behind my window, can't silence them behind the double-glazed frame, for I'll be simmered, stewed by the heat absorbed all day by the limestone of which this house is made. It has no air conditioning. Mine is one of the households that still resists, still hanging onto a postcard Amman, a childhood Amman that occasionally deploys electric fans to soften the occasional heat wave. Times changed. Climate changed. And I keep my windows open, waiting for the chilled breeze that hesitantly arrives, easing the pressure, cooling the sweat. Now other things arrive with crudeness: the scourge of returning neighbors.

Feeling sullen, I watch them right across the street. Their exhaust fumes penetrate my nostrils, their second-hand lies seep into my ears, their gesturing hands slap my face.

"Such a waste," I tell myself, "millions of years of slow, strenuous evolution, down the drain." Look at me. Now I'm talking to myself. "Going crazy is a good measure to maintain sanity under these circumstances," I convince myself as I walk away.

They talk for the entire first half of their summer break. Two months of nonsense until their SUVs carry them back to Riyadh. There, the blazing sun, the heavy dust, the dull house-ridden life, will get even for me. But it is July now, another month to go, and I've tried many things. I talked to them. I complained to the police. I splashed brake oil on their cars and placed screws under their tires. I blasted Sin Dios out of loud speakers in their direction. I threw the contents of a cat's litter box in their garden. ("The strong smell of cat's piss will drive them into their house for sure," my friend, the cat owner, said.) Nothing seems to intimidate them. Nothing seems powerful enough to put an end to my misery.

***

Sitting out in Amman's cool summer breeze, they play cards, and pollute the air. "Mom, can you bring the embers?" the girl was shouting at the top of her voice. I could picture the mom inside, near the stove, cooking shisha embers for the gatherers outside in the small front garden of their ground-floor flat. Back in Riyadh, there is no sitting outside, for outside is an inhospitable climate. There they keep inside walls. They breathe artificial air. Even the underground garage of their building is air conditioned. And when they go out, in the air conditioned car, to the air conditioned mall, they stay enclosed in their black robes, cautious of the ever watching eye of the mutaw'a, the Islamic virtue bureau officials, who spurt out of nowhere, saying as if addressing the air: "Adjust your head cover ya hurma." Or, if an accompanying man is with them (necessarily a father, brother, or husband; no other men are allowed), they'd address him: "Tell your hurma to cover herself properly."

So nothing is like this two-month vacation stretch they spend back home in Amman, staying up till the break of dawn, then sleeping well into the afternoon. "I wish we could stay here forever. That's the life, man," shouts a girl, overjoyed, while the call for Morning Prayer was sounding from the nearby mosque. In Amman, they are free.

***

"That's the life, man..." A high-pitched shout and I awaken, startled. I was drifting on this current of background noise, floating on prickly needles that poked lightly at my brain: that borderline dream on the edge of waking that keeps you fixed to sleep, that pause button keeping the fuzz on the TV screen, freezing the rigid face of the reporter broadcasting live from across the sea just as he finishes his last sentence: "...but the ships keep coming."

They keep coming as the bombardment goes on, the killing goes on, the plundering, the hefty legacy of colonialism, slavery, impoverishment, leaving behind its unhealed wounds. And the wounded take to the sea, to the "West", running away from oppressive tyrannical governments supported and maintained by the "West"; running away from the military and political interventions of the "West"; running away from IMF-imposed "structural readjustments" and "market reforms" that leave them impoverished, unemployed; running away from Zionist settlements and walls and the "refugee status" in countries that perceive them as a demographic threat; running away from Saudi-sponsored sectarian Sunni militias; running away from Iranian-sponsored sectarian Shiite militias; running away from globally-sponsored compromises that claim their lives on a daily basis. *Go West, life is peaceful there*, the song says. But is it? And at what cost? The boats keep going, pushed to the depths of the sea by the humanitarian hand of disregard and lack of admission.

Those dreams of water, of the drowned, of life jackets, of the sea as a vast cemetery, keep haunting me.

Like they do tonight. And then comes the blow. The ship is overturned and I'm stuck right beneath it. I hover around, haven't really drowned but am able to imagine myself drowning in a few minutes. The thought suffocates me even more; I want to break the surface. "How the fuck do I get to that transparent, shaky light above?" I think, but the only answer is the reporter's calm, unwavering voice: "The death toll is on the rise," as a neighbor releases a plume of smoke in the air. It takes much more than that to lift a drowning person out of the cold water.

***

When all the excesses have been consumed, leaving behind gluttonous bodies lying on the chairs, covered in complete silence, they go on talking in my head. Or, my ears suddenly wake up, they—slowly, thoroughly—scan the space for a fluctuation, a word, a cough, a breath, a stab to ignite my anger, a spark to tense my muscles, a prick to start my teeth grinding, as if crushing their heads in a trap of sharp cusps and deep fissures.

Die, motherfuckers, die. The speakers are blasting again, and I close the door of the room that now feels like a cell in Guantanamo, complete with sound torture and all. I close another door, and move to the kitchen on the other side of the house. I can feel the collapse. I can sense it. The trembling at the beginning of an earthquake, the insects running out of their hiding holes. A preliminary warning, to them, to me. The message is clear, but there's nobody home to accept it. Other signs keep popping out of the blue, raising their heads from behind the wall: birds flying overhead in ever-expanding circle formations; stray cats gathering the collective courage to attack bewildered passersby; trees discarding their fresh green leaves and immediately sprouting ones anew. Something *is* going to happen.

The nightly summits across my window continue, and more cars arrive. Their doors bang like prison-door latch locks, telling me all hope is lost, telling me that this is only the beginning, telling me the future is roman numerals carved with a makeshift knife onto the fatigued concrete wall of a cell. The future is counting days until they leave, until they are no more.

But you can't entertain guests in your cell, or can you? I call her. "Come over," I say, "there's champagne, your favorite." I pop a bottle of Baron de Rothschild, a generous gift sent by my brother who lives in Europe (an executive, not a refugee), with his blessings in a note that read: *This guy financed the colonization of our land, and the killing of our people, so we might as well drink his goddamn champagne*; and I sip it from between her lips as we make love on the couch.

"Don't hold back," I say as her moans get louder. Those bastards across the street: I want their men to get horny, their women embarrassed, and their children inquisitive. But the next day, I still wake up with the same headache, short of breath, attacked by never-ending nightmares that I don't usually remember, though I feel their heavy footprints on my brain.

***

It's late September. The sky is steely. The wind, cold. Can you hear it? Can you sense it? The rain is coming. Heavy rain. It will wash everything away. I hope.

THOSE EYES OF HERS

Set in Chicago, where her family made home after leaving India in the 1970s, Samina Hadi-Tabassum uncovers a childhood mystery, which transforms her memories of envy and longing into something entirely different.

SAMINA HADI-TABASSUM

SAMINA HADI-TABASSUM is an education professor who focuses on language, race and culture. Born in Hyderabad, India, Samina migrated to Chicago as a young child in the 1970s and moved throughout the United States during her adulthood. Her first book of poems, *Muslim Melancholia*, chronicles life growing up in different spaces and places. She has three children who take up most of her time, and whatever morsel is left, is for writing. saminahaditabassum.com

The calls always came around midnight. We were all asleep so the story was told only from my parents' memory. A man with a deep, husky voice called several times throughout the night, my father having to get up and answer it each time as the ringing from the old rotary phone was maddening. At first, the man on the telephone started to just scare them, telling them about how dark men were going to come into their apartment and rob them at any time of the night, and that this was not a safe neighborhood to live in for good Muslims like them. That they should move out of the apartment immediately. Then the man on the telephone said that these dark men were going to break through the doors and set their apartment on fire. "Who is this?!" my father yelled through the phone, half awake in his white cotton undershirt, hair disheveled, ready to pull the phone out of the wall.

Sometimes the calls came on weekdays and sometimes on the weekend, but always around midnight. When they came, my mother would get up and stand next to my father, keeping a watchful eye over our bedroom where all three of us slept. Eventually my father figured out from the voice that this man must be a desi like himself, and switched to Urdu after a dozen threats. When he spoke in Urdu, the man on the telephone paused for a bit, but then continued tapping those t sounds with that British English accent, refusing to acknowledge that they were tied to some Muslim brotherhood. Nonetheless, my father started cursing back in Urdu like a 1970s movie villain, sisterfucker and motherfucker, and threatened to find this man on the telephone and beat him senseless with his shoes.

My mother, my two siblings and I had moved into that second-floor corner apartment when we arrived from Hyderabad, India in 1975. My father had been living in Chicago for a few years, having come with his younger brother, both engineers. The apartment at Lawrence and Kedzie was a step up from the deplorable bachelor pad on Devon Avenue, in which seven to eight Hyderabadi men all lived together before their wives received green cards. My father and uncle had both left India during the recession and trekked first to Tehran, where engineers were needed and the Shah's money flowed. Once talk of revolution hit the streets, the young Indian men had gone back home and looked for another way out of dire poverty.

My father picked this apartment because it was near the Jewish kosher markets where we could get halal meat. The building owner was an old Yugoslavian man who brought over beaten up furniture before we arrived: a few gray-threaded sofas, a wooden table with a loose leg, four mismatched chairs and a chest of drawers. No armoires. No charpoys. Everybody in the building was an immigrant, fleeing all kinds of horrors back home, from the Koreans to the Slavs to the Muslims. None of us knew English and spoke in that lingua franca English of untethered migrants. All our mothers congregated in the courtyard and watched over each other's children while hanging washing on the lines and ironing clothes on the cement back porch near the laundry room. But the Muslim mothers kept to themselves and only smiled at the Koreans and Slavs. The children played without boundaries in the alleyways and carried on conversations from Hibbard Elementary down the street.

Every morning before school, even when there was a blizzard covering the streets of Chicago with knee-deep snow, our mothers gathered in front of the building to walk the children over, clad in summer saris over rubber boots, knitted sweaters poking out of their midriff winter coats, and cotton dupattas wrapped around their heads so the cold air did not seep into their ears. To protect their children's ears was even more sacrosanct, and all of us looked like criminals walking down the street in windproof ski masks that left our faces wet with sweat. Most of us were pulled out during the day for ESL services, and there were enough of us to also have an Urdu teacher who talked to us like our mothers and asked about our day, and what we still did not know and understand in English.

Sadiya Haq was my best friend in Mrs. Huntley's first grade classroom. She lived in the same building as me and she was pulled out for both ESL and Urdu. Her family was from Pakistan but only a generation ago they had migrated there from Hyderabad, after the partition that split India into three separate countries. Sadiya had long, thick dark brown hair and the fair skin that all our mothers coveted for their own daughters. The light hazel eyes were from her mother, who had worked in a factory in Pakistan so she could pay for all her sisters' education.

We had never met a Muslim woman who had worked outside of the house, so my own mother was quite curious about Mrs. Haq. She often thought about how her own life would have been different if only my grandfather had allowed his six daughters to work instead of being pushed into arranged marriages to men in faraway places. And here, in our building, was a Muslim woman who had walked to the garment factory by herself in a sari and not a burka, made her own tiffin lunch, and smoked cigarettes on her break. None of the other women believed her until Mrs. Haq took out the tattered black-and-white photos of herself sitting under a banyan tree, a puff of smoke circling about her own beautiful mane of brown, braided hair.

Sadiya looked just like her mother and had that same bravado that I did not possess. I was the introvert to her extrovert, the id to her ego. Sadiya walked with confidence in the shalwar kameez outfits that her mother sewed on the Singer machine we could hear constantly buzzing down the hallway. I coiled myself into a shell whenever my mother would make me wear the gaudy sequin outfits she had sewn, clashing against my gray gym shoes. Sadiya had learned to double jump rope before the rest of us and could sing Queen Bee while jumping. She knew how to chase boys on the playground without our mothers ever knowing. She raised her hand in class all the time while the rest of us pressed our hands under our thighs, looking at our feet when the teacher asked a question. Sadiya was also the first one to bring sandwiches to lunch while the rest of us suffered through lamb meat dolloped inside wheat parathas that had been sitting in our metal lockers since 8 am. Sadiya was *the* All American Pakistani girl that we dreamt of being.

The closer I came to Sadiya, the more her mother wanted Sadiya to stay away from me. At first, I thought Mrs. Haq did not like any one of us children since Sadiya was an only child and one was enough for her. But every time I came closer to Sadiya I saw Mrs. Haq whisper something into her ear and Sadiya standing there for a minute before coming over to play with me, her mother's cold hazel eyes staring back at my black eyes, greasy hair and dark skin. Once I told my mother about how Mrs. Haq did not like me, but my mother just thought it was all in my head and recommended that I bring a bag of candy to entice Sadiya to play with me, since after all, she was so beautiful and all the children wanted to play with her.

But there was something about Mrs. Haq that I never told anyone. It was my seventh birthday and my mother invited all the Muslim families over to our apartment. My mother and her sisters baked pans of lamb biryani, fried beef samosas in a deep vat of peanut oil, sliced and cubed onions and cilantro for the yogurt relish, and soaked cooked rice into pots of creamy, sugared milk for the kheer. There was enough food for everyone, and the Pakistani women commented on how delicious the meal was even though it was not from their own country, where raisins would have been thrown into everything.

The families brought small wrapped gifts for me, and then my father placed the gifts in their bedroom and closed the door after the last guests had arrived. Just when I was about to blow out the candles on my birthday cake, my mother announced that her water had broken and she needed to go to the hospital to deliver our next and last sibling, the only American born one, my Gemini twin. In the midst of chaos, the families decided that they would leave quickly so there was some peace for quick decisions, and it was Mrs. Haq who said that she would stay behind and watch the children until my father came back from the hospital. I was overjoyed at first, knowing that Sadiya and I would get to play with my new toys and have time to jump on the bed in the bedroom, even though I shared it with my younger sister.

"Sadiya, let's open up my presents and play in my room!" I shouted.

"Oh no, no," said Mrs. Haq. "I will keep them in a safe space in our apartment so that none of them gets broken. You can open them when your mother comes back from the hospital. She will enjoy you opening them very much."

I watched Mrs. Haq walk into my parents' bedroom, scanning the walls and trying to measure the worth of the room with her eyes, the gifts bundled tightly under her arms. When she left the front door slightly ajar, she looked back at me with those eyes of hers. I don't remember when she came back into the apartment. My brother, sister, Sadiya and I played hide and seek in the apartment until it got very dark outside and we finally retreated into our bedroom to play board games, falling asleep on the floor. For dinner, we ate the rest of the birthday cake and avoided the biryani and no one cared. Mrs. Haq watched television the whole time and only took breaks to smoke cigarettes on the back porch.

In the morning, we woke to the smell of my father, the formidable bachelor, trying to cook eggs on the skittle while wearing the same suit from last night.

"Come in for breakfast Sattar, Rubina and Samina," he shouted. "Your mother had a baby boy last night. Faisal. And he will join us soon." We were so excited and kept asking my father all sorts of questions. What did he look like? How fat was he? Did he cry the whole night? With a look of exhaustion, my father asked us to eat quietly and get ready to go to the hospital to see for ourselves. As we were leaving, I saw the stack of gifts from my birthday party in the corner of the living room, only a smaller pile, with some missing. I did not think about Mrs. Haq again for quite some time.

Soon after we brought Faisal home from the hospital, my father decided it was time for us to move out of the city and into my uncle's townhouse in the suburbs. Maybe my paternal grandmother would come join us and help take care of the children, he said. And she did but only for a few months. On Saturdays we returned to the city, to Devon Avenue, to shop for all the groceries we needed for the week. We had lost touch with the Muslim families in that apartment building and only saw them occasionally, when we went into the city to pray during Eid at McCormick Center, along with thousands of others.

Eventually all of us went onto colleges in the Midwest and then spread out in radial fashion to various parts of the country: my older brother Sattar went to medical school in New York; my younger sister Rubina ended up a lawyer in Beverly Hills; our younger brother Faisal was a social worker in Boston, and I ended up a middle school teacher in Houston. When I came home for one Labor Day Weekend, my mother and I decided to go to the Islamic Foundation's annual convention in the far suburbs and shop for clothes and jewelry, at a giant open market with stalls from all over the world. At one of the stands, a dark-skinned, stocky man kept staring at my mother from a few feet away and would not look away. I nudged my mother, but she said that she did not recognize him as anyone she knew. But it was now too late and the man was putting his taqiyah on his head while walking over to us. We said our salaams and he began with an apology.

"You do not know who I am but I know who you are," he said. At this point, my mom's ears began searching for his voice and trying to remember where she had heard it before. "I am embarrassed to say this but, almost 20 years ago I used to call your apartment in Chicago and leave threatening messages." We were both stunned. My mother could not remember when the calls had stopped but now she remembered his voice. The apartment. The late night calls. Their naiveté as recent arrivals.

"My name is Maqbool," he continued, "and I am the nephew of Mrs. Haq. Do you remember her? She lived down the hallway from you in that building on Kedzie. Well, my aunt really wanted me to move into that apartment of yours so I could be near her and Sadiya. To help out. But she knew that you would not leave since you were pregnant at that time. So she had me make those calls. To scare you, so you would leave the apartment. I feel really bad about it now but I was just 15 at that time and I had just come from Pakistan. So I did what my aunt asked me to do. You know how she was." Then he chuckled. Neither one of us spoke. We just stared at this man for a few minutes, then walked away. It was the last time I would think about Mrs. Haq and the way she stared at me with those hazel eyes of hers. The same hazel eyes Sadiya possessed. The eyes I would no longer covet.

DOING THE WOOL

In Andalusia one Ramadan, Medina Tenour Whiteman tries a new lifestyle tending sheep, and deepens her connection with God in the process.

MEDINA TENOUR WHITEMAN

MEDINA TENOUR WHITEMAN is a British-American Muslim writer, poet and singer based near Granada in Spain. She is the author of the poetry collection *Love is a Traveller and We Are Its Path* (Ecstatic Exchange, 2016), *Huma's Travel Guide to Islamic Spain* (2016), and *The Invisible Muslim: Journeys Through Whiteness and Islam* (Hurst, 2020). Her work has appeared on *BBC Radio, Critical Muslim, Sacred Footsteps*, and other international platforms, as well as being anthologized in *A Kaleidoscope of Stories* by Lote Tree Press. She is cofounder of the Muslim Writers' Salon and regularly holds creative writing workshops online and in person.

I found the first one slumped on the floor in the storeroom by the water reservoir, her neck twisted at an awkward angle, her yellow eyes with their slotted cuttlefish pupils open, gathering dust.

Usually, as the sun began to set, the sheep trotted of their own accord to the barn, which was cobbled together from old doors, wooden pallets and bed frames, roofed with corrugated iron. This evening, one was missing.

It was August 2012, south of Granada in Andalusia, Spain, and temperatures were soaring to 46°C. The sheep hadn't been sheared for two years, and wore their death sentence in thick, butter-yellow coats. We were housesitting a cortijo, a country house with a slate patio (perfect for scalding bare feet) with a gnarled wisteria over one end, set in one corner of a flat piece of land 7000 square meters in size. This could only be irrigated using a well, so we'd been piping the water sparingly to the young olive trees. Now the land in between had become a blond, flammable expanse of dry grass that crackled constantly with crickets. Around the borders there was a thorny lemon tree, a pineapple guava tree with fragrant, edible flowers, a loquat tree, some sour grapevines, skinny psychedelic cacti and pomegranates, their scandalous red flowers swelling as they fructified. A few walnut trees provided shade. Otherwise, the plot was a huge, terrestrial frying pan, slowly sautéing the sheep alive.

The owner of the flock, an elderly German man whom I will call Augustine, had driven them down from Germany to Spain in the boot of his car as lambs. But after being diagnosed with Alzheimer's, he had found it too challenging to look after them alone. The ram had butted him and knocked him over; wild dogs had broken through the fence and turned the barn into a bloodbath. With his night blindness, Augustine hadn't been able to fend them off.

That's where we came in.

Ali and I were newlyweds. I had divorced only a few months prior and was bringing two kids who'd recently turned four and two. I'd needed to get out of the house my ex-husband had built. It was a marvel of green architecture, complete with hemp bricks and burnished lime plaster pigmented with yellow earth dug out of a nearby cliff. But its arches followed the exact curve of the misery that still woke me up some nights like a jinn pressing into my throat. The few years we'd lived in that lovely house had marked my lowest point, when I started to believe that if I were to disappear, everyone would be better off.

It was no place to begin a new relationship; it was haunted with old versions of me.

Augustine knew the man my new husband had been housesitting for and had asked us to look after his cortijo and flock. No rent, just an exchange of labor. The farming life had a salt-of-the-earth allure for me. Perhaps, I thought, this was where I would crawl out of my spoiled Western persona, so constricting in its self-consciousness and fragility, my mind clarified with good, honest graft. I was convinced that we modern humans were disastrously disconnected from the sources of the things we consumed, erasing millennia of human experiences that were coded into our genes as surely as those crinkly filaments of wool were spun into the fabrics we'd depended upon for our survival. Not only did this leave us with an acute sense of alienation, surely contributing to our avalanche of mental health problems, but it also allowed for all manner of abuses, both of workers and of natural resources, in which our present economic model is so deeply entrenched.

So, engaging with these ancient practices in a hands-on way would surely return me to a pre-industrial idyll, my pallid English face flushed to a wholesome rouge, my monkey mind finally tamed. Here I might finally become, like the Sufis whose words I'd been reading all my life, "the child of the Present."

Another reason for settling in this area was that a good number of Muslims who lived here belonged to Sufi tariqas. Many of them had been advised by their spiritual teachers to go back to the land, and now tended olive groves, fruit orchards, beehives, horses, donkeys and herds of goats and sheep. This landscape had been the last place that the Muslims of Al-Andalus lived, apparently in harmony with the natural world. Rafts of Andalusi poems, songs and philosophical treatises exalt Creation as a stage for contemplating the Divine.

What still delights me about this approach is that a physical act of the humblest dimensions takes on extraordinary dimensions of meaning—working with wool being one of the most significant of them to me. Both of my grandmothers taught me to knit, and my mother to crochet; much later, my sister would gift me a drop spindle. The transformation of a heap of matted, burred fibers into yarn, and its further transformation into pliant, warm textiles still strikes me as nothing short of alchemical. Even more mesmerizing is frogging, in which you pull out lines of "live" knitting into mounds of telephone wire curls. Dampening them and hanging them to dry, the crimped shapes slowly release, like mermaid's hair.

The spiritual path I had been born into also took its very name from this humble fiber. Tasawwuf, anglicized as Sufism, is an enigmatic term that hints at suf, or wool, probably because the woolen cloak was a mark of asceticism and nonattachment to the dunya, the transient world. It may also refer to safa, or purity, itself linguistically related to wool, perhaps through the association of lambs with innocence. There are Sufis who describe the process of felting wool as a metaphor for the individual being united with the Divine, each individual thread woven into a state of oneness—hence the tall, felted hats of the Mevlevi dervishes.

Sufis have not been the only ones keen to return to a naturally spiritualized way of life in this valley. It has drawn throngs of hippies, organic farmers, permaculturists, and burnt-out city folks, who set up flea markets, health food shops, several attempts at alternative currencies, a home birth midwives collective, musical groups, theater groups, alternative schools, and clinics for every imaginable therapy. With copious quantities of home-grown marijuana—organic, of course. Entrepreneurial folks make jewelry, shoes, soap, clothes, and wooden spoons for sale or trade. I once saw a poster requesting space to park a van where a middle-aged American psychic could paint the feline interdimensional visitors he received, in exchange for acupressure sessions.

As entertaining as these observations could be, I felt people here might actually be on to something. A rejection of capitalist materialism and cynicism; the pursuit of healing and whole(some)ness, freedom to think outside the box, to make art and babies, and remember our original integration into Nature. Building a society in which no-one falls through the net.

This was how I came to be straddling a ewe, face to tail, laying bodily along her well-padded back, staring at close range at a rear end ochred in a perpetual bloom of poo. As they came one by one into the milking area of the barn, barging past their sisters eager for that extra ration of oats, I had to tie one of their back legs to a post, loosely knotting it so as not to hurt them.

Then came the slippery part. My hands lubricated with Vaseline, I gave the hot, heavy udders a gentle massage, and then pinched the top of the teat between thumb and first finger, trapping a small amount of milk inside it. Firmly closing each finger successively, ending with the pinkie, the trapped milk was squeezed out through the orifice at the bottom. It made a satisfying squirting noise against the wall of the bucket.

***

That year Ramadan fell in August. My parents picked up my son to go to iftar at our local mosque, for the fast breaking and nightly festivities that continue all through the month. Kids race giddily around in the starlit gardens while adults grow euphoric as their veins are newly flushed with dates, watermelon and coffee.

Usually I would give the sheep their own iftar of alfalfa, oats and water at sundown, and enclose them safely inside the barn. But that evening, I'd tried to count them up and kept reaching the wrong number. My little daughter was yawning and rubbing her eyes, dinnerless but determined to "help" me. In that peculiar, panicky delirium only experienced in the last few minutes of a Ramadan fast when there are still urgent things to be done, I ran up and down the hectare of land looking for the lost lamb, feeling a little like Hajar, the wife of Abraham, seeking water in the Meccan desert for her baby Ismail.

I was holding down the fort. My husband was away cooking falafels at a trance festival in Portugal. I had to keep it together.

Of course, I didn't. In a mad flap I tried to find the right course of action. I rang Augustine to tell him a sheep was missing. He averred that there wasn't anything to do but wait for morning.

After discovering her motionless body by the reservoir, I was faced with the task of what to do with it. I asked some friends to come and bury her. Being faced with a dead animal roughly as large as a small adult is an experience to sober the most enthusiastic back-to-the-lander. I had been responsible for her and failed. Dyed-in-the-wool farmer I was not.

After the guilt and the grief came the vexation. Why had Augustine left us with his sheep when we had zero experience in shepherding? Why had we been so optimistic as to take on this ambitious task? Was it the exhilaration of starting a new life together, or a burst of motivation to rectify our woeful lack of self-sufficiency skills? Did we think that sheep farming was something that any idiot could do? Or was it meant to be a shortcut back to our fitrah, the innate human sense of God-consciousness described in Islamic sources?

I wondered, too, about this crazed attempt at fasting, alone, in one of the hottest summers I'd ever experienced, while also trying to keep my attention on eight sheep and two small children. Ali insisted that mothers were already in service, which was equivalent to worship. Did I feel I still had something to prove? Or was attempting to recreate a bucolic scene from Al-Andalus my way of reconnecting to a faith community from which I had at times felt distant?

***

It's not hard to see how a sheep, capable of producing meat, dairy products and fibers to keep our hard-bitten ancestors warm with clothes, bedding and even tent cloth, might be exalted to mythological status. From the Sumerian shepherdess-goddess Duttur to the Ancient Egyptian shepherd-god Khnum, believed to form human bodies from clay and place them in the womb, since the birth of civilization sheep have been associated with fertility and abundance. For anyone who has walked along the razor edges of survival, abundance must surely be linked to goodness: in Chinese mythology, sheep are associated with filial piety, while the characters for "good" (shàn, 善) and "beautiful" (měi, 美) are based on the pictogram for sheep, 羊. I am reminded of one of the words for "beautiful" in Arabic, جميل (jameel), which is derived from the same root as the word for "camel", جمل (jamal).

I wonder how our ideas of goodness and beauty might be derived from our new symbols of value: the purring sleekness of a powerful car, the effortless efficiency of a smartphone, or the understated elegance of a truly expensive suit. Since our iconic embodiments of wealth are no longer alive, our relationships with them seem to me somewhat drier; though the word "brand" originates from the marks humans used to stamp livestock as their own, the symbols we honor today are a far cry from a living, breathing companion, born slippery and bleating, capable of death.

In the Abrahamic religions, lambs have come to signify more than simply fertility or material abundance (and hence beauty and goodness), but rather innocence and purity, hence the Lamb of God, whose holy mother is deemed protectress of sheep. In the Qur'anic telling of the story of Abraham, after seeing himself sacrificing his son Ismail in a dream, he consults with Ismail, who agrees that it represents his father doing so and is willing to be sacrificed. At zero hour, Abraham is told by

God that this was a test, and that he should slaughter a sheep instead, an act commemorated each year by Muslims during Hajj celebrations.

The Prophet Muhammad was raised from birth by a widow named Halima, who is said to have been the poorest member of a village of shepherds. As per the tradition of the Arabs of Mecca, babies were given to wet nurses in the mountains, as they believed the air was cleaner and babies would be stronger. An orphan, Muhammad was taken in by Halima, whose sheep were thin and had almost no milk; when he arrived, their udders miraculously filled.

The first time I milked a ewe, I had a rush of what I imagined to be a primordial astonishment, that grass should, unfathomably, be turned to milk inside a sheep's living body. Here was a trade as old as the prophets, as old as our earliest sedentary ancestors—producing milk for yogurt and cheese, to feed myself and my family. But when I looked out across the field and saw a ewe munching dry grass with a benign, vacant stare, turning her head to look at me with her ears out at comical angles, I couldn't help but laugh at her goofy appearance. I suppose the privilege of not depending on them for my survival tempered my reverence.

***

My turn as sheep-sitter was already looking pretty bad when a few nights later, just as I'd just got my children to sleep, I heard a tremendous clattering and baa-ing going on in the barn. In my striped pajamas and flip-flops, with a feeble bicycle lamp in hand and a jangle of trepidation in my chest, I crept out in the dusk to the barn.

I was not prepared for what confronted me. One of the lambs, really a full-grown ewe, was lying on her side, running madly, her feet stretching out horizontally. Her hooves scraped the wooden side of the barn in a futile gallop. She ground her teeth, foam frothed at the side of her mouth, and her head was thrown back, eyes swiveling in white-edged terror.

Stunned, but strangely pragmatic, I went back to the house in search of Bach's Rescue Remedy—a flower essence medicine, the only thing I could think of that might soothe her, as it has done a hundred times on my tantruming kids. I managed to get a few drops into her open mouth; the gallops started coming in waves, interspersed with peaceful lulls during which she panted in a paralyzed trance.

I also did the other thing that often came to mind when trying to calm my children, and softly sang the last few chapters of Qur'an, in a lullaby voice. Slowly the clopping of her hooves became less insistent, the pauses for breath more protracted.

Squatting down in the straw-strewn barn, watching as the movement of her legs gradually slowed to a canter, then a walk, I was reminded of an experiment on cats in which scientists removed the part of the brain responsible for paralyzing the body during REM sleep. Sleeping cats were filmed carrying out all the actions they were obviously dreaming about—running, biting, hunting. The thought crossed my mind, as I stroked her forehead: is she dreaming? Or is she dying? The dim atmosphere of the scene, musty with dung and hay, struck me as strangely calm, prehistoric, Biblical. The other sheep were relaxed now that their shepherdess was there (I appreciated their confidence in me, as ill-placed as it was) and carried on blithely munching their alfalfa.

Meanwhile, the ewe's legs became stiffer and stiffer. There's a Spanish expression for dying: 'estirar la pata' (literally, to stretch out one's leg). In my tangled mental web of Spanglish, I remembered our own expression for the same thing: 'to kick the bucket'. Perhaps both phrases were born in a barn, with a disconcerted shepherd(ess) witnessing this very scene.

It was abundantly clear now that the ewe was dying. The first death had prepared me somewhat, though I'd naively thought it was a fluke. A powerful sense of peace descended on us. In my tearful, sleep-deprived, Ramadan state I felt almost as though I was witnessing the birth of Jesus, in a barn that had landed on the wrong continent in a malfunctioning time machine. And I recalled the words of the Prophet Muhammad, peace be upon him, that a sheep sees the gates of Paradise when it is sacrificed, which is why it begins to run.

Eventually she fell completely still. The peculiarity of the experience ebbed to the sort of stoical acceptance worthy of a weather-beaten peasant farmer, or even, perhaps, of a sheep. Barns are places of feeding, sleeping, mating, lambing, milking, and now, dying. Two thresholds, opposite ends of a roll of film, only double-exposed.

***

A few evenings later, I was dismayed, though better prepared, to see another lamb wobble dangerously on his feet as he came down to the barn, collapsing as he arrived. I grabbed him under the belly and hoisted him into the shed, but he stood there in a daze, not rooting around in the boxes of hay as usual.

The kids were picked up by their dad that evening. I sprang into action, making phone calls and racing into town to find rehydration salts. En route I co-opted a friend who obligingly came down with her son at 11 pm to help lift the lamb's head up while I squeezed a syringe of liquid down its throat. Over a liter went down in 40 ml doses, sometimes trickling out straight away as he had lost the strength to swallow. His teeth chattered against the plastic of the syringe; fever had already set in. He lolled his head back, panting, dragging his legs back and forth across the grass, making straw angels in the dirt.

At midnight we all withdrew. There was nothing else to do, short of sleeping on the manure-trampled earth beside the barn to keep watch over him. I'm afraid I couldn't muster up the saintliness for that.

As soon as I woke up the next morning, I went over to check on him. He was exactly where I'd left him, immobile, open eyes dusty and frozen, his coat of wool coated in cold dew. The vet would tell us later it was septicemia.

In the week since the second sheep had died, we'd had the rest of the flock chipped and tagged. We couldn't simply bury the lamb we'd affectionately named Rambino; the body had to be officially removed.

Andalusian bureaucracy being phlegmatic at best, actively callous at worst, and non-existent in August, two days after his death the carcass lay under an old plastic window blind on the edge of the land, rotting in the stifling heat. We couldn't go outside for five days. It was a miracle the campsite next door didn't complain of the stench. When the truck finally arrived to take his cadaver away, all that was left of him was a skull, legs, and a wooly pelt.

The time had long passed for us to call on professional help. The sheep were sold to a stumpy, gnomic shepherd from up the mountain, Ricardo, who came down to shear the remaining ewes. This, too, proved to be a task that required more skill than I was prepared for, as sheep do not recognize the health benefit of being shorn and tend to avoid it however possible. Hanging onto the collar of a particularly brawny ewe, Ricardo was dragged for several meters across the dry grass. Finally managing to overpower her, he tied three legs together with repurposed plastic twine to keep her still. Tie all four legs together, he explained, and they would suffocate.

Using my kitchen and sewing scissors, we snipped at each dense, two-inch thick layer of wool encrusted with mud and shit. For an hour and a half, we bantered about drugs and divorce and farming and brain tumors, turning the bewildered sheep over gently and snipping until my hands blistered. Afterwards I washed the greenish lanolin off the scissor blades.

Shearing, I started thinking, is a physical embodiment of letting go of the accretions of ourselves, the burrs and thorns we pick up, the colors that life paints on us. It's like a rebirth. A lost sheep was recently discovered in Australia after wandering for 10 years in the bush, covered by 200 pounds of his own matted wool. He almost couldn't see out from under it. This is how we go, in our most sheeplike states, burdened with what has grown out of ourselves for protection and warmth, but which we don't need forever.

After the shearing was done, I took a cold shower—the boiler was broken—and floated to the market, drifting elatedly uphill. Weightless, as though I was the one who'd been shorn. As inept as I had been as a shepherdess, it had certainly been one way to learn the limits of my capabilities; one friend who came to visit not long after saw me chase away a group of wild dogs, and was shocked that it hadn't frightened me. That wasn't the city girl who'd arrived only a few years before.

In this traditional agricultural community, while many animals are well cared for, there is also the sense that their mortality is not anathema. Aside from the obvious instances of slaughtering animals for meat, I've heard of campesinos drowning kittens in the river, presumably avoiding the cost of sterilizing cats. At a birthday party, my daughter and her young friends stumbled across a goatherd slitting open the belly of a kid by the roadside. It's a long way from pampered city pets being cremated and turned into diamonds.

Do we lose our tenderness when faced, as farmers so often are, with the inexorable deaths of the creatures under our care? Or does our experience of the everyday expand, inviting death close enough for it to shed its fearsome halo? The lives of these sheep, with blue-misted mountains for a background petalled with bougainvillea, were worlds away from those living en masse in cramped commercial dairy farms. Here life and death are surely experienced with greater intimacy and compassion, with all their textures and nourishments and odors.

Did this episode bring me closer to a primordial way of being, gloriously communing with nature in all its sacred abundances, its healing mundanity? If I were to tease out some thread from it, a yarn to spin for my grandkids, could I say it brought me closer to the humble serenity of prophets and saints?

That sounds, ironically, too pretentious. Since moving to town we have a smaller garden, with lower-maintenance plant and animal companions. I haven't heard the call of shepherdessing for a while. But sometimes, while setting the timer on my electric yogurt-maker, I get a frisson of self-sufficiency, a whiff of the dairy and its earthy embodied wisdom. That'll have to do for now.

ZUMURRUD

Hanan al-Shaykh visits a friend in Beirut whose precious African gray parrot has been kidnapped. Together, they reminisce about their comical communion with the talking bird.

HANAN AL-SHAYKH

HANAN AL-SHAYKH is the author of seven novels, including *The Story of Zahra, Women of Sand & Myrrh, Beirut Blues, Only in London*, as well as a collection of stories, *I Sweep the Sun off Rooftops*, and the much praised memoir on her mother's life, *The Locust and the Bird*. She has written two plays, *Dark Afternoon Tea* and *Paper Husband*, and published *One Thousand and One Nights*, an adaptation of some of the stories from the legendary *Alf Layla Wa Layla – The Arabian Nights*. Her novel, *The Occasional Virgin*, was published by Bloomsbury (2018), and was named an Observer Book of the Year. Her latest book *The Eye of the Peacock* (2023), is currently available in Arabic. Her work has been translated into 28 languages. She currently lives in London.

This story was translated by **CATHERINE COBHAM**, whose bio appears on page 563.

I rushed to that room where nobody wanted to live, not even cockroaches, searching for my friend. They said she'd lost her mind after her parrot, Zumurrud, was kidnapped. She'd abandoned her beautiful flat in the building owned by her father and moved to live here so she could be just a few steps away from the shops selling birds and domestic animals, in the hope that whoever had snatched her parrot would come here to sell the bird. She had made the shop owners promise to buy the parrot with no haggling and no questions asked.

Samia opened the door and hugged me, shouting, "Thank god you're safe, my dear Hanan. Welcome to Beirut. How lucky I am that you met Amal on the plane!" She embraced me again and the sight of her laughing face convinced me that the reports I'd heard were exaggerated: she hadn't lost her mind and, what's more, the room was clean, even if it didn't have a proper window and looked out onto concrete walls, rather than a street or trees, so it was a little like being in prison. As if Samia could hear the whirring of my thoughts, she suddenly burst into tears, then controlled herself and sat down in front of the same birdcage that had been in Los Angeles, though it was now empty. Artificial flowers were entwined around its metal bars, and food and water containers stood empty inside it. It looked lonely, as if it was mourning Zumurrud. Samia burst into tears once more."If only we hadn't come back from Los Angeles. Do you still remember, Hanan, when you visited us there? Life was fantastic, and now the bastards have kidnapped Zumurrud."

I heard Samia's mother's voice raised in protest. "What? Our life in Los Angeles was fantastic? My daughter, have you forgotten how we used to die a thousand deaths when we heard the news of the killing and fighting in Lebanon? Welcome, welcome, Hanan!"

Samia's mother appeared from the corridor, carrying a tray laden with glasses of mulberry juice, which she placed on the table in front of us. I stood up and embraced her cautiously, since she looked really thin, ready to crumble to pieces in front of me. I felt as if my long absence from her and Samia—around ten years—had erected a wall between us.

She asked after my husband, son and daughter, wondered if I still liked living in cold London and why I didn't visit Lebanon more than once a year.

"Do you remember, Hanan?" interrupted Samia, to prevent her mother asking more questions. "Do you remember Zumurrud?"

"Who could forget Zumurrud? Your spoiled daughter."

But Samia didn't appear to be listening to me, as she was focused on opening a biscuit tin, inside which was an untidy heap of papers. She took out a card and skimmed over the words, muttering to herself until her voice suddenly grew louder. "I've fallen in love with Zumurrud just like you," she read. "Christian Dior must have designed the feathers on her face and chest himself, a lace ruff, for he wanted Zumurrud to be like the old queens of England. The white around her eyes reminds me of Mademoiselle Chanel's two gardenias, and her eyes are two pieces of lime green quartz. And the gray feathers on her body, delicate as the color of cigarette smoke, ensure that her scarlet tail takes us by surprise and draws us to examine it at length."

I wanted to laugh at this exaggerated description of mine. I'd written this card to thank Samia for her hospitality while I was in Los Angeles during a US book tour. I had been surprised to see my friend and her mother in the audience, and a feeling of warmth and affection had swept over me, then sheer happiness, and we'd agreed that I'd visit them the following day. The moment I entered Samia's flat it was as if I'd walked into a theater, where the only actor on stage was the parrot. Perched on the metal bars of her cage, she changed accents as she answered the phone. "Hallo, hallo, the line's busy, dear," then switched to imitating the whirr of the sewing machine, gesturing with her head, lowering it and raising it, moving from one side to the other, going in and out of the cage. Suddenly she was mimicking someone sipping hot tea. "A little honey, please," then yelling, "Mama Samia, Mama Samia, I need the toilet!"

Samia hurried towards her, Zumurrud jumped from the bars of the cage onto her shoulder, and the two of them went into the bathroom. I followed them: Samia held Zumurrud under her wings, or her armpits, over the lavatory, and as soon as she had peed, Samia shouted, "Bravo! Well done, you clever girl." She held a piece of biscuit up to Zumurrud's beak, while Zumurrud continued to repeat "Bravo, bravo, clever girl," hoping for a second or third piece of biscuit, until finally the doorbell rang and Zumurrud called out, "How are our neighbors today?" When Samia opened the door, a Lebanese woman entered, choking with laughter. "I heard her, I heard her!" The woman then turned to Samia's mother and asked, "How are our neighbors today?"

Samia introduced me to the neighbor, Violette, who joined us to watch Zumurrud's performance. Violette was just asking me whether I lived here in Los Angeles, when Zumurrud's voice drowned her out, imitating a police siren, then an ambulance, then the ringing of a phone. She hopped from the bars of the cage onto a wooden perch nearby, trying to interrupt our conversation, while Samia told us—when I asked her whatever had made her think of buying a parrot—that she'd wanted to help her mother feel less isolated.

"We went to buy a canary and came home with Madame Zumurrud."

"It's fate, my daughter," interrupted her mother. "Pure fate."

The two of them were in a shop that sold pet birds: big birds and little birds of all colors, shapes and varieties, who twittered, shrieked and jumped around in their cages. Samia's mother almost tripped on a step and cried out, "My god, what's happening to me?" and a voice came back to her like an echo. "My god, what's happening to me?" Their astonishment turned to laughter and admiration, and a sudden rush of love for the parrot who'd imitated Samia's mother. The shop assistant asked them what language they were speaking. "That's the first time this parrot's imitated Arabic," commented the shopkeeper. "But what do you think? Did she do well?"

"One hundred per cent," replied Samia. They learned she was an African gray parrot, and that these parrots live till they're seventy, maybe a hundred years old. Hearing this, the two women immediately paid a thousand dollars, cash down.

"My god, who's going to look after her when we're dead?"

"Don't worry, Mama. I'll try my best to live to a hundred for the sake of Madame Zumurrud."

The sound of Zumurrud imitating the bubbling of the shisha made us laugh again, especially when she called out in the voice of Samia's mother. "Come on, daughter, bring more hot coals. Ayyy, how good this tobacco is!"

I still remember how Samia's mother stood up and asked us to excuse her, and how Zumurrud imitated the squeak of the door. Then a few moments later, as Samia's mother went into her room, the call to afternoon prayer rose up in the flat. "Allahu akbar, Allahu akbar." The muezzin was Zumurrud, who paid no attention to my astonished shriek, but carried on with the call to prayer, bowing her head to right and left. When she cleared her throat and coughed, Samia and Violette dissolved into helpless laughter that grew louder as Zumurrud finished her prayer by imitating the crackle of the microphone.

We all took refuge in silence, delighting in it. Peace filled my mind and heart. No, it wasn't the words of the call to prayer that comforted me, but our mute dialogue with ourselves. Our return, we four, Violette the Christian and we three Muslims, to our country when it was safe, and when it disregarded the barriers between the religions that had now transformed it into a hotbed of militias and opposing fronts fighting one another, destroying daily life and forcing us to migrate from one area to another, before spewing us out of Lebanon as if we were dirty sea foam. Just because we didn't want any part in this bloody war.

The call to prayer, not on a human tongue but on an impartial parrot's tongue, succeeded in moving us and arousing our longing for our past selves in a way that no other call could, restoring us to that beautiful necklace whose beads the war had unstrung and scattered far and wide to different parts of the globe.

"Bravo, Zumurrud," called Samia, and told me that her mother had brought a cassette recording of the call to prayer from Lebanon to Los Angeles, so Zumurrud had heard it day in and day out and learned it by heart. "The weird thing is that when Zumurrud sees Mama get up and go towards the bathroom, she knows it's time for the afternoon prayer."

I stood up, utterly amazed by the bird and full of affection for her, wanting to be close to this miracle. In a flash, she moved from the bars of the cage to the long wooden perch and from there to the table where she came to a halt. But Samia scolded her and ordered her back into the cage, telling her she should respect guests like me. As soon as the parrot had obeyed her orders, Samia said to me, "That wretched parrot was really keen to bite you, Hanan! She bites hard."

"But I haven't done anything to make her want to punish me. I didn't eat her food."

We all laughed. "She's worried that you'll stay too long and I'll be late taking her to Venice Beach. She loves eating pizza there and flirting with her admirers."

Zumurrud threw me a look full of venom and then collapsed in the bottom of the cage, motionless, as if unconscious. "See, everyone! Look, Hanan, see how naughty she is, the little bitch. Madame is playing dead!"

I approached the cage where Zumurrud was lying on her back without stirring.

"Who wants to eat baked beans? Poor Zumurrud, she's dead so she can't have any."

At this point Zumurrud got to her feet and shouted, "Baked beans. Yay! Yummy!"

"You want some? Not a single bean for you unless you say sorry to Hanan. Go on, say 'I'm sorry, Tante Hanan'."

"I'm sorry, Tante Hanan."

Samia opened a small tin of baked beans and offered a spoonful to Zumurrud, who took the spoon in her claws and raised it to her mouth. "A bit more, please," she shouted once she was back in her cage. When Samia refused, Zumurrud started chattering again and imitating Samia's mother. She coughed violently and went through the actions of spitting out phlegm, then gave a sigh of relief and said, "Oh my dear, oh my god. Now I feel better, oh god!"

***

I see the same sheet that used to cover Zumurrud's cage at night in Los Angeles, now folded next to the abandoned cage, which looked covered anyway now that Zumurrud was gone. Neither the sound of car horns nor the street noise managed to inject life into this melancholy place.

"I'm going crazy, Hanan. Believe me, I'm going crazy. I took her on my shoulder as usual when we went to buy manoushe flatbread with zaatar and cheese. We were waiting our turn when someone came too close to Zumurrud and my darling got scared and flew off. I chased after her and a guy who knows us both rushed to help me, but the damned taxi driver was too quick for us. He grabbed her, put her in the boot of his car and drove off. Another boy tried to follow him on his motorbike, but it was no use. If only I'd clipped her wings. O Lord, where is she? Where are you, Zumurrud? I hear her calling me night and day. There's not a wall left where I haven't stuck her picture and an announcement about her kidnapping. Me and my friends have distributed leaflets in houses and offices, saying there's a reward for whoever brings her back, and of course I've added useful information about her, like the fact that she's microchipped, she doesn't like sunflower seeds and has a broken finger that's a bit red..." Samia sighs and stops talking, as if she's about to burst into tears.

"Lots of people have been in touch with me, even from Syria. Yes, I believed that somebody had smuggled her into

Syria and somebody else wanted to return her to me. I went to Aleppo but didn't find anyone waiting for me in the place we'd arranged. It seems they either wanted money or to make fun of me and waste my time. Honestly, I hated the world, I hated the house because every corner of it reminded me of Zumurrud, and when I couldn't stop crying I moved with my mother to this flat. You know, for five months, since she disappeared, I haven't known real deep, peaceful sleep. I lie down on the sofa with my phone and handbag next to me so that if someone finds her and contacts me I can be up and out in a flash. You know, I wish we were still in Los Angeles and I hadn't believed that the war was over and everything had settled down."

Samia's mother got up muttering. "There is no power or strength save in God almighty." Then she came back with a cell phone in her hand, from which Zumurrud's voice sang out, this time imitating Samia's soulful, expressive, kind voice rather than the throat clearing and coughing of the muezzin that the parrot had imitated in Los Angeles.

I imagine her neck feathers quivering as she moves her head up and down in time with the melody, her beak curving over her mouth, forming a question mark. On this occasion her call to prayer takes me to our quarter of Beirut, to my childhood as I played there among the houses and gardens, on the roof of our house. Everything surrounded me with warmth then, even the washing hanging out to dry on the line. When the muezzin's voice rose up without the aid of a microphone, peace and calm suddenly descended and the sound of the call to prayer dominated the other sounds around me, even the voices thronging inside me. I used to feel that the muezzin's voice absorbed the burning heat of the sun, and it no longer poured its cup of anger over us, but rather stroked us with gentle affection. It amazed me that everybody listened to one call, which reassured them and convinced them they were all in the same boat. The whole quarter took a deep breath, filling its chest with air, and we children carried on with our games, but calmly, with no screaming or shouting. Then we would all rush into the neighbor's garden: she kept hens, a rooster and some little chicks, and we were told these chicks used to start praying the moment they heard the call to prayer. We would watch them as they lowered their heads to drink water and then raised them to the sky, and we would sing to them:

"Little chicks—cluck cluck—how sweet—cluck cluck
They gather round their mother all content—cluck cluck
They drink water—cluck cluck
they say 'kha!'—cluck cluck
They raise their faces to the sky and
thank their Lord—cluck cluck."

Samia's mother brings me back to the melancholy room. "My daughter, Hanan, you have to convince Samia that Zumurrud still lives among us. When she recites the call to prayer she enters the hearts of all who hear her and serenity reigns in these hearts. Who knows? Maybe it's her fate to leave us so she can make the call to prayer to many people, not just to us, and all those people will remember their Creator."

To myself I added: *And so that we ask our minds, that drift and hover and move between so many thoughts, to settle and reflect and turn inwards and shut out the world and be still, even if it's only for a moment.*

I said goodbye to Samia and her mother. Samia laughed and as she closed the door said, "I hope Zumurrud is living in a handsome young man's house now. She always loved young men, loved them a lot."

BIG LALEH, LITTLE LALEH

Based in post-revolutionary Iran, Shokouh Moghimi tells a haunting coming-of-age tale about self-harm and sibling love that reveals how loyalty can turn to loathing and back again.

SHOKOUH MOGHIMI

SHOKOUH MOGHIMI is a poet, journalist and documentarian. She has written and created videos for several newspapers and journals in Iran as well as Lebanon. Her first collection of poetry won a number of Iran's prestigious literary awards, including Best First Book Award.

This story was translated by **SALAR ABDOH**, whose bio appears on page 563.

Everyone thought Laleh was majnoona—crazy, mad, not quite right in the head. Everyone, that is, except our father, Baba, and me. They wondered why my older sister always carried a book in her hand and would never quit reading. "Why is she always alone?" they'd ask. "Why is she always muttering things to herself and to the walls?"

I was five when Laleh's "madness" started to cause tensions in the house. She was a decade older, and it seemed like besides Baba, the whole world wanted to convince me to steer clear of Laleh or else her spirit of strangeness would enter my body too. But how could I stay away when in our household everyone was already calling me "Little Laleh"? We looked too much alike.

I loved it when "Big Laleh" would read from her books of poetry to me, even if I understood almost nothing of what she read. Other times, when she strolled by herself in the dark maze of our basement and held conversations with invisible beings, I would quietly follow and watch her. I was completely fascinated by Big Laleh.

The neighborhood had its share of the mad. Often they'd hide behind the ubiquitous myrtus trees and suddenly jump at you making faces, or they'd find the fattest lizards they could find in our boiling hot southern province and throw them at passing cars. Whenever our mothers were fed up with us, they'd threaten to hand us over to someone like Reza Salaki or Crazy Ferdows.

But Laleh, my Laleh, was not like any of these people. She was quiet. So what if she gazed at the sky rather than watch where she was going when she walked? She wasn't bothering anybody.

Mama would say, "Laleh's strangeness comes from her childhood fevers when Saddam was bombing the city." Whenever I heard her say this, I wanted to experience Laleh's fevers. Apparently I'd had a lot of fevers too at some point. I always imagined a black-clad woman associated with those fevers. Fevers made me happy, because I could then pretend I was becoming more and more like Big Laleh.

Our grandmother who hailed from Bushehr, a city even further south on the Gulf, was certain that the jinns had made a nest in Laleh's mind and body. "The mad see the devil," she'd say, "the majnoon see the jinns. Laleh talks to the jinns because the jinns want a sacrifice from us. We have to take this girl to Mamazar, the exorcist."

Remarks like this turned Laleh more and more solitary and inward. Her only friends remained Baba and me. Baba couldn't always be around though. He worked for the National Oil Company and was often gone on assignment. When he was around, that was the best of times for me, because then I could ride on the back of Laleh's bicycle without anyone giving me a hard time. We'd ride by the Karun, the beloved river that split our city, Ahvaz, in half, and I would wave at the water buffaloes wading about on the other side. Laleh and I had another name for the river too; we called it Naneh, a more rustic word for Mother. Laleh would always say, "If it wasn't for Naneh, Ahvaz would have been done for during the war. Naneh washed all the filth of the war away. That's why we can still breathe here." When she said these things, I'd let go of her on the back of the bicycle and breathe as deeply as I could. The river was life. She'd add, "Do you know why people throw themselves off the White Bridge into Naneh's waters? Because they know there's nowhere safer than her embrace."

One day I found a bloody shawl among Laleh's things. It was the first year I was going to school and I was more curious about my older sister than ever. I'd search through her stuff all the time. The sight of that blood terrified me. But I kept my mouth shut, even when I finally realized she'd tried to cut her wrist. Months later, Laleh was caught having poured gasoline all over her clothes. Our mother would not stop crying while Laleh kept asking for forgiveness. This episode caused the jinns to retreat for a while and there was some calm for a change.

Then one day leading up to the Persian new year, our mother took us girls shopping for new fabric at the bazaar so she could sew us dresses from the designs periodically sent to her from Kuwait. I loved listening for the different accents in our melting pot of a city and whispering folks' origins back to Laleh: "The fava bean merchant is from Dezful, the incense seller is Arab, the flower guy is Persian, the one hawking dates is from Behbahan, and the samanu dealer has to be a Lor. Am I right?"

We had just passed through the section mostly run by ancient Arab women who sold bras and women's underwear. Inside the fabric shop our mother began picking out cloth and haggling in her broken Arabic with "Uncle Adel." Laleh stood apart, her usual disconnected self, while my other sister and I remained mesmerized by all that sequined fabric with the gold threads lining them. Mama's sudden screams made me jump. Laleh was disappearing in the throng outside. "Grab her. She's unwell. Don't let her get away!" Laleh was running and Mama was running after her. Mayhem ensued, and all I heard inside the shop was Uncle Adel repeating "majnoona, majnoona" under his breath.

After that episode, the jinns seemed to come to our house with a vengeance. All of Laleh's books and cassettes were confiscated and she was no longer allowed out on the street. Soon she stopped going to school altogether. The only thing I could do was watch her walk barefoot day and night on the steaming hot mosaic of the courtyard without ever exchanging two words with anyone.

On the morning of my 10th birthday the jinns finally broke us. A loud thud made me jump. Our father went to the window and then immediately ran outside. Mama and my brother followed. There she was, Laleh's broken body on that same courtyard mosaic. They tried keeping me from seeing what was going on, but I saw it all—Laleh with cotton balls stuffed in her nose and ears, a piece of cloth also shoved into her mouth. She had done all that to herself and then taken the jump from our rooftop. Was it possible the jinns had really done this to her, as our grandmother always said they would? My eyes automatically went to the rooftop. There was no one there.

***

It was a Friday when this happened. My other sister and I stayed home. I had a lump in my throat, but I was also angry. Mama had promised to bake me a birthday cake. Now my birthday was forgotten. What a birthday gift Laleh had given me! I was resentful. The only good thing that came out of it was that our father stayed put and didn't go on one of his usual assignments for the oil company. I kept thinking: Dad will be back from the hospital and everything will be alright. There were no cell phones back then. We kept waiting for someone to call. No one did. In the afternoon our brother finally showed up. "She's paralyzed."

It took a moment and then I started to laugh and I couldn't stop laughing. From that day on, every time I heard horrible news I would start laughing uncontrollably. In truth, after that day every one of us became majnoon in our own way. It was the madness that turned Baba's hair and Mama's hair utterly gray in no time, and the madness of the silence that blanketed that house so that I could virtually see the jinns of silence, but not of calm, dancing forever after on our walls and ceilings and making faces at me.

Yet it was Laleh's own silence that was more spine-chilling than anything. Her only refrain: "Don't be upset. Before you know it, I'll be up and running again." She had become the very symbol of jonoon, madness, for me. Why did she have to reduce the day of my birth into ashes?

They ended up keeping her in the hospital for three weeks. During that time I barely saw our parents. Once in a while Mama would call and say, "You didn't tell anyone at school about this, did you?" A lot of this had to do with saving face. One's child doesn't just go and throw themselves off a roof. I would come home from school and food would be ready, but no Mama or Baba. They'd leave us dinner and lunch and hurry back to the hospital. Maybe they didn't like me anymore! Maybe all this was because it had happened on my birthday. I wanted them to hug me and tell me it would be alright, but they weren't around.

I withdrew into myself.

Baba sounded like the saddest man on earth when he finally asked me to come with him for a visit at the hospital. At first I wanted to show my bitterness and not go, but I didn't have the heart for it. Laleh's eyes shone when she saw me. She apologized and said a belated happy birthday. I forgave her, but not completely. Not deep down, anyway. Slowly though, once she had returned home, I came to love her as I had before.

Not so, however, with my other sister and my brother. It was as if everything Laleh did, or mostly didn't do, was a bother to them. My brother was convinced no one in the city of Ahvaz would have him for a husband after what had happened in our household, and my sister kept saying that our connections with the larger family were permanently destroyed because of Laleh.

The scolding and rebukes were endless. Every other day my brother would threaten to send Laleh to the asylum if she didn't stop pissing and shitting on herself. Laleh would quietly weep and say nothing. I had no other weapon but to laugh. In the midst of that sick laughter I would try to remind everybody that Laleh's spine had been severed. "You'd piss on yourself too if your spine was gone." I wanted to help her, but didn't know what to do. Her eternal friends, Baba and I, went back to buying her all the books and cassettes we could find so she'd have something to do. I'd sit next to her and ask her to read to me for long hours. "Flower of suffering, read! Read to me."

Meanwhile, Mama had become addicted to medical news. Every day at 9 am and 7:30 pm she'd sit listening to the news and get old. She was waiting for the day the news would tell us they'd found a way to put spines back together. She'd say, "That none of our neighbors heard or saw what happened is a miracle in itself. Now there's sure to be a second miracle and my dear daughter will walk again."

After a few months Laleh was able to gain control of her bladder and bowel movement. Mama and Baba seemed to grow wings from happiness. Was the miracle really happening?

Hope returned to the house. A pair of young doctors came by and made a cast of her feet to make braces. One of the doctors had the strangest last name we'd ever heard, "Birds of Flight." Doctor Birds of Flight! Laleh and I could not stop laughing afterwards. Some weeks later Doctor Birds of Flight and the other doctor returned with their gadget. The first time they stood her up it seemed truly like a miracle. But Laleh got tired quickly and begged them to leave her alone. After a while the contraption disappeared.

On my 11th birthday we all were out of sorts. An entire year had passed since the tragedy. A year during which we hid Laleh from everyone. No one among friends or family had a clue what had happened to her. We'd say things like, "She's shy. She won't leave the house, or even her room."

This secret life was hardly easy in a midsize city like Ahvaz. Our years slowly turned into one long bout of concealment. I could no longer bring friends to the house. Friendships began and ended at school. And at school there were lies after lies that I had to tell my classmates about what a happy family we were. Every time some new pain visited Laleh, we'd spend days at the hospital where I learned to occupy myself in its busy corridors. At least the hospital visits brought Laleh out of the house and I, too, could escape that afflicted place for a while.

At some point I mustered enough courage to go up to that roof. I would take my homework and sit there watching the tall palms and the jujube trees. Those trees had been the last witnesses to Laleh's decision. I'd gaze at what I imagined was what Laleh saw before jumping. The roof was now my refuge. The final place that Laleh actually climbed to on her own two feet. Every day I would imagine Laleh leaping off that roof. I'd imagine invisible hands pushing her off—those jinns. Pushing her and laughing with their hideous opened maws bigger than the roof of the house she fell from.

***

Then Mama slowly gave up hope. My two other siblings wouldn't be found dead walking past Laleh's room. As for Baba, the oil company would not stop sending him on assignments around the country. None of us talked about Laleh. Meanwhile, besides the walls and her jinns, the only other entity Laleh would talk to was me. As soon as I'd get home from school I'd go to her room and make her do stretches so she wouldn't get bedsores. She got bedsores anyway. Her room smelled terrible. But I pretended nothing was wrong and we'd talk about our river.

"Naneh has been asking for you. The migrant birds have arrived too, you know. They fly all over Naneh. I told her you'd be coming to see her on your own two legs any time now."

Laleh listened intently. I told her of the happenings at the bazaar—what the Dezful merchants were up to, what the Arab folk were doing, the scent of incense and the Ameri neighborhood with its brickwork that must have been taken right out of the pages of the *One Thousand and One Nights*. We'd imagine that one day we'd go to Baghdad together and walk through the city gates with the words our Arab neighbor had taught us, "Iftah ya simsim!" I'd describe the majnoon guy who suddenly showed up one day in Kianpars not long after Laleh's fall. People said he'd been a masseur for the national football team before the revolution. He would put henna in his hair and wore mismatched sandals and carried with him a plastic tarp with an assortment of useless knick knacks in it. He spoke to the grass while opening his legs wide as if he were about to start doing warmups. I'd wave at him each time under the bridge and he'd just laugh hysterically and make faces.

My stories made Laleh laugh. She'd say, "You know, every person is majnoon in their own way. I guess the masseur too must have fallen off a bridge." But was the former masseur a jinn or a majnoon? I'd wonder. How could he so easily relax by our river without a care in the world when Laleh had to stay here like this?

***

By the time I turned 14, Laleh's behavior had taken a turn for the worse. She would spend hours staring at the flower patterns on the carpet. Her face changed expressions constantly and she was always mumbling under her breath. I'd find torn up pieces of paper scattered around her mattress. I wasn't sure if she was writing things and then destroying what she'd written. I never asked about it. The same way I never asked her, "Why did you kill yourself, Laleh? Why did you allow those jinns inside you when Little Laleh loved and cared for you so much?"

Soon her behavior toward me too turned odd. One day she'd be kind, the next day she wouldn't want to even look at me. She'd withdraw and I could tell she was frustrated and tired. She'd go days without eating. She stopped reading and at some point she destroyed all her cassettes. In retaliation they took her room from her. Now she had to live and sleep in the hall because they wanted to keep an eye on her at all times. What they really wanted was to be able to upbraid her at every turn.

"That bedroom is yours now," they said. "Take it."

"I don't want the bedroom," I'd answer. "I prefer the hall. I'm more comfortable here."

"Take the bedroom!" they commanded.

Home had finally turned into hell. The only escape was to stick to school as much as possible. When classmates encouraged me to reach for the stars because I had perfect grades, I wanted to pull them aside one by one and tell them, "Listen, my sister committed suicide."

I'd sit in that hall and read in front of Laleh. I'd turn the music up loud to get some kind of reaction out of her. Nothing. The storyteller Laleh of yesterdays had gone mute. She'd turn to the wall and suddenly scream at nothing and no one. Her body was declining fast. Her kidneys were failing. Some days she'd piss on herself on purpose. It was as if she hungered for the constant condemnations from the rest of the family. Laleh was ending and I could do nothing about it.

***

It was on the fifth anniversary of Laleh's fateful decision that my relationship to her finally snapped. I had just come home from school carrying the little gifts my classmates had given me for my birthday. Laleh sat on her wheelchair behind the window. Seeing me, her face turned full of longing, then sadness. That look was a kick in the stomach. Suddenly I could no longer stand her. I could not stand that she was regretting what she'd done five years ago. Until then, I'd respected her choice, because she'd believed in what she was doing. But that look of regret seemed to end whatever reserve of forgiveness I'd ever had for her. Instead there was anger and resentment for seeing five years of my childhood scorched in the bonfire of grief over what she had done to herself and to us. I stopped speaking to her.

***

Laleh died. Apparently it was hepatitis that killed her. One winter night she wailed and groaned till morning like a wounded animal. The next afternoon when I came back from school no one was home. They'd taken her to the hospital. In the evening Baba called.

"Why aren't you sleeping, little one?"

"I can't sleep."

"Give the phone to your brother please."

After talking to Baba, my brother came and stood over me. "Doctors say Laleh won't last the night. She's been asking for you."

"I'm not going to the hospital. I want to sleep."

Sleep never came.

At dawn my sister came into my room. "Laleh's dead."

I pulled the blanket over my head. "Leave me alone. I want to sleep."

The jinns finally had extracted their sacrifice from us. Laleh was dead. But why? Was it because I'd stopped talking to her? But I loved her...

We went to the cemetery. I couldn't cry. I saw her stretched out on the surface of the platform where they washed the bodies. She seemed no different than years ago. Just her legs had shrunken unto themselves. Otherwise, it was the same Laleh who was always looking up at the sky rather than in front of her. I was speechless, but wore that same dumb smile as always. When they lowered her into the grave I started laughing maniacally. Then: "Leave me alone. I want to get back to school. I don't want to get an absence mark."

Now I had two roles to play in our house; I had to be Little Laleh, and also Big Laleh but without her craziness. When Mama kissed me, I wasn't sure if it was me she was kissing or Big Laleh. Whenever I looked up while watching TV or reading a book, I'd catch Baba looking intently at me with tears in his eyes. I hated mirrors, hated anything that hinted at our resemblance. In the mornings when I woke up and saw that the books on which I'd fallen asleep had been removed, I didn't complain. Often they were books Laleh had read at one time. I knew what was happening. They all were worried for me. My brother and sister would suddenly barge into the room and ask if I was all right. I'd say nothing. Sometimes I'd talk to a neighborhood cat that I imagined carried Laleh's soul inside her. It was a game of push and pull between me and the family to make sure I hadn't gone over the edge, and one of my daily routines was to prove to everybody that no, the jinns had not yet taken over my body like they did Laleh's.

***

One day when we all were pretending nothing was amiss and ours was not a house of hurt, Baba called from across the room, "Laleh dear, come, let's play a game of backgammon." He hadn't meant anything by it. People called me Laleh by mistake nearly all the time. But that day my patience finally gave out and all the jinns inside me came screaming out. I demanded to have my books back, and all of Laleh's too that they had hidden from me. I didn't want to be Laleh anymore. I'd been nothing else since my 10th birthday. I was sick of it.

I hit the streets. Not just that day, but all the time from then on. In the fabric sellers' market where I'd seen Laleh on her own legs for the last time in an outside setting, I found a little bookstore. The bookstore carried most of the banned books in the country. The owner allowed me to come every day, sit in a corner and read to my heart's content. I devoured those books, mostly because I didn't want grief to sink me. At nights I'd return to the jinn-stricken silence of our house and sleep without saying a word to anyone. And when my schooling was finished in Ahvaz, I made a beeline to the capital, Tehran, the huge metropolis that could, and can, take in all the crazies of the world—a city where you wouldn't have to make yourself and others suffer for five years and then regret your act of jumping off a balcony because, well, you really needed to make that jump.

In Tehran I hung out in parks with strangers. Whenever someone asked about the dark circles under my eyes, I'd give them one of my stock lies: my twin sister had just died, I had cancer, my mother was in jail...

Other times I'd tell people I only had one brother and one sister. I hid Laleh from the world and tried purging her jinns.

But the jinns do return, at least once a year on my birthday. Birthdays for me will never not be a funeral, while for those jinns they'll always be a feast on madness.

This essay originally appeared in The Markaz Review.

NOSTOS ALGOS

In this brief portrait of a migratory life, k. eltinaé reflects on the meaning of home through a series of loving family vignettes, revealing his reverence for the mix and mingle of languages and continents, and his admiration for the amalgam.

K. ELTINAÉ

K. ELTINAÉ is a diaspora poet of Sudanese-Nubian and Mediterranean descent, whose work is centered around otherness, cultural/geographic displacement, generational trauma and exile. His debut collection *The Moral Judgement of Butterflies* won The Beverly Prize for International Literature 2019 (BSPG Press) and the Eyelands Book Award 2022. He is a World Literature Lecturer and an oldies and classic afro-beat disc jockey residing in Granada, Spain.

I peer into an art store as I'm finishing off my cigarette. There is a boy glued to his phone screen, sketch pads, brushes and canvases surround him. I start counting the things that are white inside and miss the last drag. I ask about a sketchbook that catches my eye, its leather the color of my skin, but he replies by showing me piles of different ones that are on sale.

When I point to the gold-colored soft pastel pile behind the counter, he calls them camel. When I point to the mauve pile, he calls them wine. The only color we agree on is black, negro he says in Spanish without making eye contact as he does the math on his calculator and waits for the bill that will end our tête-à-tête about colors.

I tear the plastic casing off my new sketchbook as soon as I find a terrace seat at a neighboring café, and begin drawing a line of pyramids in gold first, then purple, and black, before a friendly waiter shows up and takes my order. When he returns he asks if I'm drawing a fence or a border; I decide it's best not to tell him I'm drawing home. The classical Arabic word for "home" دار is the same as the Spanish verb for "give": dar. So what exactly has a home given me?

When you are raised between so many lands, cities blur into a tent of memories you migrate forward with, knowing that the only balm to soothe each new beginning is the one territory you never leave behind, home.

***

We were clearing up after dinner, when my mother brought out her little stainless steel cheese box from the fridge, balancing a tray with bananas in her other hand. The sight of this miniature steel case always made my siblings and me smirk. She had gone out and bought it one night after my father had devoured more than half a block of a delicatessen cheese she'd been saving. It came with a key, which never left her sight.

She sat beside my brothers on the far end of our L-shaped sofa and unlocked the case as my father stole glances. She lay out the portions; their different wax papers rustled like a tempest.

"Oh my god, Mom! That smells like an old woman's feet!" My older brother fussed, pinching his nose as the aroma filled our den. It smelled to me like street puddles after a rainy day, or the entryway to our home when my father's friends visited and took off their shoes.

"Perfect, I won't share any of it with you, will I?" My brothers slipped off the sofa, distancing themselves from the cutting board. Mom went to work hastily dividing precise rectangular slices onto a small plate for my dad. Hers was a larger plate, on which she sliced banana into gourmet mini-buns, each holding one perfectly sliced chunk from the assortment of cheeses. She drizzled honey over it all, and speared each delicacy with a toothpick when she was done. My father paused his channel surfing to devour his portions, while my sister found some random movie that had just begun.

An elegant man in dark sunglasses filled the screen. He was driving a black sedan on a highway, until he pulled up to the hotel. He got out, offering his keys to the bellhop, then pinched a bill into his palm, which confused me. They had hardly exchanged words, so what was the fee for? My sister sighed, annoyed by my question.

"It's a tip, dummy. It's like a monetary thank you you give to a person if they're offering a service for you, or if they've treated you well, usually at a restaurant."

We sat in silence watching the rest of the film. As I relished my banana-cheese treat, I pondered the idea of this "monetary thank you", which in my mind was a bit like gift-giving. I imagined it as a chain of kindness, a wave that brought people together. I was eight years old, so of course I had never paid attention to how my parents paid for anything when we went out for dinner.

A few weeks later my parents popped into my bedroom and asked if I cared to accompany them outside the compound to buy some fruits and vegetables from the local market. I got dressed, counting the bills I had from my allowance, rapidly jotting down the balance, subtracting what I took in case I saw something I liked.

Traveling outside the military compound where we lived at the time, in Dhahran, Saudi Arabia, was always an adventure. Several security guards ushered my parents' car out after formalities and careful inspection. Perfect green grass and identical houses no longer surrounded us. I could smell petrol, see alley cats and people dressed locally, which filled me with a dangerous thrill. My mother unfolded and loosely put on the headscarf she brought in her bag. We parked the car near the fish market, my mother cursing as she skipped between puddles to the other side of the street.

The fruit and vegetable market was swarming with families, screaming babies and nannies rotating around the different grocer stands. At first I tagged along behind my parents who were picking tomatoes and onions, refusing to buy the prepackaged boxes. Rows of grapefruit and pineapples distracted me, and on a whim decided I would buy a few with my allowance so I excused myself and walked over to the fruit stand where a man sat counting bills. Something about the way he was counting those bills brought to mind the scene of the man tipping the bellhop.

I waited until he was done and politely asked to pick the fruits I wanted. He mumbled something in Arabic, handing me the plastic bag, promising their excellence. I selected my fruit and handed him a bill, and when he gave me back the change I politely insisted he keep it as a tip.

The calm face of the man suddenly lit up with rage as he threw the change at me. He began cursing at me in Arabic, while I apologized over and over, picking up the coins as my parents swooped in, yanking me by the arm. I had never imagined that tipping was an insulting gesture in some Middle Eastern countries.

My entire body shook as my parents crossed the street, rushing me inside the car. "What has gotten into you?!" my father asked, his voice stern with shock as he started the car. My gut sank and I awaited their reprimand.

"I gave him a tip," I answered, half whispering. Both my parents burst into such whooping laughter it rocked our old green Land Rover. They shook in their seats, tears streaking their faces as I sat in the back, dumbfounded by their reaction. It became their favorite story to share with guests, who found it equally hilarious.

***

Our snoopy assistant principal patrolled the playground, eavesdropping and observing the different cliques during our recess break. I was having a conversation with a friend when a cuss word flew out of my mouth in frustration. He marched over like he had discovered a kilo of cocaine on me.

"Follow me, young man." When we reached his office, he pulled out my student file, and dialed the phone number listed, which was my mother's since my dad was usually operating.

I listened as he spoke to my mother. His southern American accent unnerved me, and all I could hear was shouting coming out of the receiver. My mother's voice boomed as it did in person, and I watched his face wrinkle up as his fantasy of busting me collapsed before him.

"I don't understand you, please stop shouting," he pleaded into the receiver, pressing the speaker button as my mother's voice echoed the same sentiment, her three languages melding into broken English. I watched in horror as he slammed down the phone and gave me a pencil, starting to dictate a 'first warning' letter.

"This will go into your student record," he informed me. When I finished, he made me apologize and promise to never speak in such a way. "After all, what's the use of receiving an education if you end up speaking that way?"

The office door flew open as the secretary yelled something out in warning.

"Where is he?" I heard my mother asking as my heart began to thump, afraid of the scene that might follow. "I want to speak to the real principal," I heard her say to the secretary.

"He's in a meeting right now," she pleaded, exasperated. I started to explain to my mother what had happened when the principal came out of his office. He greeted my mother, as the assistant principal appeared in the background like an older brother tattling, before my mother cut him off, her voice rising like a wave.

"This...man called me at work because there was a problem, and I was trying to understand him when he hung the phone on my face."

I watched the principal's face twist in surprise, attempting to calm my mother down. "I can't believe Richard would ever attack a parent of any student..."

"Ask him, he hung the phone on my face," my mother repeated, lowering her voice.

I found myself, as on many occasions, trapped between two worlds, attempting to explain the difference between the English phrasal verb and Arabic expression for the identical thing. My mother told me she would deal with me at home. I carried on for the rest of the day with a looming dread in my gut.

***

I tiptoed into the house that afternoon as my mother looked up from her newspapers and pointed at the pile of dishes in the sink. I didn't mind. In fact, I loved cleaning up, attempting to scrub off my guilt in that murky water and rinse away the fear of what greater punishment awaited me.

My father arrived in the middle of dinner, his eyes exhausted from a long day of work. I automatically slipped away with my plate to the kitchen, avoiding eye contact. He sat down and listened as my mother served dinner, recounting the story of the phone call and her heated argument, imitating the assistant principal's accent, which made my siblings giggle.

When dinner was over, I heard my father's voice yelling out my name and knew that the moment had presented itself. In the den of our home my mother sat like a Roman spectator, glasses pushed halfway down her straight nose, sunflower seeds at her side. My father, in his home jalabiya, sat beside her with a serious look on his face.

He began his speech as he always did, with some strange elaborate metaphor, this time explaining to me that I was a diplomat, and that every time I stepped outside of our home—the country both he and my mother had founded—I was representing them. He then asked me if I heard words like the one I had used at school at home, and the honest answer would have been yes, in a few other languages like Arabic, Greek and Turkish. But never in English.

Finally he handed me a plastic bag with a book inside. I hung my head low in performance and clutched the bag, attempting to slip away to my room in shame, as they insisted I take a look at what was inside. It was an Arabic translation of a book titled *The Art of Massage*. I looked up at my parents in confusion. My father asked me to start reading aloud, as they both settled back on the sofa and corrected me every time I stumbled on a word or mispronounced a vowel. Once I was finished with the title page, my parents asked me to flip through the book and start reading the techniques chapter. I let the words slip from my mouth, like slippery tadpoles in a pond I could not count or make sense of.

My father waited until I was done with the first technique before he used my mother's back as a blackboard, explaining the location and type of pressure I had just finished reading about. My mother's tense back began to relax as she insisted that my father be the guinea pig. I went to bed way past my bedtime that night, having learned four different massage techniques to my parents' approval.

The following day, I came home after choir practice and found the den filled with guests. Three different couples chatted as my mother entertained them with stories about her students and teas and sweets she had prepared. I put my backpack down, combed my hair and straightened my t-shirt, before returning to greet them as I was expected to.

One of them, a neighbor, asked me about my new talent as a masseur. I exchanged a look with my mother, who looked back at me with a pursed smile.

"I have a pinching pain in the lower part of my back," our neighbor started, offering her back to me. And with that wave-like motion began a new phase in my life, as the prodigy seventh-grade neighborhood masseur. I came home most afternoons to clients who showered me with praise, and blessings for my family and bright future, expressions that brought such joy to my parents' ears I couldn't possibly refuse them.

Thirty-odd years later, I still sweat with this fever, a condition known as nostalgia that once discharged soldiers from the war. In the middle of the night it has become ritual that my lover curls her back against my hands. I return to a living room that no longer exists, to the laughter of my parents in the car after I tried to tip the fruit vendor in Khobar, to the principal who only saw violence in words and not actions. The tension disappears in each of her muscles like those stones I flung into the Rheine River with the impetus of my youth, bringing back leisurely afternoons dripping like Kaya coconut jam from my child lips in Singapore. As my hands pass over her skin I think about the hidden milieus we collectively share but only value for their differences. Identically colorful as those rosaries, misbaḥahs as they are called in Turkey, used for zikr (to remember) but known in Greece as kompolois, to bury worries and forget. I guess home gave me shelter in a few neat languages, a kitchen where I still drizzle honey over sliced bananas and cheese in the morning to fight off the ache of maybe today and tomorrow.

SIREN SONGS

In Kuwait, on the eve of the US invasion of Iraq,
Barrak Alzaid has his first real kiss with a boy,
and is stifled by the painful apprehensions
of puberty worsened by needing to
keep secrets in a family whose
foremost concern
is reputation.

BARRAK ALZAID

BARRAK ALZAID is an artist, writer and curator. His current work in progress, *Fabulous at Five*, is a memoir relating his queer coming of age in Kuwait. It is a story of family fracture, reconciliation and finding true love in the most unexpected of places: home. He is a founding member of the artist collective GCC, whose work examines the Arab Gulf region's transformations and shifting systems of power. In 2018, he was a member of the fiction cohort at the Lambda Literary Writers Retreat for Emerging LGBTQ Voices. He lives in Copenhagen with his husband and their dog, both ongoing sources of inspiration. @barrakstar

Mama passed the fax around to my siblings and me in order of seniority, first me, then Meshari, then Hayuna. The missive on American School of Kuwait letterhead was lopsided from being fed at an angle into the machine.

...school will temporarily close from the 10th of February 2003, through to the 21st of March, 2003. This decision has not been made lightly and is directly related to growing security concerns in Kuwait, the level of uncertainty regarding military action against Iraq, and possible consequences of any such action...

That meant one week until school shut down, barely any time to say goodbye to the American friends I'd spent the last two years getting close to. Katy, Lindsay, Jen. Even Hamad.

Having them around filled the void that depression had carved out of my insides throughout the first half of high school. The weight of navigating social expectations with my Arab friends lessened around the American group. But that fax dislodged my precarious hold on equanimity, replacing it again with the void.

Mama cut through the silence. "It's for all of us to decide whether to stay in Kuwait or go to Gramma and Grampa's in Buffalo to finish the school year there. I'm comfortable going, I'm comfortable staying. It's what we all agree on as a family."

She was cradled in a corner of the sofa that had grown lumpy and misshapen from Baba's form. She flicked the lace mat she had placed to cover the tear in the fabric that stretched across the sofa arm. After years of drinking tea and Turkish coffee here, Baba's fingers had worried through to the spongy interior.

Although she was still in middle school, Hayuna was sometimes more perceptive than the rest of us. "What about Baba?"

Mama pressed her lips tight. She cleared her throat and a sigh escaped her nose. "We can decide and let him know when he's back."

I flattened the corner of the fax I'd unconsciously crumpled in my left hand. Hayuna hung her head in her lap while Meshari cracked his knuckles.

As kids, we'd been eager for anyone to get rid of Saddam "Mad Ass Insane," and older relatives spit at his name. Everyone was thrilled that George W. Bush and Tony Blair were haranguing Iraq about their nuclear weapons reports and pushing the issue to the brink. But none of us thought it would send Kuwait into another theater of war.

I felt like I was back at a Model UN conference debating security council resolutions.

"Do you think there's a credible threat if we stay?"

Mama considered my question. "I'm not sure, but I don't think Kuwait would be a target this time. We have the American military bases along the border and the no-fly zone between us and Iraq."

Meshari and I repeated the same arguments for staying and leaving. Tension tightened our voices and resentment laced our words until Hayuna interrupted.

"What about Ummah? Can she come with us if we leave?"

Our grandmother had just returned from surgery in London, and though she'd survived the first Gulf War, she'd gotten a lot more frail in the years since that humid August evening in 1990 when Kuwait fell asleep a free country and awoke an occupied state. My family had been on holiday at a Florida theme park, and Meshari and I had been fighting over morning cartoons, yanking the remote from each other, flipping back and forth between channels. Mama stood across the room with our infant sister cradled against her shoulder.

She startled out of her reverie and shouted "Stop!"

The television became an uncanny window that panned across Iraqi tanks lined up along Kuwait's coastal road. An offscreen newscaster described how they had just rolled through our unguarded borders. Those Iraqi soldiers and secret police spent the next seven months pulling young men out of their homes and shooting them in front of their parents; they conducted torturous electroshock interrogations; they kidnapped thousands of prisoners of war whose bodies lie in mass graves. Back then there was no conversation, we could not return. Ummah was the only one of our family remaining, and she traveled through checkpoints each day to protect her sons' homes from looters. When a group of soldiers barged into her home she faced them down with biscuits and tea. Even though neighbors and extended family involved her in escape plans, she always rejected them.

Ummah is deeply faithful, and years later I asked her if she had been frightened. She held her henna-covered hands to the sky and murmured, "Allah katib. God's will is written and if they killed me I would be a martyr in heaven."

After liberation Kuwait felt closer to hell than to heaven. The Iraqis retreated and set fire to our oil wells, coating the sky with streaks of greasy noxious smoke that hung there for months. When our plane approached Kuwait soil my brother turned in his seat and said, "Mama, Saddam took the sun away."

Mama always said family was the most important thing, and this time we could choose to stay together. Most of my cousins were already studying abroad, and now Khalid and

Lulu were leaving until their high schools reopened. If our part of the family left we would miss a month or more of Ummah's Thursday lunches. None of us could imagine her sitting alone at the head of her long mismatched dining tables, pressed end to end to hold all of our relatives.

Meshari nodded slowly. "If Ummah won't leave, then we shouldn't either."

***

The first time an air raid siren went off we ran to Meshari's room and waited. We'd taped the seams of his windows to prevent fumes from biological weapons creeping in, and the one gas mask Baba managed to secure lay unused between us. There were no tanks, no troops, no signs of war except a tense monotony punctuated by periodic air raid sirens.

We adhered to our family routines, and every Thursday piled into Baba's red Camry to eat lunch at Ummah's. We were merging onto the second ring road when the wailing cry of a siren pierced the car. I jolted forward against the seatbelt. It pressed against my chest and bile rose up my throat.

"Take us back home Baba, it's not safe." It didn't matter that we could die at any moment, the relative comfort of home felt safer than the exposed streets.

"Ten minutes, Barrak. Ten minutes, we there." Baba's clipped English broke down when he got anxious, and I watched his lips curl around dry unsympathetic words. *Be a man*, they seemed to say. My precarious barrier of self control collapsed. I shrieked, pounded my hands on the car window, causing Hayuna to burst into tears and Meshari to glower.

Baba's arms stiffened and pulled the wheel towards the exit back to our house.

After a few weeks we all gave up the pretense of safety in favor of a sense of normality. We acknowledged we were at the mercy of outside forces but it still exacerbated the sense of gloom. One afternoon a siren competed with the quacking and whirring of my internet modem logging onto the net. The familiar endorphin rush surged when the bright green ICQ messenger icon whirled on screen. My chat window with Hamad stayed blank. I'd been waiting for days for his reply, so I flicked open a new chat with Melina.

Hey Mel, how's college?

Uni is tough but good. How are you? Surviving the situation in Kuwait?

My fingers hovered over the keyboard, clenching, unclenching. Fuck it, Christine knows. I told Taiba already.

It's really bad Mel. I can't stop obsessing about my friend. He ignores me unless we're hanging out in a bigger group. I've been journaling like crazy. Feel like I'm getting carpal tunnel syndrome LOL.

Is it a friend thing? Maybe you want something more.

I thought of the powdery white stripes that wrapped around the nude torso of Hamad's translucent green bottle of Le Male Gaultier cologne. So many other guys had that cloying scent hanging off their clothes, but the reaction between the scent and Hamad's creamy skin was the only one that shot longing through my heart.

I just want to be loved, by a guy, a girl, doesn't matter. It doesn't have to be romantic. Prefer if it wasn't.

Is there anyone in Kuwait you can talk to?

No.

A few minutes later Melina messaged from a group chat.

Antoine, meet Barrak. Barrak meet Antoine, you two have lots in common, plenty to chat about.

Hai Barack! Pleasure to meet you!

Heya Antoine! What are you doing in Kuwait?

I graduated from the French school in Kuwait last year. Been at Uni since Autumn term. Worried about mum being alone in all this mess, so I took a leave of absence for her.

Our conversation lasted for hours. It was so, so different from the gay chat rooms I've prowled on Yahoo Groups or mIRC. In those spaces we peppered our messages with endless "Age/Sex/Location?" We exchanged fake photos, jerked off, logged out.

It became perfunctory, a hidden part of my release, until Baba barged into my room and caught me browsing pictures of hairy naked men. I scrambled for a cover story.

"I was curious about puberty, it took me to this site."

To berate me would be to acknowledge my heinous actions, so instead he fell back on a threat. "My friend's company give us this internet, so they're watching everything."

Like every other Kuwaiti of his generation, Baba was preoccupied with reputation. Our parents threatened us and instilled in us a sense of constant surveillance. We were held captive by the knowledge that any poor choice of judgment in word or action could diminish ourselves, and by extension our family, in the eyes of others. When my cousin kissed a boy in first grade my aunt told her she would kill her if it ever happened again. As a guy with an American mom I could never threaten our family's respectability, not like a girl supposedly could. But that night I still slid into bed racked with worry that whispers of my misdeed would echo across Kuwait.

Sitting at my computer, chatting with Antoine, I could ignore those societal expectations and all the ways I needed to conform. Instead, I hung on every emoji he sent.

Rainbowsuncloudumbrellarainbowsmileyfaceshearts.

My heart fluttered.

My fingers grazed the keyboard. Fuck it, what do I have to lose?

Wanna hang out?

Oki! But I actually have to run for dinner with my mum, chat soon?

***

The afternoon Antoine came over I had a pile of clothes covering the blue and white checkered comforter covering my bed. My Abercrombie button-downs felt too formal, but a simple t-shirt didn't feel cool enough. Despite acne scars and a few lingering pimples I wasn't self conscious about how I looked. I was more worried if he'd like my personality; I definitely didn't want to be needy like I'd been with Hamad.

The doorbell rang and I slid across our slick marble floors to greet Antoine, but Mama was already at the door armed with snacks that I was quick to unload. Baba rushed past us toward the mosque with a gruff nod, "Salaam alaykum."

I juggled the sweating juice bottles and crinkling bags of chips, trying not to stare. Antoine's head was covered in adorable tight brown curls. I wondered if they were thin and wiry or thick and soft. He exchanged pleasantries with Mama, and spoke with a light English accent that bumped along a French cadence. It turns out he and my sister overlapped at figure skating years ago. I shifted my weight from one foot to the other while they reminisced.

"Okay," I interrupted, "Let's go to my TV room?" Whenever a non-Kuwaiti friend visited I felt embarrassed by the size of our house. It was typical by Kuwaiti standards, but luxurious by any other.

There were fewer entertainment options than the basement (no video games), but the tradeoff was more privacy. Plus my blue Ikea loveseat was a good size for cuddling. So I was disappointed that he grabbed a pillow and splayed his legs across the floor.

I perched on the sofa's edge and munched salt and pepper Kitco chips. Greasy crumbs coated my palms and without a tissue handy I dusted them off in a flourish.

"Want to watch *Moulin Rouge*?"

Antoine's eyes lit up. "Oh, yes! Love that movie!"

"Oh my god me too. I've seen it like 12 times."

He tucked his arm under his chin, nodding along to the music like a kid wrestling with a young man's body. When we got to "Elephant Love Medley" I couldn't stand the distance any longer. Ewan McGregor was yearning and playful, Nicole Kidman was flirty and coy. He wooed her, she seduced him, I slid onto the floor to stretch out beside Antoine. We sang both parts loudly with big gestures and giggled and folded our legs over each other.

At some point one of us nudged up against the other and the movie fell to the background. His curls beckoned me, but my hands smelled sour. I needed to make some type of move before the movie switched from romance to tragedy. Baba's frequent rebuke thrummed through my head. "Barrak! Catch the opportunity!" I wiped my palms on the rug and kept my legs wrapped around his. Obviously Baba never meant for me to apply his maxim to my sexually charged circumstances. He wanted me to be successful and instilled a sense of ambition. But I needed to channel the impulse, gather my courage anyway, kiss Antoine. I'd kissed girls before. But those felt more like handshakes than romantic gestures. On screen the hero sang a final ode to his lover and I pressed my lips to Antoine's. His mouth tasted like the last sip of carrot-orange juice, dregs of crystalline sugar melting off his tongue and washing over the sour remnants of chips in my mouth.

My desires shifted from pixels and empty yearning to those of an actual teenage boy. Even though I craved having a "boyfriend" I knew we had a clear expiration. That didn't stop me from transforming the monotony of my days and the drone of those sirens into the backdrop for a romantic tryst.

Since my family was constantly around the house I usually went to his apartment while his mom was at work. That gave us plenty of time to watch movies and play video games, always pressed against each other. One afternoon sirens pierced his room while we watched *Buffy the Vampire Slayer*. We lingered at first, but the sirens persisted, so we hauled our horny teenage bodies into their safe room and onto his mother's bed. It was so clandestine, daring and delicious. I wanted to get totally naked with him, but didn't know how to ask. I wanted to try all the things I'd watched on my computer. It felt treacherous to close that gap, to actualize my desire in the most pure sense of what gay desire could be.

Baba's "catch the opportunity" refrain rang in my head and I rolled over a lacy throw pillow to face Antoine. "Isn't there a vacant apartment downstairs?"

"You don't think we'll be caught?"

"I've never seen or heard anyone in there. I tried the door on my way up to your place. Guess what? It's open now."

We prowled the empty property and fumbled our way towards the back, pulled our cargo shorts down and tore our shirts off. I noted all the new places on his body I could touch. He was hairier on his bottom half than his top, like the satyr I played in a performance of *The Chronicles of Narnia*. Without our clothes our smells melded; some spots held wisps of cologne, others radiated deodorant. Everything was amplified and it all smelled of longing. We were so preoccupied with the fresh sweat beading along every crevice and curve that we didn't hear the front door click open. But the grating register of teenage boys jostling and cursing in Arabic did reach us. I recoiled from Antoine's sweating body and leapt away from him and grazed my knee against the low pile carpet. The friction burned a rough patch that prickled against the cool air. We couldn't get dressed and walk past those guys. If they found us together in any sort of intimate configuration they might assault us. We couldn't protect each other from the inevitable, so we hid in the closet. I bumped my knee and it was tender, but it would heal. Antoine held me and the garrulous boys laughed their way through the apartment and out the front door.

We'd climaxed together, we'd survived a brush with danger, but I wanted more. I hadn't had a sleepover since freshman year, and even then it was always with my brother in tow, headed to our cousin's house for video games and late-night KFC. I felt bold enough to invite Antoine to spend the night.

Even though rules were suspended in this time of war, I still wasn't allowed to lock my door. We were two guys, we weren't supposed to be sexual beings, so there wasn't any reason for

Mama and Baba to consider our privacy. But I still worried they'd find a reason to barge in. Baba to remind me my Arabic tutor was arriving, or Mama to offer us pancakes for breakfast. I set an early alarm to allow Antoine to crawl out of bed into the sleeping bag on the floor.

In bed his lean body was soft and comforting. He asked if I wanted to try oral, and I strained with the weight of his suggestion. He held one hand against my head to guide me down, whispered where to place my lips, how to wrap my lips over my teeth. Tangy sweat cloyed to my mouth. A salty spray of ozone shot across my taste buds, and I dashed to the bathroom to grab the mouthwash. During elementary school Baba told me not to touch anyone who scratched or cut themselves. A few years later sparse hair littered my chin and a mustache trailed above my lip, but Baba forbade me from getting a straight razor shave at the barber, even though every other guy did it. The contagious quality of even the tiniest amount of human fluid settled into my consciousness. It wasn't until years later that I realized his was a paranoid, unwarranted repulsion against the threat of HIV.

I slipped under the comforter and we slept in an embrace until my alarm rang with the morning athan.

Later that day I found a pair of underwear in my pile of laundry. I didn't recognize the brand, so I pressed it to my nose and inhaled the sour scent of a man's body. A secret treasure, a prize of conquest, a way to relive our sensuous night.

Sex was still roiling around in my groin so I slipped the underwear on and connected to ICQ to share this illicit discovery with Antoine. There was a pause, and I imagined a coy smile on his face. I clicked through a few porn windows, and his chat window pinged.

It's not mine, I only wear briefs, not boxer shorts.

A few minutes of mental gymnastics and I realized: they belong to Baba. Only I'm too far along. I clicked out of the chat, watched the writhing men, and climaxed.

***

Antoine's departure and my start date at school got delayed another few weeks. American troops finally went into Iraq, who retaliated with 12 missiles launched at Kuwait. Most were knocked out of the sky by Patriot missiles, and two landed in rural areas without causing injuries. Number 13 was a Silkworm missile that skimmed across the water's surface and shattered glass doors, crumpled drywall, and twisted steel beams across the interior of the movie theater at Sharq Mall. One person suffered light injuries while hundreds more strolled through to witness the impotent climax of a month-long siege on our daily lives.

Even though he was leaving, and there was no practical way to do a long distance relationship, I wanted to woo him, to offer him a singular unforgettable romantic gesture he'd cherish for the rest of his life. Since *Moulin Rouge* was our movie it made sense to cook him a meal set on my roof and serenade him with "Your Song". I knew the words, and could even mimic Ewan McGregor's accent. But no amount of rehearsals could fix my tone deaf ears.

I simplified everything down to lunch in my TV room: green apple and rocket salad with spaghetti bolognese. Now I had to orchestrate it so that my family would be out of the house, and the only time that ever happened, when I knew exactly when they'd leave and return home, was Thursday lunch at Ummah's. But Mama and Baba wouldn't let me skip out to hang out with a friend. So I lied. I told them I'd lost a bet to Antoine, so my punishment was to cook him a meal. I laughed it off as an awkward inconvenience, but I had to keep my word!

Before they left Mama came up to me at the stove to ask if I needed help. The tomato sauce was bubbling and burning on the stove top, not unlike Baba's Turkish coffee.

"I'm fine, I'm fine!" My voice got a little too loud, and she ushered my siblings out the door.

For weeks Antoine had sprawled his body across mine, laid out in countless configurations against my gray Ikea loveseat. But this afternoon his knees bumped against the scalloped wooden edges of my low coffee table, pulled almost flush to the sofa, his lap overburdened with the meager offerings of my final romantic meal. The greens were fresh when I put them in, but the dressing weighed them down, limp and scattered on the embossed porcelain plates. He took his last bite and spun around to face me, lifting his left leg onto the couch, drawing his knee close to his chest. His smile was warm but lacked its usual tingle of affection. Maybe it was the meal's formality or his impending departure, but there was no finale-worthy or show-stopping intimacy. Instead, we embraced like friends and I let him go.

Before Antoine, depression had carved an empty space inside of me. Fulfilling my carnal desires, I felt whole. When he left, those feelings of pleasure stole away with him and the void returned.

***

A dry wind blew dust off of just about everything and irritated my eyes. Our entire campus is outdoors, and I paced outside Ms. Salah's classroom, way too early for religion class. The air around me was sweltering, rivulets of sweat trickled around my armpits and down my sides. I peered through the windows at the twin air conditioning units pumping cool air across the empty desks and chairs. The large glass panes were separated by white painted borders that bled splatters across the dirty surface. I pressed my palm against one pane and a sharp jab of heat seared my palm. It grew hotter, and instead of recoiling, I pumped my hand into a fist. Once, twice, three times and it smashed through. Shards tinkled into my hair, settled on my shirt, sliced through my wrist. I pressed the wound to my mouth to stanch the blood even though a part of me wanted to press further, to annihilate myself, reduce myself to a teeming morass of nothing.

The school bell signaled the end of lunch, and my first conscious thought was Baba's insistent voice. "What will people say?"

For years Baba warned me against others with exposed wounds, but now I was the untouchable one. I cowered, folded into myself, but before the whispers could gather any force, two of my classmates flanked me. The boys placed their arms around my shoulders and against my lower back. They ushered me along to the nurse while glass crunched between our bodies.

"What will people say?" Baba's voice again, but this time I have my own response. They'll say, "Your son needs you."

I had tried, whether consciously or not, to annihilate my void with physical pain. And yet over time my skin knitted itself together, revealing that my capacity to heal was far stronger than any impulse to self-destruct.

THE UNBELIEVER

After her youth spent straddling a dual-continental context—born in Nigeria to Bangladeshi parents—Abeer Y. Hoque moves to the US as a teen, struggles to define her identity, and eventually carves her own path home to her heritage.

ABEER Y. HOQUE

ABEER Y. HOQUE is a Nigerian-born Bangladeshi American writer and photographer. She likes counterculture, coloring inside the lines, and contradictions. Her books include a travel photography and poetry monograph (*The Long Way Home*, 2013), a linked collection of stories, poems and photographs (*The Lovers and the Leavers*, 2015) and a memoir (*Olive Witch*, 2017). She has won Fulbright, NEA, and NYFA fellowships, holds BS and MA degrees from the University of Pennsylvania's Wharton School of Business, as well as an MFA in writing from the University of San Francisco. olivewitch.com.

I can pinpoint when I started losing my religion. I was 15, freshly ensconced in the strip mall suburbs of Pittsburgh, thousands of miles from my childhood home in Nigeria. It will come as no surprise that I was uneasy in my teenage skin, nor that stridence and angst marked my manner.

Our Sunday Islamic school had just taught us about the inheritance and witness laws of Islam. These laws treated—and still treat—a woman as worth half a man. A woman inherits half that of her brother. Two female witnesses equal the weight of one male witness.

"But why?" I asked my father, all teenage bellicosity.

"You have to understand," he replied, "before Islam, women weren't even allowed to own property. Even in the West. It was a revolutionary shift."

This explanation fobbed me off for a few more years, and then only because my parents had never shown any signs of treating either me or my sister as worth half my brother. In our family at least, nothing less or different was given to or expected of daughters. Indeed, with his less than stellar grades, my brother was often compared unflatteringly with us, his older sisters.

But let me start at the beginning. One beginning anyway, set between two tragically resonant countries. In 1972, my parents moved to the small university town of Nsukka in southeastern Nigeria, Biafra land. Just two years earlier, the Igbo people of Biafra had lost their separatist bid in a terrible civil war that had killed hundreds of thousands, and millions more from famine. My parents were from Bangladesh, a country that was merely a year old, after a successful but just as devastating liberation war, which was followed by famine that also killed millions.

The south of Nigeria is mostly Christian, the north Muslim. When I was born in 1973, Nsukka boasted two churches, but no mosques or temples. It would take another 15 years for my father and some of the other Muslims in town to raise money and secure space to build a mosque. Yet my father would never get to pray in the mosque he helped build. The year before it was completed, our family moved to the States, and other than a brief journey I would make 25 years later, none of us has been back.

The Nigerian landscape and weather were spectacular and sensate. Mornings and evenings were cool enough to wear blazers, while afternoons were roasting. There was a thunderstorm every afternoon during the rainy season, when the sky would turn black and roar. Then the rain would come. The dry season was called harmattan, after the desert winds that traveled thousands of miles from northern Africa all the way to the West African coast. Then there would be no rain for months, and the ground would thin, losing its red skin to the incessant wind. Dust blew everywhere, and we swept twice a day, otherwise our feet left footprints on the floor. Our lips cracked and our limbs turned ashy in the dry heat.

My best friend at my school was Nigerian, and I understood Igbo even though we had never been formally taught the local language. But at home, we spoke Bangla, we ate Bangladeshi food and wore Bangladeshi clothes on special occasions. Every Sunday in Nsukka, my mother sat my younger sister and me down to write letters to our grandparents in Bangladesh. *Dear Nana and Nanu, how are you? I am fine. Dear Dada and Dadi, how are you? I am fine.*

The letters to Nana and Nanu went to the capital city of Dhaka, where my mother had grown up in a bungalow with an overgrown garden buzzing with crows, and a pond so big you could hardly see the other side. The letters to my paternal grandparents went further, to a village called Barahipur in southeastern Bangladesh.

My mother also taught us Bangla folk dances and songs, and made sure that we learned our okkhors, the Bangla alphabet, using a large poster from Bangladesh as a guide. I still remember the pictures on the 52 squares, one for each letter of the alphabet. Kaw: kaw-la (banana), khaw: khawr-gauche (rabbit).

We also had notebooks in which we copied down short suras, prayers from the Qu'ran. We penciled the Arabic transliteration on the right, the English translation on the left, and memorized both. Oddly, my favorite sura back then was Sura Al-Lahab, *The Flame*, which started with the word "Perish!" and dealt a series of terrible curses on an evil man and his wife.

When we left Nigeria in 1986, it was for what seemed like another dimension—the suburbs of Pittsburgh. What I didn't realize at the time was how both geographies were going through a kind of existential crisis along with me. In the late eighties, Pittsburgh was slowly and painfully sloughing off its industrial identity, while Nsukka was undergoing a different kind of turmoil, one of political unrest, student strikes and staple shortages.

I processed none of this. All I knew was that I was having to start over in a new country, at a new school, and everything sucked, from my Kmart clothes to the casual racism of Rust Belt America. And now, this set of religious rules that had guided my life thus far, this bubble of Islam that my family had lived inside, was breaking down, insofar as my ideas of gender and justice were concerned.

Even the landscape was like alien ground. No more thundering rainstorms, red earth, jungle insects, desert winds. Instead, Pittsburgh's weather swung from bitterly cold to muggy hot, and the sun barely showed from behind the clouds and smog. The rusted sprawl of the dying steel industry lay everywhere, factories flaming into the ominous sky, others emitting foul odors despite years of disuse. The very air was gray and pungent, masking the stunning landscape of the city: three rivers coming to a point, two thousand bridges, hills upon hills.

Pittsburgh was—and still is—a racially segregated city. We moved to a township that was almost wholly white, although this is something I barely noticed. I was already used to being different, but more overwhelmingly, everything else was a sea change from before.

One of the many casualties of our uprooting was language. English was now our main mode, for school, work, TV, movies, books, everything. I forgot Igbo almost immediately. There was no one speaking it around me anymore, and my already limited ability faded like in a dream.

More slowly, we lost Bangla. My parents didn't realize that if they didn't keep speaking Bangla to us at home, and most importantly require us to speak it back, we would forget our first tongue. And we did. How much we forgot was in direct proportion to our ages. My sister was 12 and forgot more than I did. Our six-year-old brother lost the most.

We were warned not to take any Nigerian art items with us when we left, so as not to be accused of stealing artifacts, and so we ended up with almost no visual evidence of our years there.

There was no internet in those days, and the international postal system was often unreliable. I soon lost touch with every single friend I had grown up with, despite a dogged Victorian commitment to letter writing. It was as if this part of my history had been severed, and I had traveled to another world carrying nothing but my memories.

Despite all these paradigm shifts in geography and culture, some things remained the same. We still ate rice and daal at home, and attended weekly dawaats, or dinner parties, at the houses of other Bangladeshi immigrants while wearing Bangladeshi clothes. My mother still sang Tagore songs in our strange new American life, though less frequently.

It's a truism that immigrants cling to certain practices more than if they were still home. My parents immigrated, singly and together, to five countries after leaving Bangladesh: West Pakistan (now Pakistan), Iraq, Libya, Nigeria and America. But the household that my siblings and I grew up in was resolutely Bangladeshi and Muslim.

My parents made sure we continued our Islamic education at the nearest mosque, a 45-minute drive away. Every Sunday, my siblings and I would grumblingly attend three hours of Quranic and Arabic classes. It wasn't just the time that we protested. It was also that many of our classmates were equally unhappy with their required attendance, and eager to show anyone up. My sister and I were older than most of the other students, so we were generally left alone. But my brother, traumatized by his snotty peers, developed a hatred for Islamic instruction that followed him into adulthood. Ironically, he has also grown up to be the only one of us who prays.

As I grew older, my fights with my father about my romantic life began, even as our careers converged. He retired from a career of teaching and consulting in geology to start writing novels, a few years after I left business for creative writing and photography. His efforts to force his religious morals on me led to a slow cataclysmic burn.

"You know we don't recognize dating in our culture," he told me when I first revealed I was with someone.

"But I love him," I burst out. I did. I was in hopeless velvet love.

"If you marry him, or someone not of our faith, let alone culture, understand this: you will no longer belong in this house."

"You would choose your religion over your own child?" I exclaimed, no less prone to dramatic statements than my father.

"I would."

This exchange was so potent and traumatic that it would take me years to articulate and manage my feelings of betrayal. It would take longer still to reject the religion that turned my own parents against me.

Other than when I visit my family in Pittsburgh, I haven't been to a mosque in years. I often find them unwelcoming spaces for women. Before the new mosque in Monroeville was built, my family visited a hodge-podge of buildings around Pittsburgh, each repurposed for prayer: a university's gleaming basketball court, an old ground-floor store still displaying a storefront window, a cramped two-story single-family home, now empty, the bedrooms upstairs filled with children learning lessons from the Qu'ran. These spaces made it difficult to keep the sexes separate and thus, women, rarely prioritized in any religion, had to make do with backdoor entrances, cramped female prayer halls, judgment about dress and practice abounding.

When I moved to Bangladesh in my thirties, the space left by religion was amply filled by the country's syncretic social traditions. I participated in festivals like Pohela Falgoon and went to weddings, markets, readings, and cultural shows galore. I reconnected with my extended family, and created a stalwart network of friends, many of them spirited single women.

It helped that women never go to mosques in Bangladesh—too many of the public spaces are still patriarchal and male dominated. But this social stricture actually helped me feel more Bangladeshi without the pressure of having to be Muslim. I could feel like I belonged, at least in all the non-religious ways. Which in time made me feel like I belonged altogether. And perhaps that's all belonging is, feeling like it. The sense of multiplicitous identity and comfort persisted even when I returned to the States after a few years. I hadn't added layers so much as settled into what was always already there.

More than a quarter century later, my conflicts with my father about my love life continue. He now has Alzheimer's, and his slow progressive memory loss has destroyed any hope of talking through our differences, logic and flow breaking down sometimes inside one conversation. It would be funnier in the moment if it weren't so devastating in the big picture, but he can remember my living-in-sin state, though he can't always recall where it is I'm doing the living and sinning.

My mother is, as always, more forgiving of paths different than her own, but she would rather I settle down in a relationship sanctioned by law and/or Islam, preferably both. Both of my parents have lived outside Bangladesh long enough to have given up on the hope of Bangladeshi partners for their children in America, where there just aren't enough of us to make a "love marriage" feasible.

I often wonder if my stance against marriage and the performance of organized faith is worth my parents' grief. In most ways it's not, and I acknowledge the stubborn selfishness of my refusal. But in one way, I'm fortified. That a Bangladeshi girl in Nigeria, a Nigerian teenager in America, an American woman in Bangladesh might live undefined by her marital status or religion. That women before me made these paths, and those after me will continue to widen them. Representation is a powerful thing.

Sura Al-Kafiruna, the prayer of the unbelievers, is the only Muslim sura I still recite without guilt. As a child, I used to like it because it repeated a line, which meant one less line to memorize. Now the prayer has become a shield against those who would spurn me, on religious or other grounds. To you be your way, and to me mine.

Sura Kafiruna: The Prayer of the Unbelievers
Say, O ye of little faith
I worship not that which ye worship
Nor will ye worship that which I worship
And I will not worship that which
ye have been wont to worship
Nor will ye worship that which I worship
To you be your way, and to me mine

CHASING HOPE, LOSING OMAR

In a story set across Turkey, Qatar and England, Indlieb Farazi Saber unfolds her husband's cancer diagnoses in an ensemble of tender, stolen moments, capturing their bond and honoring the process of loss—or rather, her process of losing.

INDLIEB FARAZI SABER

INDLIEB FARAZI SABER was born in London, then raised and educated in Ethiopia, Nigeria, Libya, the Netherlands and finally, the UK again. Her global upbringing led her to work as a writer, editor and producer for several news organizations including *Al Jazeera English* and *BBC World Service*. She's also one half of the rap sensation "Kiddo and the Widow" at all other times.

One month after diagnosis

Like floating embers, her words drifted through the doorway. "Sorry, do you mind helping me?" Although barely a whisper, they stopped me mid-stride.

I needed to get back to my husband. I'd only left him for a quick toilet break and only then because his sister was with him. But the words drew me towards her room.

Like others in this whitewashed clinic on the seventh floor of an office block in Istanbul's bustling Sisli district, the room emitted an amber glow—perhaps from the light of the treatment machines inside. It too had a hospital bed with starched white sheets. At its center, propped up on a pile of pillows, lay a woman so slight she looked like she might disappear among them. Her face was beautiful, framed by tufts of cropped mousy brown hair. She reminded me of a hatchling.

"Sorry," she said again. "There's just this song playing in my head and I need to listen to it on my phone... But I don't remember who sings it, or what it's called. Can you help me?"

"How does it go?" I asked, reminded of a childhood game where relatives would play me clips of music and I'd have to guess the song.

She started to hum the tune. I'd heard it before but couldn't place where, and like her, I had no idea who sang it.

You need to get back to Omar, a voice in my head reminded me. But I knew I wouldn't leave the room until I'd helped her. I reached over, took her phone and began pulling names from somewhere in my subconscious and typing them into Google: Peter, Simon, and Paul. Lucy, Peter, and John. Then I remembered where I recognised the tune from—an old advert for a British DIY chain. A quick Google search—"theme tune from Homebase ad"—and I'd found her song.

The woman squeezed my hand. I smiled. She was in her thirties and dying of cancer.

She had two young sons back in the UK. She was hoping to be home for Christmas, later that week, but wouldn't be allowed to see her boys as her immunes were low, and they had winter colds.

As I turned to leave, her tired voice sounded again with another question. "Do you think I'll make it?" she asked.

"Of course you will," I assured her. I believed she would, just like I believed that Omar would, that everyone who had traveled to this clinic in the hope that it could heal their broken bodies, when doctors in their own countries had told them there was no hope left, would.

She smiled, wiping away tears, and said she was just being silly. Then she put her headphones on to listen to "Young Folks" by Peter Bjorn and John.

I can tell there's something goin' on
Hours seems to disappear
Everyone is leaving, I'm still with you.

One month before diagnosis

Mine and Omar's journey to Istanbul had started two months earlier—or perhaps long before that without us even knowing it.

We were in London, at my parents' house where I had been staying with our son since the summer. Omar was visiting from Qatar, where he had been born and raised and where we'd met and lived for most of our married lives.

It was an autumn afternoon, and we were about to leave the house to meet one of my cousins for coffee. "Habibti," he said in that gently lilting voice with his accent that was so hard to place, "just give me an hour, ok?" He wanted to sleep for a while. "You go and I'll catch up later, Andaleeb," he added, pronouncing my name like honey, thick and sweet, not the way I'd often quickly mumble it, 'Ileeb,' as though I were unworthy of staking a claim to all the syllables in my name.

As a British Pakistani and part Cypriot girl, growing up I'd hated my name. The quicker I said it, the quicker people could forget it and me, I'd reasoned. When I was a student, I'd rented a room from an elderly lady who collected porcelain figurines that she displayed in a cabinet in the front room of her terraced house. She could never remember my name but would sometimes invite me down to keep her company over a meal of salmon and buttery mashed potato. Once, when she asked me about my name, I'd told her that in Arabic it means nightingale. "Ooh, I shall call you Flo then," she'd declared, delighted. "You know, Flo like Florence Nightingale."

It was Omar—a Palestinian who'd never been to his homeland and had grown up without the nationality of the country where he'd been born—who'd helped me embrace my own name, and identity.

It was Omar—who never cared what anyone thought of him and always spoke his mind, who was, in so many ways, my polar opposite, who showed me that it was ok not to be ok, that I didn't need to make other people feel comfortable at the expense of my own comfort.

But now it was Omar—a martial artist who'd just turned 40, father to our two-year-old son—who was regularly carving out time to sleep at the strangest of moments.

He'd always blamed his work shifts for playing havoc with his body clock and often missed appointments, family gatherings and meals to catch up on sleep. I'd learned to accept it and had grown used to doing things by myself.

But now, I knew something was different. His sleep had become more sporadic and an agonizing pain in the pit of his stomach that he had mentioned over the past two years had started to pulsate through the rest of his body, stealing the moments when he tried to rest.

One afternoon a few days earlier, we'd watched an elderly couple at a Costa Coffee. They must have been in their nineties. He pulled out a chair for her to sit on; she stirred his coffee for him. I'd imagined us at that age, still together, sitting next to one another, arms interlocked. But Omar had confided in me that he simply couldn't see himself getting old.

Earlier that week, he'd come with me for the first time to the cemetery where my grandmother is buried. It felt familiar, he'd said, as we walked past the towering redwood trees towards the graves of other family members.

Just over two months later, on a gusty January day, I would be back there. So would Omar.

11 days after diagnosis

"Ma'am," the air hostess leaned across our seats, "please can you ask your husband to sit up in his seat?" She tried to mask her unease with a smile, but her distress dripped into her stilted words.

Omar was sat slumped in the footwell, silently writhing in pain. With each jolt of his body, I readjusted the blanket draped across his aching shoulders, soothing his forehead, our son curled up in sleep and blankets beside me. But now I was signaling to the air hostess with my eyes and gently maneuvering my way out of my seat, careful not to disturb the two pieces of my heart that lay there.

I walked her back to the galley behind the burgundy curtains on that almost empty early morning flight from Doha to Istanbul. “My husband isn’t well,” I told her, quietly, then paused, swallowing back the words I feared saying out loud because speaking them might make them true.

“Ah, yes ma’am, your husband isn’t eating anything,” she replied.

“He is in a lot of pain. Listen, please just let him sit for now where he is most comfortable,” I answered her, with the quiet assertiveness that had creeped unexpectedly into so many of my conversations lately.

“Does he have a broken leg?” she asked.

“No, he has cancer,” I told her, speaking the words I’d wanted to avoid, the words that sent her into a panic as, teary-eyed and frantic, she began to explain that we shouldn’t be on board.

So there, 35,000 ft in the sky, I held her and reassured her that we had permission to fly, that we were traveling for treatment, that we had a letter from the hospital, and that Omar. Would. Get. Better.

Two weeks before diagnosis

On Omar’s hospital bed table were two flasks—one of tea, the other of traditional Arabic coffee. Omar had insisted. There was a steady stream of visitors—friends Omar had known since childhood—passing through each day. They’d sit and talk. And drink.

They’d also eat. “Dates please...but not just any dates, habibti. Can you make sure they are the nice ones, either ajwa or sukri, you know the ones I mean?" Omar's sense of hospitality, even while himself in hospital, required his visitors to be well looked after. So, beside the flasks of tea and coffee, there were dates—the nice ones.

Omar had been admitted to Doha's state hospital shortly after we'd returned from London and the pain had become unbearable, spreading from his stomach to his back. He hated being there and hated being expected to follow the rules. So, somehow, he charmed the staff into letting him leave for a couple of hours each evening. He'd visit his mother to reassure her and then return to our home for a few hours of rest. Oftentimes he'd curl up and fall asleep next to me on the couch, and I'd watch him, peaceful. An intense protective love had taken over—one that felt like it transgressed this world and the next—making me feel closer to him than any time before.

By dawn he would have to leave and return to the hospital, where doctors tried to determine the cause of his pain.

One week before diagnosis

In the week after Omar was discharged from hospital, we took afternoon walks through the park in slow motion—partly because, by now, he was unable to walk as well and partly, I think, because he was trying to absorb every last drop of those moments.

In between sporadic naps and pain numbed by tramadol, he wanted to go on nighttime dhow rides past the shining skyscrapers of Doha as well as drives through some of the older remaining back streets where he'd played as a child. Underneath the apartment block he'd once lived in still stood the small convenience store where he used to buy cans of Shani and packets of Pafki crisps, or Chips Oman.

He wanted to know the most mundane details of my life—where I would eat with friends and what I would order—as though he needed to gather a lifetime's worth of details in a matter of days.

While our son slept, we would watch nineties sitcoms and talk late into the night—the kinds of conversations you might have with a long-lost friend with whom you'd become unexpectedly but joyfully reacquainted. I'd share with him the prayers that brought me the greatest peace and he'd share with me his dreams for our son's future.

"I can't do this without you Omar," I'd tell him. And he'd reply: "You, my love, are stronger than you know."

12 years before diagnosis

Omar had a roughness about him, that on first inspection seemed to need sandpapering down... But shuffle slightly closer, you'd find out he had the kindest heart beating.

The first time I really spoke to him we were in the canteen of the drab office building where we both worked. That was the day he proposed.

He had collected the office's lunch order that day, as he often did because he was that rarest of things in an office full of foreigners who relied on taxis to get around—someone with a car. The canteen was empty apart from Omar and the remnants of other people's lunch when I arrived to collect my salad, ordered less for the lettuce than the cheese quesadillas that came with it. He asked if he could speak to me about something important, which was when I noticed the single gardenia on top of the cardboard box, which seemed like an odd side for a salad.

"If a guy likes a girl," he began to talk to me, his eyes lowered and his voice uncertain, "how should he tell her?"

"Oh god, I hope he doesn't mean me," the voice in my head said, as my mouth spoke different words entirely. "Umm, it depends, culturally. Like in England you'd just tell them, but here maybe it's different. Not sure I'm the best person to ask," I muttered.

"I mean us... You. I would like to ask you if you would marry me?"

I choked on the water I'd been slowly sipping in a bid to maintain some kind of composure.

"I mean, may I speak to your father and ask his permission to marry you?" he continued.

"My father? Oh Lord."

"Listen Omar," my words eeked out like air escaping from a broken bagpipe. "Umm, I'm hugely flattered, and really surprised too, I mean you don't know me, why would you even want to marry me?"

"What I'm trying to say is, will you get to know me for marriage?" he replied.

The penny dropped. I'd figured him out. Like some of the other men I'd work with in the office, he must have assumed that a single woman on her own in a foreign country was easy prey. "Listen, I'm not going to be your girlfriend," I told him.

Offended, his voice rose slightly now. "I didn't ask that. I asked to speak to your father. To be my wife."

I looked at him—he was tall and athletic with a handsome face and a voice that could have warmed the sun. But that didn't change the fact that I didn't know him. I told him I wasn't sure I was interested so there'd be no point speaking to my dad.

I got up to leave, thanked him, and then tripped over the leg of a chair.

There was a hint of a smile now. Just a chance, he asked, to get to know him.

"What if I did get to know you and then decided no?" I asked him.

"I'd ask again," he said, the smile spreading. "And if it was a no again, I'd ask again, and again until you say yes. Andaleeb, listen... you might not yet know this, but you're going to be my wife."

Five years after our canteen conversation, Omar and I were married under the second bloom of magnolia in my parents' back garden.

The day of diagnosis

The three doctors stood separately in the windowless consultation room as Omar and I sat, hand in hand—each of them avoiding our gaze.

It wasn't shingles (as a doctor in the UK had suggested), nor an ulcer (as another doctor in Qatar had said), they told us, but advanced pancreatic cancer that had now spread its tendrils into Omar's stomach tissue, his lymph nodes, his spine.

The doctors kept talking. But I didn't hear them. White noise—like the static from an untuned TV—filled my head. If I let it grow loud enough, it could drown out their words altogether and none of what they were saying would be real. But they kept talking. And time slowed down.

Omar sat in silence, absorbing their words, occasionally nodding his head. He pulled gently on the end of his beard as he often did when lost in thought. Then he refused their offer of a PET scan to help stage the cancer and of chemotherapy to help treat it.

As we walked back to our car, his voice as reassuring as ever, Omar explained to me that he wasn't giving up, that he would fight the cancer, but that he would do it on his own terms. Desperate to sidestep my husband's death, I decided then that if this team of medical experts couldn't save him, I, as his wife, would. I wasn't prepared to live a life without him in it.

The days immediately after diagnosis

Even the most fleeting look online would reveal that Omar's type of cancer, pancreatic, has a three percent survival rate. But as I searched for hope, the facts didn't mean a thing. We weren't alone. Studies have shown that many patients who are told of advanced cancer don't always fully comprehend it, and some wilfully choose to ignore it.

Omar said he wanted to fight the cancer, but "naturally". Our first point of call was a homeopath friend. She prescribed some remedies and recommended a Qatari herbalist, who ultimately took over Omar's post-hospital protocol. There was a masseuse and an acupuncturist, with hair so long her braid swished around her calves as she walked, who I demanded leave our house after she asked Omar how old he was and upon hearing declared that, "Yes, people who are close to death often look older than they are."

There were dietary changes—turmeric was added to everything, there were pressed carrot juice shots, ground up apricot seeds, and all sugar was eliminated—although Omar could barely keep any of it down.

Around us, people did not speak directly of death, but instead of ways to make him comfortable, reduce his pain, ease his ailments. They hadn't promised a cure, but I didn't hear the things that were not said.

Still, I wanted to try anything I could to save my husband. So, in between preparing magnesium baths and coffee enemas, I'd scour the internet for doctors I could get a second opinion from. But each response was the same: it's incurable, they'd tell me.

Then two doctors from the UK told me about the same clinic in Turkey.

11 days after diagnosis

The doctor in Istanbul sat behind a large, glass-topped mahogany desk. He was younger than I'd expected—in his mid-thirties, perhaps, with mousy-blond hair and a tall frame he carried around purposefully.

He examined the medical notes we'd brought with us from Doha, then after a few moments of quiet, shuffled the papers and declared: "You've left it too late." Every day Omar had, he said, would be a blessing.

A fan of metaphors, he explained that Omar was like a broken car, delicately balancing on the edge of a cliff. He could topple over at any moment. But—and this was all I needed to hear—the team at the clinic would do everything they could to pull him back. That included hyperthermia treatment, where Omar would lie in a chamber that heated his body to 40 degrees, a hyperbaric oxygen chamber, IV vitamin drips and an insulin-based low dose form of chemotherapy. He was put on a keto diet with occasional days off, when he was allowed to savor the sweet mangoes and watermelons he longed for.

Two weeks after diagnosis

If Omar wanted mangoes and watermelons, it must mean that was what his body needed, I reasoned. If I could find them, he'd get better, the voice in my head told me as I scurried down the narrow Istanbul street, past boutiques selling leather goods and bakeries full of glutinous fruit-topped cakes painted with syrup, custard tarts and colorful macaroons. The cakes called to me, offering up warmth and comfort on that cold December evening, but my internal voice was relentless. Omar. Must. Have. Mangoes. It shouted. Then it would whisper the next part: Otherwise, he'll die.

(I'd return to the bakeries later, on those rare occasions when Omar and our son had fallen asleep at the same time, and take my purchase back to the apartment we'd rented just minutes from the clinic, where rather than savoring those delicacies as they deserved, I'd devour them in the dark in search of a moment of relief.)

But, for now, I needed to find watermelons and mangoes in order to keep my husband alive. The first greengrocers I found didn't have either fruit. The second explained that mangoes weren't in season. But they did have watermelons, so I heaved one into my rucksack and trudged back to the apartment. I watched as Omar enjoyed a couple of mouthfuls, hopeful that it was somehow healing him, but worried that the missing mangoes might be our downfall.

On other days, while Omar rested, I'd take our son for walks along the same small high street where I'd searched for the fruit I was sure could save my husband. We'd take deep breaths of the cold winter air, play "it" along the pavement and then I'd break off small, soft pieces of freshly-baked pide for him to eat.

On the way back, we'd pass by a large gray stone apartment block where an elderly woman was always sitting looking out the window of the ground floor corner flat. The window was filled with purple, pink, and white orchids and deep green, rich terrariums, all competing for space on the overcrowded sill. The woman had heavily kohled eyes and wore a small floral head scarf tied at the nape of her neck. In her hand she always held a cigarette.

Although she'd leave her small top window slightly ajar, I'd wonder how her plants thrived, blossomed in fact, in that stuffy, smoke-filled room. I wondered how they survived when my husband was dying. Why they were granted life when he was not.

Two and a half weeks after diagnosis

Omar had asked to visit the Bosphorus. He wanted to escape what we had come to Turkey for, even if just for an afternoon. The sea air would do him good, I reasoned. After all, I'd read that it was rich in iodine. So we found a spot at an outdoor café overlooking the choppy, gray water. As we sat in silence, wrapped up against the cold, I watched his face find recognition in something beyond the sea.

I followed his gaze to the murmurations, not the beautiful dance of starlings just before sunset, but to the cacophonic chaos that was the movement of a small dark bird skimming the water's surface like a locust cloud.

We were spectators to their show—Omar sipping his black, sugar-less coffee, me holding on to a glass of sweet Turkish tea left otherwise untouched.

I silently willed him to just keep breathing.

Three weeks after diagnosis

The clouds had been a constant backdrop to our time in Istanbul. I'd observe them each day on the short journey from our apartment to the clinic and watch them from the floor-to-ceiling windows in the room where Omar would have his IV drips. But this was the cloudiest day yet.

Omar had a stent put in at one of the private hospitals the clinic had sent us to, and the doctor was now briefing us on the results that I interpreted as positive. Relieved, I left the room to get some water from the cooler in the hallway. But then I heard a door shut and the familiar clacking of the doctor's footsteps behind me. "Indlieb, may I talk to you?" he asked, gesturing to a side room where I'd seen staff taking their coffee breaks.

My mind raced to the new information he was about to give me, the updates and advice on ways to cure my husband. Instead, he told me I needed to ask Omar where he wanted to be buried.

At that moment, I hated that doctor. At that moment, I cried for the first time.

The next morning, I looked out through the clinic's large windows, watching the pedestrians below us, oblivious to what was happening seven floors above them, as they ran gauntlets across the city's congestion. I turned to take in Omar who was sitting, hooked to drips, in a large blue hospital recliner.

He still had his fist-full of beard, but his body was starting to let go of him. He'd always been so physically strong but now his legs struggled to carry his weight. His movements were slower. Everything had become an effort. Soon, he'd only be able to get around in a wheelchair.

I breathed in as though I were about to start a conversation just like those we'd shared so many times in the moments before sleep, where plans and dreams had merged into one blissful moment imagining the lives we hadn't lived. But I knew this wasn't like those conversations. And Omar knew it too.

"The traffic is crazy here," I said. "I keep thinking I'm going to get run over by a car or something. If I die, can you please send me back to England?"

He reached for my hand and held me with those hazel-green eyes that always smiled before the rest of him and then, with a tenderness he reserved for a few, said, "If I say the UK too, jaan, will you visit my grave?"

I'd live beside it, I told him.

December 31st, 2017, five weeks after diagnosis

In his last weeks, just before his family arrived in Istanbul, we'd sit in the stillness of the night and talk. He'd use words that seemed as though they'd floated down from the ethers, from another world. Powerful words filled with honesty that felt like treasures.

He reminded me of his favorite motto: You meet your destiny on the road you took to avoid it.

Just three and a half weeks after arriving in Turkey, in the sacred hours before sunrise, Omar took his last breath. They say the last sense to go when someone dies is their hearing—I wonder, did he hear his mother's tears?

Did he hear me dialing for an ambulance, or begging him to come back to me as I knelt beside him, hands holding his? Did he hear my staggered recitations of prayers for the deceased, as I feebly understood but still didn't accept?

***

We had never "built" our home, never used the good glasses given to us as a wedding gift but always kept at the back of the cabinet, never unboxed the cooking pots collected as a wedding dower by my long-deceased grandmother, never hung the Palestinian wall art I'd bought to impress him, that Omar said we'd put up "when we get the right house, habibti." We were always waiting for life to begin.

Now, as I returned to London with my parents and son seated beside me, Omar too was on the plane.

Just hours after he'd died, his body—washed, prayed upon and carefully wrapped in a white shroud—had been placed in a coffin that lay in a special container in the space beneath us.

As we entered the yellow-lit corridors of Heathrow airport just before midnight on New Year's Eve, our son, climbing across my branches like a little bird, chirped, "Hello Baba, I see Baba."

Looking directly above us at the confetti of light streaming from the ceiling, seeing something that none of the rest of us could, he pointed, "There's Baba."

A version of this essay was first published by Al Jazeera.

HANDS WITH FADED HENNA

Saeida Rouass lingers on memories like beautiful old photographs in this moving tribute to a friend, confidante and protector, whose past demons took her life too early.

SAEIDA ROUASS

SAEIDA ROUASS is a British writer of Moroccan heritage. She is the author of *Eighteen Days of Spring in Winter* and *Assembly of the Dead*, and has written for *Newsweek*, *The Independent*, *Skin Deep* and other culture magazines. She spent 10 years working internationally, living in seven countries, and was awarded a Churchill Fellowship in 2019 to travel to the USA to research why women join hate groups and their reasons and avenues for leaving. She is inspired by oral history and how stories are altered as they are told, and sees the Moroccan diaspora experience in Europe as a space for creative growth.

“Oi, leave her alone!” you screamed from over the balcony. I looked up at the fourth floor landing where the world lived in miniature. Those gray London clouds above you cast dark shadows over lives, a feature of this new world our parents had not predicted. The Moroccans at number 41, the Bangladeshis at 42, the Turks at 45 and the Somalis at 48, all our parents wrapped us tenfold against the bitter cold of Britain. Escaping war, poverty or the pursuit of employment and opportunity had brought us all together. The journeys our parents had taken over oceans and land both ended and began on that balcony, the meeting point of their collective dreams and the jumping off point for new beginnings. Dislocated from their motherland with their extended families living under one roof, food eaten off a shared plate, clothes passed down from one child to another, they created a surrogate family so that they might weather the harsh conditions together. A makeshift family that for us would last a lifetime, until the day I would wake to find a message on my phone telling me you were gone. I knew at that moment that whatever our parents had run from had finally caught up with us, demanding payment from you for a generation that had dared attempt escape.

I looked up at you as the menace in your voice boomed across the council estate, shattering the nerves of my bullies, and felt your protective shield envelop me. I turned to them with a new confidence that goaded them to pick on me. You can’t touch me now. All it took was “Oi, leave her alone!” or a threat to knock on number 48 and call for the assistance of siblings of circumstance. We were sisters bonded by dreams forged thick by our shared displacement, our culture and unpronounceable names.

As I sit here listening to the imam call us to pray, my mind wanders to those early memories of you. As the bodies move around me, women claiming their spot along the prayer line, I feel them looking over at this strange group of mourners. I wear my grief like a barricade. I won't let them turn your entire life into a learning point for me. You already taught me so much. I utter the words I am supposed to utter in a language that sits heavy on my tongue, but my thoughts are not where they should be. I fight to bring them back to this moment, to fulfill the responsibilities I have to you, but the benign takes over and my mind recollects memories once so insignificant. In one breath they have become priceless and I cling to them so that they may never fade again.

You were always in the background of my life. The world has never existed without you. As I have watched my parents age I've found my thoughts wander towards their death. What will the details be? Will it happen in this land that they came to for only two years, only to find themselves still here 50 years on? Or will it happen one day in their home country as they sit in the town they were raised in, admiring their accomplishments? Yet, it never occurred to me that one day you would not be there in the background, that you would die and I would have to don the Muslim headdress, enter a mosque that I have never felt welcome in, watch as the sins of this world are washed from your body and hand you back to Allah. How stupid of me to take your existence for granted. Everyone dies, including you. To Allah we belong and to Him we shall return.

The memories crowd around me. They tussle to take prominent place in my mind, but I fight back, insisting they form an orderly queue. I don't want to rush this. I want to linger on each memory, slow it down and give each one the time and attention it deserves. Late nights sitting in your bedroom sipping cardamom spiced tea, leaving for university and the pride on your face, dancing to eighties soul on New Year's Eve until our feet hurt and we were asked to leave, the faded henna on your hands and the smell of bakhoor lingering on your clothes. I want to wallow in them, and conjure the feelings they invoke until I lose all sense of time and for a sweet moment I am back behind your brother's office on Brick Lane on a random Tuesday afternoon, smoking a cigarette and telling you my woes and you are looking at me through frowned eyebrows, unimpressed and demanding better.

I conjure an image of you. Your elbows are resting on a table with your hands clasped. The henna on your hands is fading and you are smiling wide at me. Behind you a man at another table leans in to talk to his friend, caught unaware that his image would forever exist in my memories of you. Whenever I look at you, I look at him too, in his Omani dishdash and masar, and laugh at how when we boarded our flight home I turned to you and said, "It's a beautiful country, but I won't ever come back." Who would have thought that this country you took me to, to meet your 11 uncles and one aunt so long ago, would become my home for six years? Every time I went to a particular beach or café I would see you there with your wide smile and hands with faded henna.

I remember asking you about your teeth and why they had those yellow stains. A question uttered by the insensitivity of youth, when you expect honesty from the world without realizing that the truth can be hurtful. But you weren't hurt. You explained it all to me and though I can't recall the science behind it now, I know it had something to do with the water you drank as a child in Mogadishu, before your mother lifted you up and took you to that balcony. So much of our relationship went unspoken. You were my big sister with compassion so wide it had the capacity to love us all. We were formed from that compassion, and though the world saw our differences and took pains to point them out, our bond felt ancient and our commonality was made of something beyond history or circumstance that no human language has yet managed to capture.

You were a troubled soul, chased from the womb by demons not of your making. They lurked in the background of your life. I saw them there too. You kept a watchful eye on them. We thought we could keep them at bay by living functional lives. If I went to university I could escape them, and if you spent your days at police stations, housing offices, and immigration centers interpreting for people who might say one wrong word and find themselves in a cell, on the street or on a plane to nowhere they want to be, we might make amends. Fix what we did not break. But those demons played a patient game. They were stronger and more cunning than either of us anticipated. When your resilience finally crumbled and the vice they had over your heart gripped so tight that you broke, I was not there. I failed you.

We were born out of displacement and raised in the confusion that ensued. We inherited the suffering of our forefathers, but had no way of locating what caused our pain and dysfunctions. Our parents watched with fear at the consequences of their choices and the disruption to their history they had caused. Their superstitions followed them to their new lives and lived in the shadows of their homes. They looked on as a generation was lost. Raised on foreign land with no place to tie us to, they told us stories from another world in an unpopular tongue. They sought to ebb the flow of cultural obliteration unleashed by the pursuit of their own hopes, but they were, in the end, the masters of their own destruction. While they cocooned us in homes that became memorials to the cultures they left behind, outside we faced an onslaught of rejection. I remember the hurt and anger on your face every time you were called Mojo. Our neighbors thought their defense for their racism would hold up, that they gave you that nickname because your actual name sounded similar and it had nothing to do with the color of your skin. But we knew. I remember you helping to clean up the dog shit from our doorstep and wiping off the racist words scribbled on the wall. With a wet cloth you wiped their hatred away and turned to me, eyes filled with rage, and said, "If anyone uses those words to your face let me know." We were caught between the fears of our forefathers and the hatred of our peers.

The world has no right to expect perfection from us. Our lives were never simple, our choices were never free of the contradictions we were forced to carry. We will be who we have to be to survive the reception we have received in this world. Our contradictions and hypocrisies, our selective belief is our prerogative. It may make them uncomfortable, but it is a discomfort for others to bear. We have enough of our own and I will take the judgment of God over the judgment of people.

I have fought to climb over that balcony, and even after all these years the world treats me as if I am either living above my station or selling my heritage cheap. How do I continue to fight for my own agency when I have lost a comrade to the battle? You were always in the background of my life. You always threw a protective shield around my aspirations. And I took your continued existence for granted. I assumed that you were still fighting your way through, still strong. But, the world broke you in the end, sucked you into its abyss until you were surrounded and beyond reach. I always took your hennaed hands, coco-buttered skin and perfumed neck as signs of your strength. Perhaps I was wrong. The things you took pride in were the things that offered us all a false sense of security. I took that sense of security with both hands; it was easier to believe you were okay than to confront the darkness that has always surrounded us. We sacrificed you in order to continue to live our false lives, worshiping false gods. We all have our sins. To Allah we belong and to Him we shall return.

There are prayers I should recite and words I should repeat. There are attitudes I should adopt and philosophies I should preach. Death demands its own decorum. It is Allah's will, her time has come, we have to be strong, we will all meet our maker one day, let's pray for mercy for her soul, this is a warning for us all, the dead suffer when you cry for them, the dunya is fleeting. I should be thinking of you, but even now I can't help but be selfish. I am in mourning for myself. I don't want to pray at your grave or purify it with water. I don't want to be philosophical about your death. If you are gone to teach us all a lesson, surely it is that the world is cruel and unfair. They say when the mourners take the fifth step away from the grave the questioning begins. Who is your Lord? What is your religion? What is your faith in regards to Mohammed? If I camp at your tombstone can I keep those inquisitive angels away? But, if I flounder and make my way back to the world, leaving you in the earth, just remember they taught us the answers. When the angels come, think back to what they taught us in Quran school, as they held the book in their right hand and the cane in the left. We revised together for this test. You've got this.

I want to make it up as I go along, like we have always done. But, I suppose I already know what I will do. I will pray the funeral prayer, I will stand back as the men put you in the ground, I will feed an orphan, dig a well, plead for mercy on your behalf. And if I ever make it to Mecca I will utter your name while touching the black stone. Where I failed you before, I will make up for in my devotion to the rituals of mourning. I will perform all the rites, donate to charity, visit your mother, and I will do my very best not to cry for you because I have to give you the best chance. I will pray to Allah that we meet again in a better place.

Really, I believe in your version of religion. The version you told me one day when I asked you if you felt yourself Muslim. A Somali woman was shepherding her flock back to her camp, so went the story you told me. She had never been to school, was unread and knew very little of the rites of religion. She would often stop to pray. Having never been taught the movements to make or the words to utter, she would look up at the sky, point to her flock of goats and say, "I pray to the God that made these goats." One day she was stopped and scolded for praying incorrectly. She replied, "The God I pray to hears all prayers, regardless of the form in which they are delivered." I will pray to that God.

And, when no one is looking I will also talk to you at your grave about my abysmal love life, wear a bold red lipstick in memory of you, perfume my home with the scent of your favorite bakhoor and walk with a feminine pride. And I will paint my hands with henna for no particular occasion, except in celebration of you.

AMI BESHI KOTHA BOLI (I TALK TOO MUCH)

Daring to speak openly about shame,
Lydia Abedeen finds the courage to temporarily
revive the past, in order to break the
cycle of intergenerational trauma,
with the hope of healing

LYDIA ABEDEEN

LYDIA ABEDEEN is a rising junior at Emory University. But more importantly, she is a writer—a poet and prose thinker. American-born, Bangladeshi by origin, she aims to illustrate the underrepresented in her work. Her heart on her sleeve, she always makes sure it bleeds into her work. Her passions include writing angry poetry, scarfing down tacos, a good crying jag, and fighting the patriarchy. She mostly keeps her writing to herself, but she's gradually coming out of her shell. @lydia_abedeen on Twitter.

"On March 26, 1971, West Pakistan launched a military operation in East Pakistan against Bengali civilians, students, intelligentsia, and armed personnel who were demanding separation, eventually resulting in the nation of Bangladesh. According to Bangladeshi sources, two hundred thousand women were raped, and over three million people were killed. These women were deemed "birangonas" (war heroines) by the Bangladeshi government after the war, but are to this day ostracized and their stories are ignored."

—Tarfia Faizullah, *Seam*

There comes a span of time in the early mornings when the sky bleeds.

You may see it, sometimes; you're driving to work, your eyes bruised from lack of sleep, and the sky splits open, the sun rises, bleeding crimson, then orange, then pink, then blue. The sky heals itself, right in front of you.

I wish it were that simple.

The very word "heal" reverberates, makes your skin glow, swims beneath your skin like a fish that has never before seen the surface until it dies, weightens, rots—until health turns to hell and optimism turns to depression, oppression. When the sky bleeds you never think the morning is going to come. Sometimes you think you will stay stuck in that puffy-pink shade of healing, or bleed back into the crying crimson. I mention this because it was only during those times each day, as I sat at my laptop, recording my research and thoughts for this project, a project meant to show the permeation of trauma stemming from the Bangladeshi Liberation War, that I found my mind increasingly turning to sickness, illness, and promise; to the beginning of days, and the ending of pain.

For when the sky bleeds, it is not just the beginning of the past, but also its momentary return.

***

Immediately, the first thing that comes to mind is the rain, and the fever.

Spring break, 2018. Orlando, Florida. It is nighttime, and the guests are just now leaving my house. I watch them go. It is cold outside, but, standing in front of my open front door, the scents of dhaal and shutki permeating the air, it means nothing—the warmth wraps around me like a blanket, and my cheek burns like a furnace.

Only after my uncle had struck me had I felt the heat.

Shut the fuck up! You talk too much!

The guests are just now leaving. I look at my mother. She is smiling, but the exhaustion in her eyes betrays her. Her shoulders sag downwards. It is pouring overhead, and the two of us stand in the rain to bid the guests goodbye. My father and brothers stay inside, because that is just the way it is, has always been. I have had the flu for days. She had been preparing for this dinner for weeks, and yet, it took one question of mine to unravel it.

The guests are just now leaving the house. The men shoot me dirty looks. The women are too scared to. I feel light-headed. I haven't eaten the whole day, waiting hand and foot on these guests for the past eight hours. The rain soaks into my headscarf, cool against my feverish forehead. I want to curl up where I am and sleep.

It is freezing. The guests are almost gone. My knees begin to shake. My mother has long since gone inside, but I stay where I am. I am not willing to face my transgressions just yet. But my grandmother grabs my hand. I turn to hear her whisper.

Yes, it happened to me.

***

The night the guests left, my father came to talk to me at the dining table.

Mamoni, that took courage. But you have to realize that they aren't mad at you. They are ashamed.

I looked at him curiously.

Those were their mothers, their grandmothers. The unloved offspring of those unions are their sisters and brothers, their husbands and wives. They aren't mad at you. They are ashamed it happened. For how could they have stopped it if it had been coded in their collective blood?

***

My grandmother's sister also came to visit that day the guests came. A delicate older woman. Ninety years old. She held her hand in mine the whole time, her skin paper-thin. Of the matter, she only said this:

All I remember is the pain. Don't you know that they made us watch each other die? That they made us, made us, made us?

***

When they found her she was not about to wake.

Dhaka ports, Bangladesh, 1971. A rice farmer with skin the color of charcoal awakes to harvest the bhaat from his rice paddy.

My grandmother pauses to take a trembling sip from her milk cha. I look at her hands, wrinkles threaded like etched glass.

My hands were once smooth like yours, she tells me. *But even then, they were wrinkled. Waterlogged.*

The farmer found a pink sari, the color of bleeding spring shapla petals, unfurling in the water, seeping into the grass. Found a bruised blackandblue woman who remained enshrouded within the cloth like an afterthought.

A pregnant pause. Then I hear her murmur:

Honestly, Lidi. I would have let him do anything to me by then.

I looked at her, unsure.

If no one sees a wound, does it truly bleed?

***

Regarding the issue, my mother was quiet. She watches my youngest brother play in his high chair.

Rape is genetic. It carries to every generation. Not just for Bengali women. The birangonas had their share, and they gave birth to unloved daughters and sons who were pestered by monsters who used their existences against them. Those people will give birth to children who don't know how to love because their parents didn't either, and will fall for people who'll abuse them.

My mother looked at me.

It's why nobody wants to talk about it. Because they refuse to believe it's important, even to this day. The birangonas aren't just those women. They're every woman, ever since then.

***

The next day, my grandmother flew in one of her old friends from Bangladesh, whose children live in Boston. One of her friends from the war.

I remember how frightened she was of everything. When I came to embrace her, she flinched. When my father came to greet her, tears sprang to her eyes. I remember how she watched my infant baby brother play in the shade of palm trees outside with a clenched jaw and even more clenched fist.

For this reason I did not take active notes while interviewing her. She spoke the same way I remember her, in a blur:

We didn't even know what was happening. They asked me if I was a Bengali or a Muslim and I said both both they took us dragged us bruised us beat us we were animals forced to feed from their hands we were sisters best friends sworn enemies and of course they hurt us hurt us hurt us and we fed from their hands. We'd betray each other for these men's fancies just to suck the mango sap from their hands. We were hungry but more importantly our babies were hungry my daughter grew inside my stomach like a lychee when she was born I cupped her in my hands the same hands she died in. But it wasn't me it wasn't me it was one of her fathers I think I say fathers because I never had sex with the same man. I say sex because by the time she was born I had started to want it, by then. To this day I remember the beating. They beat us the way the river runs don't you remember that old poem Lydia? The river runs that way, slithers this way, that is always the river's way. They dumped me in the river that day. But it didn't take me, and neither did my family. I could never conceive again. I am still repenting for my sins even to this day.

She passed away three days ago, as of typing this. They say there was a smile on her face. When they found her, she wasn't about to wake.

***

There comes a span of time in the early mornings where the sky bleeds.

You may see it, sometimes; you're driving to work, your eyes bruised from lack of sleep, and the sky splits open, the sun rises, bleeding crimson, then orange, then pink, then blue. The sky heals itself, right in front of you.

Or maybe not. Maybe you lie in bed as the sun cracks the sky open, as it oozes orange, yellow, and gold, lightening into pink hues, then blue, you want to curl up and disappear. The sky heals itself, right in front of you, and yet you are still broken. You have been left torn into.

The very thought of healing reverberates, makes your skin glow with shimmer, swims beneath your skin like a fish that has never before seen the surface until it leaps, lightens, glows—until hell turns into health and oppression and depression turn to optimism. When the sky bleeds you always know that the morning is going to come. Sometimes you think you will stay stuck in that weeping crimson, but before you know it you've risen into that puffy-pink shade of healing, and you are. I mention this because it was only during those times each day that I found my mind increasingly turning to healing, love, and redemption; to the beginning of days, and the ending of pain.

For when the sky bleeds, it is not just the returning of the past, but also its ending.

Or so I say. After all, I talk too much.

REVERENCE

Duaa Randhawa assembles memories of her grandfather, centered around his garden in their ancestral home in Pakistan, as she charts her understanding of love and grief and how we access them through the divine.

DUAA RANDHAWA

DUAA RANDHAWA is a writer born and raised in Queens, New York and currently based in DC. Her work and research are in international and diaspora development, specifically with issues of migration and refugees. Her writing is a combination of creative nonfiction and prose-poetry, which meets at the juncture of experience, identity and community. Her work has previously been published in *New Moons: Contemporary Writing by North American Muslims Anthology* published by Red Hen Press.

My paternal grandfather was always very meticulous about his garden. The garden was a section of grass probably six yards long and five yards wide, lined with plants and flowers along its perimeter only, with a large mango tree in the corner. When I think of words to describe the old mango tree, I can only come up with adjectives I would use to talk about my grandfather. It was tall, but more importantly it was grand. It was a little bent over, but it was oh so dignified. It was the biggest thing in the garden and it looked over all the smaller plants from its post in the corner. Every year when the old mango tree would bear its fruit, the mangoes would be collected and given to my grandmother, who would save a small portion of them for the family and distribute the rest to our neighbors.

I remember the last time I was in Pakistan when both my grandparents were alive. My grandfather and I were sitting in the garden on lawn chairs. As hard as I try, I can't remember what we were talking about. But I remember Scooby, our golden Labrador (misfortunately named by my little cousin) was running in between our legs. Well not so much running as pacing—he had grown old and slowed down—but he turned circles around us and would stick his nose through the little holes on the sides of the chairs, trying to snuggle his head into my lap while I pet him, absentmindedly. I remember we were facing the old mango tree and I asked him something about it.

"They're not ripe yet," he said. "I don't let anyone touch them until they're ripe."

Then he leaned in and whispered to me, "I think that girl Aisha's been sneaking some away." He was referring to the maid. "She's a clever one. She hides the pits in my big plant pots around the house." Gumle, he called them. Somehow the word captured the majesty of those pots in a way that "big plant pot" never will. "But I find them all," he said.

"What're you gonna do about it?" I asked him, almost as a challenge.

"Nothing," he said, straightening back up into his chair. "I can scold all I want, but these girls never listen."

Years before that, when the house was still relatively new and the garden wasn't all that it later became, there was a mound of mud and soil in one corner that looked like the beginnings of a construction project. The mound leaned against the wall that split our house from the neighbor's and it was large enough that we could climb on top and look over into the neighbor's lawn. Except for me. I was shorter than my cousins who were eight and ten at the time (or maybe they were nine and eleven) and my five- (or maybe six-) year-old body wasn't tall enough to make the cut.

One time, a few days before Eid-ul-Adha, or as we called it, Bakra Eid, my cousins were standing on the mound peering over into the neighbor's house and one of them screamed, "Look! They have bakre!" I ran over and climbed the mound to see the goats they were talking about. I hopped up and down hoping to catch just a glimpse while I was mid-air. If only I was *just a little bit taller!* My cousins taunted me, discussing the goats amongst themselves. One of them was black, the other white with black spots. *Is it a goat or a Dalmatian dog?* I thought to myself. "I'm going to tell Dada Jan," I yelled at them, once I realized my hopping was futile. Just then, a loud *Out of my garden!* sounded. We all looked at each other, alarmed, eyes wide, all yelling and taunting forgotten. *How did he always know?* We all thought the same thing without speaking it and scattered off the mound and out of the garden.

As the years progressed, the garden did too. My grandfather hired a gardener, a poor old guy who came by nearly every day. He was the only one allowed to touch the plants. Not that that stopped any of us. When he would come over, we would run circles around him yelling his name, which was Mali Uncle (Gardener Uncle) as far as we were concerned. Mali Uncle was a frail and bald man who wore a loose turban around his head. We would tease him by stealing his turban and then dropping it back on his head. We would pluck leaves off some of the plants and sprinkle them over him like rose petals over a bride during a wedding ceremony. We even sang wedding songs. Yet Mali Uncle never got mad, or frustrated. He let us play around him and tease him, and he never even told on us about the leaves.

I don't remember when Mali Uncle stopped coming by, but I remember that he and my grandfather built a stone path at the garden's entrance. It was the most beautiful touch, one that my grandfather was very proud of. I remember that my cousin and I wanted to contribute to the garden so on more than one night when we sat with my grandmother eating fruit, we spit our seeds into our hands, mine from my oranges, his from his apples. We hid our hands under our thighs as our grandmother sliced the fruit, handing it to us with her eyes on her favorite TV channel, StarPlus. We collected the seeds until our hands were full and we ran outside. We dug littles holes with our hands in the soil on one corner of the garden and shoved the seeds into them. The next morning, we would run to the same area looking for the new plant that should have been there. We pouted when we found nothing, and then we would forget about those seeds altogether. I wonder now, if maybe the rain washed away those superficially planted seeds, or maybe Mali

Uncle found them and threw them out, or maybe there's a small orange tree growing there now. I've never thought to look.

My grandfather potted motia in that garden (*Jasminum sambac* or Arabian jasmine), but I only know it as motia, and as my mother's favorite flower. Every morning my grandfather would do the forbidden—pick something out of his garden. He would pick a cluster of the motia and place it in a glass bowl on my mother's bookshelf. Every morning we would wake up to the most beautiful smell in the world. Every morning there were fresh motia in the bowl. I think a lot about my mother's loneliness in that time; of the loneliness of all of our immigrant mothers. And when I do, I find comfort in their friendship.

It's been six years now since my grandfather passed. Five since I started recounting this story on paper. Five also since he appeared to me in a dream. In the dream I woke up from another bad dream. And in that bad dream I found my grandfather alive. We embraced and I clung on to him. When we parted, he said:

"Duaa, why do you cry over me all the time. I do not miss you at all."

Three and a half since I was at Cornell getting my master's degree. My advisor introduced me to a friend of hers who was also a Pakistani writer. Before meeting her for dinner, I picked up her book, *City of Spies*. I remember a scene in it in which the main character's parents attend an event at the American embassy in Islamabad because her father is a WASH specialist for the government. She says that the embassy was the only place in Pakistan where drinks were served openly. I remembered my father, and my mother alike, speaking on multiple occasions about how principled a man my grandfather was. "He worked with Americans his entire career and never smoked or drank a day in his life." I called my mom. "Where exactly did Dada Jan work?" My grandfather was retired for the duration of my conscious life, but I knew he had had an American job in Lahore. At an American bank maybe? Some position that allowed him an American visa and citizenship for my father and family. "USAID" my mother said.

I spent a moment in silence, letting the existential shock permeate; wondering if my mom had also just connected the dots; marveling at how God works; feeling incredibly stupid; not knowing whether to laugh or cry. "Do you know what USAID stands for?" I asked my mom, whose extent of understanding of my degree and career path was vaguely that I "work with refugees." On a good day she could remember that the title was "international development," but the good days were relatively infrequent. "United States Agency for International Development," I told her. Three years since I discovered that I was following the footsteps of my beloved, and a lot more closely than I had known.

On the morning of my graduation, which was in fact canceled because of the pandemic, I woke up from another dream in which my grandfather appeared. He stood on the green grounds of my university in an all-white shalwar kameez. Into the frame walked my mother's father, dressed the same. They stood over my grandfather's brother-in-law, who, in my dream, sat in a wheelchair. He was another gentle warrior who, alongside Dada Jan, advocated on behalf of my mom for her father to allow her to pursue a master's degree in a different city. The three men, gallant, mighty and tall, looked at me in proud silence from within my dream, the hems of their white kameezes blowing in the soft wind.

Three years, nearly, since I submitted my master's thesis. The dedication reads, *To my grandfather, for whom is everything. And to my Lord, without whom is nothing.*

I don't visit the garden anymore. In fact, I don't even visit the house. It no longer feels like a home I'm welcome in. Five years ago, I made a visit to Lahore and the big house for the first time, 10 months after his death. Everyone calls it 37D after its address because no one wants to acknowledge its ownership. It no longer makes sense to say Dada Jan's house with both my grandparents gone. It doesn't make sense to say it's anyone else's either, when we all grew up, cousins, under the same roof, now all feeling estranged.

Whenever I traveled back to Pakistan from the US between the ages of eight and 18, my grandfather would be standing in the marble driveway, cane in hand, patiently awaiting the car returning from the airport before the grand gates to the house had even opened and the car made its presence known. My grandmother, with her bad back, bent nearly in half, would be pacing back and forth. Five years ago, when I pulled into the driveway, it was dark. No one waiting. It was as if the house had no presence, even though one of my uncles and his family lived there still. A canopy had been built for cars to park under, which split the driveway and the garden, and suddenly the garden was out of sight. When I entered the foyer, there were massive portraits of four generations of the family's eldest sons, my grandfather amongst them. They had always been there, but I could only notice how they somehow appeared uncentered, misaligned.

In one corner of the living room there was still a long console that my grandfather had dedicated to my achievements. It held a series of certificates that I had received in seventh grade, all framed, with pictures of me in between. I read through them: President's Award, Achievement in Math, Achievement in Social Studies, Debate Team. All meaningless in the long term and yet he never missed an opportunity to be proud. I remember how jealous it made one of my cousins when my grandfather decorated that corner. Upstairs, next to her room, she had created a mantle of her own. My grandfather's room, which used to be filled with piles of books and newspapers—neatly organized hoarding—was empty. His rocking chair, in which he sat everyday watching the news, seemed suddenly so small. How did my giant of a grandfather ever fit on it? How did a house, made so grand and eclectic by his presence, suddenly become full of chipped paint and dirty walls?

Grief is strange, isn't it? We hold it close to our hearts like a badge on our lapels to, through our pain, honor and keep alive those who have left. I remember the feeling when he passed. I was aware that he was a 90-year-old man who would not live forever, and yet I was so afraid of losing him that I was convinced it would never happen. I would repeat to myself God's promise: *He does not put a burden on a person that the person cannot bear*. And I was so sure I would never be able to bear his death, that I had so much faith God would not let it happen.

And yet years pass anyway. When you think the world could not possibly go on without stopping to acknowledge the depth of the loss you've just borne, it goes on anyway. And eventually, with the seasons, and despite the feeling of betrayal, we too fall into the rhythm of orbital resonance. Degrees obtained, cities changed, love fallen into and out of; after all the wear and tear of the heart, it still goes on.

I'm reading back something I wrote five years ago, during my year of mourning, when, between death and breakups and some existential angst, everything felt lost. It says, "I think being in love is the closest we can come to worshiping a living being." I think the feeling I was trying to understand at the time was the divinity of love. Why, no matter whom I loved, my grandfather, my baby sister, my Creator, or my lover, love all felt the same. In all its simplicities and complexities, all its intensities, it was just love. Rumi says: *Whoever falls in love passionately, a radical love that spills over, finds God.*

A common phrase in the Islamic tradition is to love someone for the sake of God. I never understood this growing up because love was a joy I wanted to be selfish with. Love was a filling of the heart to the brim. It was the synergy between anguish and calm. If I were to love someone for the sake of God, wouldn't it rob me and the object of my love of the intensity and volume of what I felt? Somewhere in the past five years, God became the object. And the avenue. The medium and the means of love.

Love now does not feel like a worshipping, it feels like a reverence. Like a respect so deep that I have to turn to God for you. And yet I do not even ask God *for* you, but I ask him on behalf of you. It feels like the greatest transgression in love would be the delusion that it is just you and me, that we are anything to each other but a cosmic intervention, a divine assembling. It feels forbidden to think that you are anybody's but God's and so I keep finding myself on my knees asking Him to hold you, to care for you, to be the river and the current that lulls your floating heart. It feels forbidden to ask for forever, to ask for anything to stay the same, to ask for the current to stop its movement for even just a second. We are simply a meeting.

It was six years ago now that with the grief of my grandfather's death I carried the grief of another, very much alive. I had never mourned the living this intimately before.

And now, six years later, I find myself again at this juncture, having loved and lost. But it does not feel the same at all. It is not mourning I feel, only a very deep missing, to which the word *missing* does no justice. And every time the thought of you crosses my mind, a prayer leaves my lips. How can we talk about loss, when through love, we've found God?

I think time becomes less linear as you grow older. There are no longer seasons of hardship and seasons of joy, but everything, all together, all at once. There is another Quranic verse:

Surely, with hardship comes ease. فَإِنَّ مَعَ ٱلْعُسْرِ يُسْرًا

It is often interpreted as the light at the end of the tunnel, the rainbow after the rain. But God did not say after hardship there is ease, He said *with*. The good and the bad, they happen all together. And grief never leaves you. It changes the landscape of your heart, and you find yourself loving and losing all at once.

ISLAM AND THE END OF THE WORLD

Youssef Rakha recounts an existential crisis coinciding with 9/11, which forces him to reexamine his life and the rise of fundamentalism in Egypt.

YOUSSEF RAKHA

YOUSSEF RAKHA is an Egyptian novelist and essayist who writes in both Arabic and English, thinking about Egypt, Arabs and Islam. Born and raised in Cairo, he graduated from Hull University, England, in 1998. He has worked as a cultural journalist, literary translator and creative writing coach since then. His first novel to be written in English, *The Dissenters*, is forthcoming with Graywolf Press. He lives with his family in Cairo.

The world ends suddenly on the night of September 6, 2001. I am alone with my filmmaker friend Islam when it happens. Something beautifully orgiastic is unfolding on the TV screen.

The taut, small-breasted torso of an impossibly desirable Brazilian undulates over a man on his back. Her skin is fawn, her partner's white. And Islam just can't forgive him for repeatedly losing his erection, as porn actors sometimes do.

The end of the world is a barely perceptible event, but there can be no doubt that it takes place. In the blink of an eye, all that is good or real or meaningful vaporizes, leaving behind a black pit as vast and formless as outer space.

We are at Islam's artsy and perpetually dusky flat at the time: cool company in a cozy setting. Islam wears his curly hair long with a sprawling black beard. He likes to smoke cigarillos with his cognac, which he sips slowly but interminably. Balanced on one of his batik-draped ottomans, he cuts a squat figure in the basketball jersey and tailored shorts he wears at home. You can always spot crystals of perspiration glittering on his upper arms no matter what the weather is like.

But tonight it isn't alcohol that's making Islam hot. On my advice, he is holding a small bottle of chilled mineral water in place of his usual snifter.

This isn't a dirty movie, he keeps saying, pointing the bottle at the sky in the window. This is an innocent young woman innocently enjoying herself. Why must he ruin her fun? I mean, Islam almost weeps as he speaks, do you see how beautiful she is?

His earnestness doesn't surprise me. He asked me over because he wanted to try ecstasy for the first time. It was too soon after the last time I took it, but I over-eagerly obliged.

And for hours, in this place full of ethnic and exotic things, we've shared the uncanny openness and connectedness it brings.

I am in a good place to start with. I have no work the next day, and everything at my girlfriend's and my parents' and the office is taken care of. I am healthy and in good spirits, confident I know what life is about and that I am living it well enough. Then I turn to the window.

I don't know what makes me want to see the spot where Islam's water bottle was pointed like a lighthouse in a seascape. At that moment the nymph is arranging herself on all fours while an unequivocally erect penis—a different one?—edges into her inner thighs. But when I turn back to the screen she is no longer there.

Strange static quickly resolves into the apocalyptic image of a plane flying into a skyscraper. Dark clouds trail tiny figures, some of them on fire, jumping out of windows at enormous heights. You can see the debris of civilization gathering right there in front of you. There are sirens and screams. For a moment I can make out both Armageddon and Beauty on her Knees. Then the static returns, Portuguese murmuring marks the movie's resumption. But by now it's too late.

Even then I can tell Islam has seen nothing. But by the time I gather enough focus to stand up and explain that I don't feel too well, I have no doubt the world has ended.

For a while I wishfully think that this darkness, this centrifugal black despair might be a bodily malfunction: an overdose or reaction, perhaps quite serious? But then I notice I am awake and breathing normally. I can walk, talk and ponder. I can see light and color. And when I leave, as I soon do, to Islam's ill-concealed consternation, I have no problem driving home.

The stairs, the pavement, the steering wheel—the surface aspect of reality hasn't changed. Yet the world as I've known it, as I've liked and trusted and taken pleasure in, is no more. In a few seconds it was replaced by a transparent hell of terror and dismay, like the existential abyss incarnate. And the fear—the fear is so primal it eliminates space and time.

Hell is neither hot nor cold. It is neither white nor black, though I shall always remember it as a kind of translucent blackness attached to the world like cling film. Hell doesn't look or feel like anything because it *is* everything. Every waking moment it dissolves the infinity of perceptions that is reality into a single, horrendous experience.

That night I eat Naima's no longer soothing phad thai. The next day I stay at my parents', as I've done periodically since moving in with N., so I can place myself in my mother's no longer comforting presence. I work, I socialize. For weeks I try to slip back into the rituals and routines that form my map of reality. I still have no idea where I am, or why it has to be so awful. No matter what I think or do, I can't find my way back to the world. I am 25.

Sometimes I like to think I saw 9/11 before any images of it could be broadcast, that I saw it on Islam's TV screen like a precognitive episode in a science fiction novel five days before it happened.

It's true there was no way I could've known, but I will gradually come to see 9/11 as a cosmic echo of my own situation. I've blocked out my dismay and indefensibility regarding my father's death and my falling out of love with Naima. Perhaps the Muslim world has done something similar regarding its discontent with history and descent into fundamentalism?

As the weeks then months progress and I finally see a psychiatrist, I begin to acknowledge the facts of the case.

It's been nearly a year since my father died in October 2000. First I convinced myself that I wanted him to die, not out of hatred so much as convenience. He had become a burden, for decades he hadn't enjoyed life. So, instead of telling him I loved him, I sat him down and yelled at him. On more than one occasion mother needed my help to transport him to the hospital or be by his side while she was out, but I didn't answer her phone calls. Later, while my mother fell into a severe depression, my hashish intake became greater than I pretended I could handle.

Although my girlfriend never smokes, by September 2001 my bloodstream has been saturated with THC for a solid four years. In the last year I've been taking whatever else comes my way too, perhaps to break out of a hashish trance that is becoming unbearable. I never thought there was any reason to worry about safe drugs like ecstasy. But perhaps I haven't been as cheerful or in control as I've thought.

In a way, the most devastating part of the end of the world at Islam's is how it forces me to give up hashish.

I remember lighting up the next day, just as I'd done every two hours or so for years on end. I remember doing it in the unassailable conviction that everything would be alright after a drag or two. And, four or five joints later, I remember facing the shocking truth that everything was still not alright.

Hashish isn't the panacea I've taken it to be. It isn't a safe conveyance through every leg of the journey. If it were, it wouldn't see me through to the existential abyss, would it? To find my way out of hell—this is my eventual epiphany—the first step is to let it go.

Giving up hashish is like being parted from a person, the person I love more than any other—more, in some ways, than myself.

In the buildup to the millennium, this person opened up vistas. He took me through the winding alleyways of Fatimid Cairo. (For better or worse I can only think of hashish as a he.) Sitting with my back against Mameluke ruins, I was not a middle-class tourist but a sipper of sweet tea in empty lots. To the squeaky sound of early Umm Kulthum songs on a rickety cassette player hanging from a nail in the unpainted wall, I melded into a ring of working-class smokers sharing the vegetal paradise in the dark.

Hashish slowed me down enough to appreciate the opera-like art of Quranic recitation: a single vocal apparatus acting out the holy dramas in sublime musical modes. It's a magic I'd been deaf to, partly because of its association with funeral rites. But in hashish's company death isn't as repulsive as it used to be.

The pigeons wheeling over the minaret-mottled skyline at sunset reconciled me to Egyptianness.

His hand was on my shoulder then, too. So I was more than happy to overlook the behavior patterns he had inculcated in me. I took a considerable cut of every lump of resin or raw opium I bought for others, with no compunction. He persuaded me there was nothing wrong with that. People no longer mattered anyway. They existed only as conduits to him or servants at his table. No social effort was worth making that didn't bring him closer or keep him longer. Except for potential sex partners—to be fucked at his instigation and under his surveillance, of course—people had stopped being interesting. Even the people I loved had lost the privilege of my compassion.

I blamed my mother for her grief, abandoning her in her hour of need. As amphetamine energy flooded my THC-honed senses, I made love to N. with only pretend passion, without tenderness or togetherness, almost without her being there. Lost in the time tunnels and numinous oneness into which he took me, I remained wilfully blind to the horror shows unfolding all around.

The rise of fanaticism and the fall of the middle class sound like general, abstract concepts. So does the failure of postcolonial nation building.

But my father had been suicidal since 1952 because of the way the July Revolution had brought political freedom to an end. People were tortured and killed for embracing political Islam, but this didn't stop religion from co-opting public space, leaving no room for personal freedom either. Having dreamt of a literary career, I had to pay the publisher who put out my first book, and still nobody paid any attention to it.

Is this why I've wound up in hell at Islam's?

I don't know at what point I realize I am molting. Hashish has given me an armor, a hard skin by which to make sense of the world. In four years this has become the only self-image I recognize: my persona, the sum total of my ego. If not for that night at Islam's I might never have known how brittle it is.

Now it is peeling off me, exposing my bloodied flesh. One by one, I get to see the skeletons buried underneath: bottomless grief for my father; remorse towards my mother; resentment of N. and, more and more, self-hatred for staying with her; a deep, unacknowledged despair with career and country and the world of human beings at large. But, most importantly of all, I get to see the severity of my anxiety about hashish dependency and a directionless life…

Cairo is a charnel ground of the soul. Millions of psyches lie about at various stages of decomposition, denuded, devoured by the necrophiliac beasts—sectarian, jingoistic, self-hating—that roam the urban humus.

Perhaps it's this otherworldly drama that, in spite of incredible crowding and chaos, makes Cairo a limpid space. You look around and you see the city that lives inside you. You walk down the street and it's like moving through the corridors of your soul. Cairo shows you nothing consensual or reliable, only what you have to see.

Between religion-propelled planes crashing into Manhattan skyscrapers and a Cairo journalist dealing with his father's death there is no obvious connection. But, while I sought to ameliorate hell by thinking of it as one of many possible Cairos—a painting, or a film—I grew convinced the two events were in some sense identical. (For me, they had become.)

I had to have my own 9/11, a mini meltdown not so much about global politics as personal history. I had to experience that kind of abysmal horror before I could start anew.

It will be another 10 years before, ecstatic in the midst of millions-strong demonstrations that promise a new career and country and renewed hope in human beings, I feel a tremor comparable to what happened at Islam's. By now I've reclaimed hashish's gifts, sober: Sufism and Quranic recitation are abiding interests. I've had relationships in which the passion and tenderness were so real they broke my heart. I've traveled. I've grieved properly for my father and cared for my mother. I've written the book that would make me proud.

Besides, Egypt is being born again and my filmmaker friend Islam is somewhere around the city center fending off tear gas with his camera. I am 35.

It'll take only a few months for me to realize my excitement is unfounded. So, after becoming a revolutionary, I will have to shed my skin again. This time it won't be nearly as painful, though I flatter myself that it's just as profound. And for a few months, as far as I'm concerned, the middle class is rising again, fanaticism falling and a more viable experiment in nation building being kick-started. Who would've thought?

Revolution is raging on the streets and I am part of it. Life is beginning all over again.

THE ICE MERCHANT

In 2003, Ameena Hussein finds a second home on the northwest coast of Sri Lanka, and gains acceptance in the more conservative Muslim community there once she befriends a Muslim man who is much more of a traditionalist than herself.

AMEENA HUSSEIN

AMEENA HUSSEIN is a writer and publisher. She lives in Sri Lanka, where she divides her time between running the Perera Hussein Publishing House in Colombo, which she co-founded, and her coconut and cashew farm on the northwest coast of Sri Lanka in Puttalam, where she lives off the grid. Her novel *The Moon in the Water* was longlisted for the Man Asia Literary Prize, and her short story collection *Zillij* won the State Literary Prize. Her most recent book *Ibn Battuta in Sri Lanka* won the State Literary Award in 2021. She is a fellow of the International Writing Program at the University of Iowa.

The man on the other end of the phone was excited. He stuttered a phrase, the line crackled. I removed my mobile from my ear and squinted at the unfamiliar number on the screen. "Hello! Hello?!" I shouted into the phone. Once again, I could hear him only faintly. I stood at the entrance to my house hoping to get a stronger mobile signal. Unexpectedly, the line became clear. "Hamdoon is dead," I heard. The line dropped.

***

When we returned to live permanently in Sri Lanka in 2003, my husband Sam and I spent two years looking for a property that would become our second home, away from the busy capital, Colombo. Our search was confined to the northwestern and southern provinces, which were located a safe distance from the civil war in the north of the country. We had no idea what the perfect piece of land would look like, but we were convinced it existed. We found it in Puttalam, a small old-fashioned town on the northwest coast of Sri Lanka. Puttalam has a large conservative Tamil-speaking Muslim population, with neighboring villages that are Catholic, Hindu and Muslim. Our little cashew and coconut estate was within a Sinhala Catholic village, but we frequently had to head to the main town, 13 kilometers away, for our farm and household supplies.

Puttalam was a traditionalist place, where nearly all the men sported long beards and the women draped flowing black Saudi-styled cloaks. I was reluctant to reveal to the Muslim traders I did business with that I too, was a Muslim, as I was not like any Muslim woman Puttalam denizens might come across. My head was bare and my arms were often bare too.

I wore trousers and skirts, and drove a double cab truck. In short, I appeared to be the opposite of the standards set for Puttalam Muslim women. My reluctance was further encouraged by my previous experiences in many parts of the island, of general astonishment that I belonged to the Muslim community. But I met a man who changed my relationship with the town and, in lesser ways, the town's relationship with me. As I stood there with the phone still against my ear, trying to process the news of his death, I realized I had lost a friend.

***

Our farmhouse doesn't have electricity, which means we don't have a fridge. Our solution was to construct a crude cement container that functions as a cool box. The only requirement for it to work well was that we go regularly into town to buy ice blocks. Hamdoon was our supplier, our ice merchant as I called him. But in reality he was a dairy merchant, selling milk, ice-cream and yogurt, and incidentally blocks of homemade ice, shaped like the ice-cream boxes he sold. Week after week, month after month, we would frequent his shop for ice. He would usually be seated behind an undersized desk that emphasized his girth, backed by two large freezers that sat at the end of the small room. Most often he was examining small, scribbled-on pieces of paper, or reading the Tamil-language news.

Hamdoon was a middle-aged Muslim man sporting the trademarks of his conservatism—a bushy long beard and a prominent prayer scar on his forehead. He almost never engaged me in conversation, except for a brief smile that flickered across his face when he caught my eye. When he smiled, his normally sober face brightened considerably.

While Sam conducted his business inside the ice shop, surrounded by other male customers, I preferred to sit in the vehicle and watch people—black-garbed young women teetering precariously at the edge of the drain to avoid a dairy truck that took up the width of the entire street; a grandmother wearing a colorful sari with one end draped over her head, escorting her grandson, tightly clutching his wrist; a group of young women, their faces completely veiled, standing uncertainly outside an abaya dress shop at the corner.

One day, two years after we bought the farm, I had to run errands without Sam. Knowing I would have to also buy ice that morning, I dressed conservatively, in my white linen trousers and blue shirt, and drove into town. As usual, Hamdoon was immersed in a newspaper. I greeted him as I entered, and at first he didn't realize it was me. Once he did, he appeared confused. Recovering quickly however, he broke into a smile and said, "You say assalamu aleikum just like our people." I smiled back and said, "But I am one of your people. I am Muslim too." Puzzlement flitted across his face, but he immediately composed himself and attended to my requirement without any more conversation. As I drove off, I could see him in my rearview mirror, standing on the stoop of the shop, watching after me.

The fact that I was a Muslim had broken an unacknowledged code within Hamdoon. It soon became apparent that he didn't care that I dressed or acted differently, it was the commonality of our faith that was most important to him. On our ice excursions I began to enter his shop with Sam, and we began to chat more. My mother, on one of her visits to us, encouraged Hamdoon to speak Tamil to me, so that I could improve in the language. We gave him pomegranates from our estate, he gave us fresh prawns caught from the lagoon. It was the beginning of a slow series of small steps towards becoming friends.

Several weeks later, during the month of Ramazan, Hamdoon spontaneously invited us to break fast with him and his family at sun down. Just before sunset, Sam and I presented ourselves at Hamdoon's home. In the first room was a small table set for two, neatly laid out with dates, water, fruit and bowls for rice cunji. I wondered if he and Sam would eat here, and if I would be asked to join the women. But that was not to be at all. Instead, we were told we would be breaking fast here, by ourselves, while Hamdoon and his family ate in the inner room. I felt a twinge of sadness. Here was a man and his family who shared the same faith as I did, yet he was still treating us as honored guests, as strangers, foreigners. We continued standing and looked unhappily at the laden table. After a pause, Sam asked Hamdoon if he would join us. There was a moment's hesitation, then he asked his two older sons to join him and the five of us broke our fast together. We chatted comfortably as we ate and afterwards, to my delight, his two daughters came out from the screened-off quarters at the back of the house to say hello.

It would be at least a year, after the first visit to his house, until I met his wife, though I already knew a little about her from her husband. I knew that Safire was a trained teacher, that she and Hamdoon shared a birthday, and that they liked to cook together. He disclosed their ambitions for their children to become professionals, unlike him. Often, while I sat on a stool in the shop sipping flavored milk or a cool Necto,

Hamdoon would tell me their dreams for his eldest daughter. She was sitting for the medical entrance exams and he was so very proud of her. When she was accepted into medical college, we gifted her a stethoscope. As the years progressed, the break fast during Ramazan became an annual tradition. Hamdoon and his sons, and later his married daughter and her husband, would join us in the ritual ceremony.

Soon, we began to depend on Hamdoon for a number of things regarding our living in Puttalam. The pharmacist, the fishmonger, the egg seller, all entered our lives through Hamdoon. If I needed a banquet cook to serve lunch to 60 of my relatives, no problem, he seemed to conjure one. When I wanted to buy three niqabs for a theater-play, Hamdoon accompanied me to all the niqab shops in town until I found the perfect ones. Dig a well, rent a generator, find a plumber, batteries for the solar system, the list went on and on. Hamdoon was always there for us. Our relationship with the town began to change too. We began to be recognized, people hailed us on the street, and stopped us for chats. Hamdoon came to visit our estate. He came with his wife for lunch, met my family, visited my home in Colombo with his younger daughter and even asked me to accompany her to the hospital in Colombo when they needed support. At that time, I knew it would have been uncomfortable for him to describe our relationship as friendship, but one thing was certain—we could depend on each other whenever needed.

Towards the end of October, we drove into town. The lagoon shimmered in the morning heat. The rains were impending, but it was a sticky, warm light-filled morning that promised a muggy day. A salt tinged breeze floated over the lagoon towards me. The egg seller had a new kitten sitting on his table. The shop's cloistered walls were painted lime green with a band of red running round the mid-way point. The young man running to fat looked up at me and smiled as he picked up the scrawny kitten and stroked it. I asked him if the kitten had a name. He looked puzzled and said, "Kitty." I practiced my halting Tamil, my clumsy tongue trying to remember words in the language my grandmother spoke. Twelve eggs. Pathirendu. "Are you going to the wedding?" he asked. I nodded in excitement. Hamdoon's daughter was getting married.

The marriage was arranged as was customary within the community. Out on the farm, I carefully draped my sari in the style of my grandmother, and Sam placed an embroidered skull cap on his head as we entered the wedding hall. It was a lavish affair and Hamdoon's sons, who had shunned their daily western clothes for north-Indian finery, looked like Bollywood princes. After lunch, Hamdoon escorted us upstairs to shake hands with the bridal couple. His daughter was wearing a beautiful gold and red sari. She sat on a bedecked throne decorated with jasmine and sparkling lights, while her western-suited husband hovered beside her. We stood for photographs with the beaming couple before we drove home through the deep purple of dying heat and haze. That was the last time I saw Hamdoon. Barely six months after his daughter's marriage, I received the disturbing call from Puttalam. Hamdoon had passed away. A mysterious ailment had claimed him.

With his death, our contact with the family lessened. Most often the shop was closed. The few times we went in, they had run out of ice. Many times I thought the shop would close down, but it survived in a desultory fashion.

And then all our lives changed. On April 21, 2019, Easter Day, amidst prayer and celebrations, six suicide bombers detonated themselves. More than 250 people died either praying at church or enjoying Easter breakfast with their families. The country's 10-year peace was rent asunder and all Sri Lankans, regardless of ethnicity and faith, were horrified at what had happened. When I discovered the bombers were Muslim extremists I was devastated. It was not a scenario I had ever envisioned happening in Sri Lanka. The unjustifiable violence, and the senseless destruction, shook me to the core.

Five days after the attack, we went up to the farm. As we drove into Puttalam, an air of grief and fear hung over the mostly Muslim town. White flags wreathed buildings and many shops had hung the national flag in a show of solidarity. The traders were silent as they served us and didn't engage in much conversation. Shop hours were erratic and people rushed about, occupied with other concerns. Hamdoon's family entered my mind fleetingly, but I was not ready to face them. I didn't even want to speak to them over the phone. At that time, I thought it was people like them—conservative, insulated, seemingly devout—who had paved the way for these young men to become suicide bombers.

When the month of Ramazan began early May, I was still not ready to face Hamdoon's family. And so it wasn't until the last weeks of Ramazan that I decided it was time to go into town to meet Safire, who always helped me get my food packs ready for distribution to the needy—my annual tradition since Hamdoon's death. Safire answered on the first ring; our call was short and to the point.

Waiting for us at the shop, we saw someone we didn't recognize at first. There, with a wide grin on his face, stood Atif,

Hamdoon's eldest son, who had been away in Qatar. He was now a mature, young man and had married two weeks ago.

That year, marking four years since Hamdoon's passing, we received an invitation to break the Ramazan fast at Hamdoon's house once again. Because the invitation had been so unexpected, I had no appropriate clothes to wear for the evening. I borrowed a sarong from Sam and paired it with a long floaty blouse. As we climbed the stairs to the rooftop, I wondered how the evening would turn out. Would we pretend as if nothing had changed? Would they be bitter about the resulting mob retaliation against Muslims in some parts of the country? I had no idea how to act and it was making me anxious.

A long mat was rolled out on the floor of the terrace, laid with bowls of rice cunji, dates and short eats. Atif had asked other family and friends to join him, and we watched the sunset over the lagoon together as the azaan was chanted from the minaret.

Our conversation was sober. Sitting all together, both men and women, eating our cunji, we could speak of nothing but the bomb attacks. They were as horrified and shocked as I was. They, too, couldn't understand how it had happened. Together, we spent much time trying to understand how such violence could have been perpetrated by young Muslim men, men who seemed to have everything going for them.

And then, they expressed their fears. The same fears I had. A revenge attack seemed inevitable, for only a short distance away in Kurunegala the Muslim community had been attacked by reckless Sinhalese youth—a retaliation that appeared planned and had spread to other areas. We sat in sadness and quiet reflection, long after the meal was over.

Eventually, we spoke about Hamdoon and how we missed him. Safire sat by my side and as her eyes teared up, we held hands and spoke about how special he had been to us. An ordinary man, living an ordinary life, showed me with his extraordinary heart the real meaning of being Muslim. I then realized that between us, nothing had changed. We were two very different kinds of Muslims, breaking bread together at the end of the day and collectively feeling the grief and sadness of our country. On my return home for some minutes I sat still, looking out. A tear marked a path on my cheek. A bow of moonlight fell lightly on the lagoon; there was a sorrow in the air, for our friendship, our faith, and our country. Perhaps Hamdoon and I were a mass of contradictions, but we had drifted into a friendship on a wedge of melting ice.

Much later, sitting in the dying light of the moon, I remembered one of the conversations I had with him. My brother-in-law had unexpectedly passed away and I described the memorial services we had for him to Hamdoon. "We don't do those sorts of things," he remarked with a gentle smile. "I know," I told him, "but we do." I knew that Hamdoon, like some other Muslims, believed that practices like these—having prayers for the dead, feeding the poor in their name and having memorial services—were heretical. "It doesn't matter," Hamdoon reassured me, concerned I would be upset by his remark. "Whatever is done," he said, "if it is done with a good heart, it's ok." We stood there smiling at each other. It would have taken him a lot of effort to accept an alternative view, but he did. I nodded at the man before me, both of us unaware at that time, that he too would meet his maker in less than a year.

Hamdoon the ice merchant had understood the spirit of Islam that embraces all those who profess its creed, regardless of appearance or lifestyle. Gray clouds slid softly past, the sea wind lifted along with the long mellow note of a night bird, and a small yet profound joy overcame me. I am so glad I knew him.

THE FLAMINGO CHRONICLES

While visiting a classmate's hometown in Western India in 1980, H. Masud Taj brings to light his particular Muslim experience within a Hindu context. His parting gift: the extraordinary fruit of what might have otherwise become an ordinary journey.

H. MASUD TAJ

H. MASUD TAJ, Architect-Poet-Calligrapher, lives in Ottawa with his family. The previous edition of this book carried his essay, "The Sufi & The Architect." His writings can be freely accessed on Academia at tiny.cc/taj.

Some names in this story have been changed for privacy.

"Men, animal and bird, all complement each other in the world of the Almighty."

Inscription, Royal Bird Feeder in Bhuj
(demolished in 2001 earthquake)

Captain

In 1980, I stayed in the house of—bear with me now—Captain Jadavji Bapubhai Buddhbhatti, Personal Aide-de-Camp to His Highness Maharajadhiraj Mirza Maharao Shri Sir Khengarji III Sawai Bahadur, Maharao of Kutch, Personal Aide-de-Camp to Queen Victoria. The Captain's black and white portrait on the wall was unsmiling but serene, with his groomed parted hair and upwardly turned curved ends of his handlebar mustache. He wore his chest candy with pride: two medals from Buckingham Palace received at the coronation of his king in 1937.

Indeed, his demeanor displayed "Courage and Confidence," standard words on the Kutch Darbar's Coat of Arms, which also included a sailboat. The Captain had two yachts made for his king: *Nagmati* and *Rangmati*. A man with a well-stocked library, he sponsored a mosque in the Muslim pastoralist settlement, Hajipir. A poem began to percolate in my head:

I have walked where you walked
Slept where you slept
I have held your books
Read your face
In much that I touch
There is a trace of you

Other courtiers coveted the Captain's talents and closeness to the king. But, as with accomplished men under challenging positions, the subjects loved and feared him (handlebar mustaches are paradoxically popular with valiant army officers and Bollywood gangsters). Rumors persist that his untimely death was not accidental; his ending ended my poem:

You dispersed into memory
Spread over the land
Piecing them together
Lead me to you.

Googling the king "Khengarji III" throws up 15,000 hits, but "Jadavji Budhbhatti" produces no results.

Chai

The Captain's grandson Nari, my classmate, invited me to his ancestral house in the walled city of Bhuj in Kutch, Western India, because I wanted to see flamingos.

Kutch comes from the Sanskrit kaccha, meaning "a bank of any ground bordering on water; a marsh". Kachhapa means a turtle. Like the turtle, the geological amphibian Rann of Kutch is a vast low-lying desert flatland prone to saltwater flooding during the monsoon as the tides roll in, ankle-deep. But, on the other hand, rivers like Luni and Banas also flow into the Rann of Kutch. This coincidence of opposites, sweet and brackish water, proliferates plankton and algae that flamingos feast on as they build salt-encrusted, damp-mud cylindrical nests.

Nari received me at the Bhuj railway station. As I had traveled overnight from Bombay, we went over to a tea stall and ordered chai. When friends order tea in Kutch, they always specify "cutting chai" brewed with tea leaves, ginger, crushed cardamom, and milk. The waiter gets one cup of tea and pours half into a saucer. Nari offered me the half-cup and took the saucer. Throughout my stay, we had cutting chai, each time insisting that the other have the honor of drinking from the cup.

Cook

Outside the station and across the road lay an open field with a mosque at the other end. We took a rickshaw to his house. The rickshaw turns into Station Road, and after a while, as we pass another mosque on the opposite side, Nari told me rather abruptly that I'd need to change my Muslim name. Then, as we passed the Muslim shrine of Hajipir, Nari elaborated on his startling request: he did not have the guts to tell the resident cook, Kabiben, who was the reigning matriarch of the ancestral house, "Guess who is coming to dinner?"

The house was a block away from the Kalimata Temple dedicated to the Dark Mother Hindu Goddess with red eyes, rolling tongue, a garland of skulls, and four hands, a pair of which held a decapitated head and a sword. You equally did not mess with Kabiben, who would never reconcile to the presence of a Muslim staying in the house, let alone feeding him. So, I had to take on a Hindu name for her sake. Nari had banked on our friendship and our mutual sense of humor and adventure.

Muslim names can be in any language as long as they carry a positive meaning. We needed a Sanskrit equivalent of Masud (fortunate) Taj (crown). Nari suggested Shrikant (lucky), and I added Raj (king). By the time the road crossed the Ground Road near the centuries-old lake and turned around another shrine of a Muslim saint, I was Shrikant Raj. The saint would have approved.

Soon we reached the ancestral house *Pipa Faria*, named after the Pipal Tree in the courtyard. The living quarters were on the upper floor with its dark lacquered antique furniture, library and bedrooms; the kitchen and dining hall at mid-landing level, the domain of the indomitable Kabiben.

Kabiben loved Shrikant Raj; she took to me as a mother takes to a long-lost son. We would have long conversations at mealtimes. One day she warned me about befriending Muslims. "They are not all that bad," I said. "Bad," she repeated louder, eyes widening as Nari flashed his mischievous grin.

Cousin

Nari's older cousin, Rishi, joined us the day we arrived. He was a geology student coming to Bhuj for his fieldwork. Rotund, genial, wearing a beard and several bead necklaces and bracelets, Rishi appeared to be a lapsed hippie. But the good Dr. Jekyll transformed into Mr. Hyde in front of my eyes when he smelled tandoori chicken. I pleaded guilty to importing my aromatic and delectable leftover dinner from the train into the lair of devout vegetarians. Rishi ignored me and threw a fit berating Nari.

That night we turned into a chicken disposal squad, leaving the house in a single file. Mr. Hyde led. Nari followed close behind him carrying my chicken wrapped in a complete edition of *Kutchmitra Daily Newspaper* (masthead: "Mother and motherland are superior to Heaven") inside a disposable plastic bag. I trudged behind empty-handed and penitent.

We crossed a fair with a wooden Ferris wheel, lots of neon lights, blaring music and eating stalls, but nothing deterred us from our mission. Only when we had left it all behind and entered a stretch of a field in darkness without streetlights did Mr. Hyde exclaim to Nari, without looking back but repeatedly gesturing with his hands, "Throw it! Throw it!" Nari did so with gusto. We took a different route to return, and by then charming Dr. Jekyll had returned.

I volunteered to accompany Rishi as he went from farm to farm, testing the water in the wells. We didn't appear to need permission. Rishi would lower a vial tied to a string into the well and pull it up filled to the brim. Then, he would screw in the cap and inscribe some notes. While Rishi was raising a sample of water from the well on one farm, a farmer approached us, said namaste, and asked him his name. Rishi gave his full name. The farmer raised his eyebrows, and his demeanor changed in the presence of the Captain's descendant. He folded his hands again in namaste but, this time, lowered himself to the ground prostrating himself in obeisance. Rishi folded his hands in namaste as well. By his unruffled stance, I realized he was used to such shows of respect.

At that moment, I realized the deep emotion the Captain summoned in the elders, even decades after his demise.

Cylinder

After some days, Rishi departed. Nari then began to inquire about camels to take us to Flamingo City. Salim Ali, the father of Indian ornithology, had visited it in 1945 and estimated half a million Great Flamingos. The number has since never exceeded two hundred thousand tending to their chicks yearly.

As days passed while waiting for camels to take us, we decided to visit the adobe village of Dhordo near the Indo-Pak border. Those days required security clearance, and we would need a permit from the Deputy Superintendent of Police's Office, a half an hour's stroll from the house. Nari gave his name at the DSP Office; the officer asked mine. Shrikant Raj vanished, and Masud Taj reappeared (I wouldn't dream of lying to the Law). They declined our permission, and no explanation was given. Perhaps the DSP was Kabiben's cousin. Nari argued in vain. Once outside, I convinced Nari we didn't need to pay heed to such bureaucratic niceties. Soon we boarded a State Transport bus, taking our chances with the Border Security Forces.

Half an hour after leaving Bhuj, we passed Kunaria, where Amir Khan would go on to construct his epic village movie set for *Lagaan*. Crossing Loriya, we passed a board stating: "You are passing over the Tropic of Cancer." We entered Banni.

Banni means bani hui, made up; of the land formed by sediments of extant rivers such as Indus, Luni, Banas and Saraswati, which flowed through this area from the north and east. In Banni, home to 15 different Sunni Muslim clans of cattle breeders called Maldhari, the women made embroidery marking each clan's identity, akin to tartans differentiating Scottish clans. Mirrors that Banni women cut themselves were embedded in the dresses. Decades later, while researching at Oxford, I visited the Ashmolean Museum; their Newberry Collection included Banni textiles.

On return, I thought I must remember to tell Kabiben that we had traveled the traditional pilgrim route of Muslims returning from Hajj. The Raja allowed the pilgrims gratis entry to Mecca, thereby attracting the Hajj trade but not the wrath of more powerful Muslim Amirs of Sindh to the north. Later the Amirs would use Kutch as a landing point to attack British imperialists. With the drawing of borders by the British,

Kutch separated from Sindh, and Banni was reduced from a thoroughfare to an outpost.

At bus stops, Banni women would board with their colorful motifs in sharp contrast to arid landscapes and the Rabari women in black and the turbaned men in white. Were we to chance upon the Border Patrol, they would have no trouble picking us out in our faded jeans and shirts.

Dhordo in the Rann of Kutch was the last village in the district's Banni northern region, at the edge of a blinding salt desert. When we reached there, it felt like plus 40 degrees in the sun, and we welcomed the shade of round adobe houses called bhungas, which were resistant to earthquakes. The 1819 earthquake destroyed 7000 homes, and an earthquake in 2001 would destroy one million houses, sparing these bhungas but not Nari's ancestral house in Bhuj. Even the ancient Pipal tree, *Ficus Religiosa*, in the courtyard, with its roots Brahma, trunk Vishnu, and leaves Shiva, was not spared. Kabiben would not live to see the annihilation.

Each bhunga was a single cylindrical room. The circular form resisted lateral forces, deflected strong desert winds, and enclosed the maximum area with minimum walls. It was also heat resistant due to the thick mud walls with small windows, and thatched conical roofs provided insulation.

The flamingos shaped their nests as solid cylinders of mud and laid eggs on them; here, the mud cylinders were hollow to dwell within. We traveled all the way to see the interior.

Emboldened by the village supremo Gulbeg Miyan's dictum, "Atithi devo bhava: the guest is supreme," we introduced ourselves as architecture students to a stranger we came across and requested to see the interior of his house. He promptly invited us in. He removed his footwear, and so did we.

We relished the coolness under our bare soles as we climbed two steps up to the earthen floor.

If the outside was formed following function, then inside the form bordered on fiction. Low-relief mud decoration embellished interior walls. A band of white plaster with embossed patterns studded with mirrors in their embroidery ran like a border above the window lintel level. It served as a mantle to store glistening utensils, painted earthenware, and other small items. The bottom of the edge had a pattern like ankle bracelets. Embroidered quilt, with embedded mirror work, hung from the wall. The mirrors and glistening utensils multiplied light entering through the small windows, or as Louis Khan reminded us, "Architecture appears for the first time when the sunlight hits a wall." The window had a security grill called jari (also a word for illicit relations). This was augmented reality before that word became popular parlance.

Catharsis

The following week, it rained, and we feared the worst. Nari's contacts told him the ground had turned slick. The camel's legs, long and skinny yet strong enough to bear the heavy weight of its body, protect it from the hot desert environment. Its soft foot, without a hoof, is gentle on the earth. The local camel even swims in water, but if the desert floor compacts after rain and turns slimy, the camel can slip and fracture its feet. With camels unavailable, we could not reach the flamingos. I was crestfallen. I had come to see flamingos; weeks had passed and my return booking was a few days away.

The following day, Nari woke me up with a gleam in his eyes and his characteristic mischievous smile. His sources told him that a flamboyance of flamingos in their thousands had descended on the Rann of Kutch Lake and that a jeep could take us there.

When we reached the lake, Nari and the driver waited at the shore as I folded the bottom hem of my jeans and waded into the ankle-deep water that never increased in depth, no matter how far you walked. Clear water covered the gray desert floor. Ahead in the distance, a pink carpet of flamingos extended into the curved horizon. After a while of wading, I realized I was far from my companions but no closer to the birds. Either they were in tandem drifting away from me like memories or distances in an aquatic desert were deceptive.

I broke into a sprint, a manic churning of water with a vengeance of velocity shedding Raj and Taj, Nari and Rishi, Dr. Jekyll and Mr. Hyde, Kabiben and Kalimata, Raja Khengarji and Captain Jadavji, all drowning in my turbulent wake, just as a pink tsunami began to rise in silence, higher and higher like judgment day. Pink began to peel away from gray as the flock of flamingos, thousands upon thousands, took to the sky.

I stopped running and stood still, hands on my side, bending back, further back, throwing my head back, taking in the vast curvature of a pale blue sky, fast turning into silent pink.

The City of God
Is a pink city in the sky
It alights into fragments.
Folded wings
Embrace a montage:
Ribs of a Stork
Eggs of a Heron
Webbed feet of Geese

When the City of God
Comes to rest in wet mud
Intertidal zones turn pink.
Constellation of yellow eyes.
Pairs of long legs
With opposing orientations:
One displaced ankle
Folding the sky.
The other extended
Webbing the earth
Swaying back and forth
Mapping wind tides
Laying foundations
Of a new City of Mud
Molded into mounds
With volcanic depressions
Receiving blue eggs
That turn into a white
Constellation of moons
That crack into a crackle
Of red bills and red legs
Turning black with gray bodies
The eyes of the new City
Of God, are gray
Seeking red milk from
Mother City of God
That seeks geysers
Sans salt in the sea
Boiling water
To quench thirst

Before taking flight
At night when pink
Turns gray, and the City
Of God recedes
Into vanishing points
Erasing perspectives.

PINK

In this raw story about a common experience all-too-commonly kept secret, Sholeh Wolpé illustrates the power of friendship with her unconditional support, no questions asked.

SHOLEH WOLPÉ

SHOLEH WOLPÉ is an Iranian-born poet, playwright and librettist. Her most recent book, *Abacus of Loss: A Memoir in Verse*, was hailed by *Colorado Review* as a book that "examines the masks of patriarchy in powerful metaphor and narrative." Her literary work numbers over 12 collections of poetry, translations and anthologies, as well as an oratorio, several plays and multi-genre productions. She is the recipient of the 2014 PEN/Heim, 2013 Midwest Book Award and 2010 Lois Roth Persian Translation prize. She has lived in Iran, Trinidad and the United Kingdom and is currently a writer-in-residence at the University of California, Irvine. She divides her time between Southern California and Barcelona. She writes, "I do not belong anywhere, I have an accent in every language I speak." @Sholeh_Wolpe on Instagram and Twitter. sholehwolpe.com

She was still bleeding, three days later, still in pain. We returned to the clinic on the other side of town. Her feet were put back into the stirrups, her legs pulled apart. There were pieces still clinging to her womb like strands of red algae. The procedure had to be repeated.

No, no, she sobbed. *I can't do it again.*

***

She lies on a cold hard bed, legs sprawled. She scrunches her face, bites her lower lip, lifts her shoulders and neck, arms tensing with pain, and squeezes my hand so hard I want to scream. I reach over with my other hand and brush away strands of hair from her eyes, this girl who was once the jewel of Tehran. Back then, when we were teens in Iran, she was what my mother called *prime good*. The way she blinked her green eyes and deepened her dimples, the way she swayed her hips and unbound her silky brown hair from a tight ponytail, triggered desire even in straight women.

We met when we were 11 at a summer camp at the base of Alburz Mountain. She came dressed in enviable jeans made in the UK. I came armed with copies of the new skit I had written and copied in lined notebooks. We each wanted what the other had: I, her exquisite beauty, and she, my easy wit. Yet, there was no jealousy, no competition. We folded into each other like two-paper origami. Inseparable. Boys I had a crush on fell in love with her. It would be a lie to say it did not hurt, but I knew any boy's crush on me would be wasted. My parents were very strict and wouldn't even allow phone calls from boys who weren't cousins or family friends. So I didn't mind my best friend taking them all. Beauty like that was a gift from God.

Instead, I became the chronicler of her tears, the dispenser of advice, the therapist, the silly cheer-up clown. I'd tug our old-fashioned phone cord all the way into my room, close the door and open myself like a vault to receive the blow-by-blows of her I-said/he-said drama.

Now, between her thighs, the doctor is playing a war game with her body's desire to hold on to what has been imposed—by nature, God, angels, chance. Does it matter now?

He sits in the clinic's spotless waiting room. They were once in love. Or lust. He, has two kids and a conservative wife. She, divorced, with a child. He is ambitious, while she is bitter about what life has dealt her. Perspectives make any story a playdough. You can shape and tell it one hundred ways.

Silence. Then a plop followed by a clink of metal against metal. The doctor walks over to the counter, puts the bowl in the sink, then leaves; his leather shoes suction the linoleum floor. I get up (shouldn't have) and casually wander towards the sink. What's inside that metal bowl melts my marrow—not because it's gruesome, or violent, but because it's nothing but slimy pink spit; because this is how we all begin and live lives of various lengths, between happiness and misery, love and lust, belief and un-belief; between many, few, or no sunrises and sunsets. In the end, bones are buried, burned or crushed, and time bends and bounces, always true to its own form and direction.

She moans, *it hurts*, and I don't know if she means her heart or her womb. I look away from the sink and something catches fire between my eyebrows, a scalding ache like the sting of a scorpion. I pull a blanket over my friend. She closes her eyes. Her face is swollen. Lines around her eyes and mouth spread like runaway roads to nowhere.

Making true love must be skin to skin, he had insisted, refusing to wear a condom. Pills nauseated her. She imagined she was too old to sprout his seed. He bought her dresses, a diamond necklace; delivered promises fragrant as the tuberoses he brought her every week, wrapped in golden cellophane.

I throw up my breakfast in the bathroom, yogurt and peaches that look like a whirling universe of pink starfish. The doctor comes back, and asks my friend how she is feeling. She cries. I go to the waiting room and watch her Persian lover, doused with Paco Rabbani aftershave, pay the bill in cash. The nurse says I look pale and offers me a glass of water. His wallet is black. He counts the bills one by one.

How is she? he asks.

I shrug.

He drops his head, shakes it east to west, west to east.

I do love her, he says.

I rub the pain between my eyebrows.

He looks at me, his eyes the color of burnt toast. I tell him he should go home. *She doesn't want to see you*, I say. He nods, turns to leave then stops. *Please, tell her I'm sorry. For this. For everything.*

I want to say, tell her yourself, jellyfish. But my tongue is suddenly stone. I go back to the room. My friend has dressed and is ready to go. Walking is difficult. Living is difficult. Especially today. Shame is indelible. If you let it, it will stain your forehead like a tattoo.

The doctor puts his hand on her shoulder, pats it gently. He is like that steel bowl, I think to myself; he holds within himself what he yanks out. This is his sacrifice.

He looks at me, straight at me, and I know he's read my thoughts. Or maybe every friend who comes to hold hands has the same thought, this same grateful look. Maybe he registers us all in his eyes and stows us away in the vaults of his consciousness for the days that he battles fear, doubt or fatigue. *Come see me again in two weeks*, he says, jotting down notes. *The nurse will give you instructions.*

At my friend's apartment, I tuck her in, make her chicken soup. She wants a cigarette. I give her two. She smokes five. Drinks tea. Refuses soup. I pick up her daughter from school, buy her a new backpack. The girl is happy. Life is that simple when you are nine. At Johnny Rockets, she mixes ketchup and mayonnaise, spreads it on her burger. Pink.

***

I was a virgin until I married at 19. At the university, my professor, Dr. Teal, was horrified.

You are too young, she roared. She couldn't know that, for a girl like me, living at home with her conservative parents, the only way to experience sex and freedom was to get married. While my friend defied her parents, going to wild parties where she smoked and broke our religious ban on drinking alcohol, surrounding herself with adoring men, not worrying about her virginity, I was the model obedient daughter, terrified of shaming my family. Father didn't allow me to go on dates, unsupervised, unless he was a man of good standing with honorable intentions. I, too, had grown into a beautiful young woman, still I saw myself as the awkward teenager, hiding behind my best friend. To me, beauty belonged to her only.

When I decided to accept the marriage proposal from one of my many suitors, Daddy was relieved. It's exhausting to guard a girl's virginity in a place like America. I picked the youngest and best looking of them to break down that ridiculous barrier to liberty. But my friend didn't come to my wedding. She said I should run away instead. I didn't speak to her for a year. She, who had everything. What did she know about my lack of freedom or want of boyfriends? I had never even known anyone's tongue in my mouth.

The day after, at the customary lunch party, men eyed me with playful ease. I could almost hear their thoughts. *Not a virgin anymore, eh?* They looked me up and down to see how much I had changed from the night before, as if a man's member is God's miracle rod, electricity and all. I went to the bathroom, sat on the edge of the tub and sobbed. When I came out to rejoin my husband, my eyes were two swollen globes of pink. I probably should have run away, but that kind of courage takes time to build.

***

Now, back at the clinic, the doctor is scraping my friend's womb once more. She's been bleeding for three days. *This is my punishment*, she cries. *God is punishing me for my sins.*

I want to yell, God in whose garment? Under what mask? In what country and under what law? But this is not the time for religious quarrels or philosophical demands, for reviewing our lives, mine and hers, and what has been done to us, for us. It's time for letting the body grieve, for letting the womb let go of its product of love, of fear, of accident and imposition.

FOR LOVE NOT DUTY

After a missed opportunity to connect with her father at a restaurant in Durban, South Africa, Neymat Raboobee reflects on the importance of maintaining family ties while mourning something she never had.

NEYMAT RABOOBEE

NEYMAT RABOOBEE is a copyeditor and radio show presenter when she's not writing. Born and raised in South Africa, she is a huge believer in the power of the written word and has seen education reduce bigotry and prejudice to ashes. Her novels attempt to write people like herself into fiction without reducing them to caricatures. In her spare time, she runs a blog and stalks cats on Instagram. theimperfectmuslimah.com @theimperfectmu1 on Twitter.

I breathe in the familiar scent of lemon butter and seafood that permeates the pavement directly outside one of our city's most popular halaal restaurants and my stomach growls. It's been a long day and all I want to do is plop down into a chair and place an order for a chocolate milkshake before we even look at menus. I need sugar if I'm going to stay awake until the end of this quick informal supper. I'm with an old friend and her mum, and neither of them will mind if I'm poor company tonight. But I will.

We're seated quickly but the waiting staff is slammed, and we're warned to expect a wait. I begin to people-watch as the two ladies I'm with launch into a discussion about a relative I've never met. A familiar silhouette catches my eyes and I blink hard. One of my hands comes up involuntarily to swipe at my eyes, as though that will clear the image before me. My father has just walked into one of my favorite restaurants. With...well, that must be his wife. We've never met, and I begin to prepare myself for an introduction. He—my father—had promised to introduce me the last time we spoke. He looks directly at me and I straighten, waiting.

He has no idea who I am. Perhaps it's cruel of me to expect that he should—I've donned the niqab after all and only my eyes are visible. I grope in my handbag for my phone and find his number. The shock of what I'd seen hit me so hard, I blurted out my realization as soon as my brain made sense of the image my eyes were sending it: my father, hovering by the door and waiting for a hostess to seat him. My companions leave me be, not protesting my preoccupation.

I can't help but wonder as I attempt to strike the proper tone with the message I'm attempting to craft whether his thoughts had drifted toward me, his first daughter, at all tonight. He doesn't know I sit in the same room as him right now, but he surely does know that I live within walking distance. After all, he's visited me in that home before, and had made many pretty promises while he was there.

I didn't know if I should greet you, I admit via text. Then, suddenly exhausted and heartsore, I put the phone to the side and force myself to pay attention to the women I'm with. Both of them are understandably confused. It doesn't make sense for a 20-something year old woman to be afraid of approaching her father and stepmother in a clearly public place.

But I am. I've met my father a handful of times. He separated from my mother when I was an infant and contact since then has been sparse. Once, when I was a preteen, I became curious about the half of my family I knew nothing about and asked my mother if I could meet them. I was left disappointed with the awkward, difficult encounters that followed between myself and my father's parents.

Perhaps I've watched too many movies, but I can't get rid of my disappointment. In between constantly checking my phone, I answer my friend's curious questions about my father. I don't speak about him often; I don't have much to say, beyond that we're almost strangers. His DNA makes up half of mine. I share his hair color, his skin tone, his build and face shape. I share none of his memories.

It's a struggle to stop myself from staring and ruining their meal. Instead, as I force my eyes away, my mind tortures me by recalling the high school acquaintance who immediately recognised me when she served me ice cream at a mall. She didn't even know I'd begun covering my face but she called me by name before I could reintroduce myself. If she knew who I was, why doesn't he?

From there, it's a quick trip back to old frustrations. *What's wrong with me? Why doesn't he want me? Why is it so hard to get him to even answer a text from me?* I must've unlocked my cell phone a hundred times by now, and I suddenly feel fiercely glad that my mother is in a city a six hours' drive from here. I'm going to have to go home and be a mess in a way that I just can't here in this restaurant, and she's never been able to hide her anger over my father and his lack of relationship with me.

I feel foolish, letting this consume my thoughts the way it has. I'm a grown woman. I shouldn't need Daddy's acknowledgement to make me feel good about myself.

A notification pops up on my phone and I hurry to open it, clumsily pawing at it. *Sorry to have missed you.*

I hurriedly correct the misconception. *I'm still here. I could come now?* Begging like a puppy.

I've barely eaten anything, even though the table is laden with food. My friend and her mother have left me to my worries and are politely pretending that I'm not having a mental breakdown in front of them. I've turned around so many times it's possible I've injured my neck.

Not a good idea. Disappointment crashes through me. He goes on to explain that his wife's not in the best mood. And then, as a final send off, he offers me a bone. I can walk by, if I'd like.

I would not like. Thank god, I'm not that starved for attention.

It surprises me that it hurts so much. For a long time I've known that my father doesn't place me high on his list of priorities. The few visits I had with him when I was younger always ended the same way—he'd take down my number and promise to call. And again, when we met in court because I was determined that he do *something* for me, I, once again, dutifully handed over the phone number he requested.

No calls. No messages. No letters. Court-mandated money, yes. Money withdrawn from his salary every month, just like insurance or credit card debt. Automatic transactions that required no thought or effort, effected by a machine.

I've experienced love from a father figure before. But that man—my beloved grandfather—passed years ago. These days, I have memories and photographs, no more.

I want, still, to have a father who looks at me with concern in his eyes and asks if everything's alright. *Do I need something? Am I doing okay? Did I have a good day? Is something scaring me?*

Instead, what I have is an offer to walk by his table while pretending to be a stranger so that he's not inconvenienced. I know I'm being unfair. Perhaps he's having the worst night of his life. Perhaps he's protecting me from pain. All I can feel in this moment is rejection and shame.

"It's his loss," my friend assures me.

"Never mind," her mother consoles. "You don't know the full story."

They both insist that I put it from my mind and don't let it affect me, and I try to obey. I still want to cry, but the urge fades.

In my quiet apartment, I lie back and try to organize my thoughts. I've *always* prided myself on not needing my father in my life to feel fulfilled. "*It's his loss*," Mariam agreed when I filled her in, seeking comfort.

Three people have said that within the space of a few hours. I respect their opinions. Hell, I agree with them. Still, I feel like my father hasn't been the only one to lose something tonight. Perhaps it's only just sinking in that the father I used to daydream about, cobbled together hastily from what I'd read and watched, and the interactions I'd witnessed between cousins and their parents, will never exist.

It's morbid to mourn an idea that was never truly alive to begin with, but I feel better when I'm done. I have never mourned my father before. The idea never occurred to me: how do you mourn what you've never had?

Awkwardly, I know now. In bits and pieces, feeling oddly foolish as you experience the emotions.

***

One of the annoying parts about living in Durban is the humidity that thickens the air. Today is one of those days when I would very much like to own a lycra summer wardrobe to combat the heat. I've run up and down between work and home and it's almost time for my company to shut its doors for the year, meaning that everyone is very stressed and rushed off their feet. I'm no exception, and the sweat gathering on my face is not helping my temper.

It is the worst possible day for me to get bad news. Of course, less than an hour after finally tracking down the lost courier company driver and getting back to work, that is exactly what I get. My father needs to talk to me urgently. He's at a café two minutes away from where I work and he'd like to meet me for lunch.

Logic says I should ignore him and concentrate on work, and so logic gets absolutely no say. I've technically already used my lunch break but I leave anyway. I'll work some overtime to even it out.

He's *nice*. Congratulates me on the award I won recently, asks me how my studies are going, talks to me about setting me up with a nice guy. Even fills me in on a bit of family history. It throws me off balance, this niceness. I wasn't expecting it and I'm not quite sure what to do with it. The same questions that I put to bed a few months ago start cropping up again in the back of my head. I don't voice them. I don't know if I'd trust the answers.

Tied up in all this is the fact that this man has made me promises before then broken them easily. Now, here we sit without acknowledging them. I don't know if I'd even accept an apology at this point, but I would appreciate it. It would validate the pain I felt.

The apology doesn't materialize. More promises do, however.

When we part ways, he offers to drop me off at work. I decline. Agreeing, in that moment, would feel as though I was in debt for inconveniencing him and I can't face that. I leave, call an Uber, and refocus into work mode.

Why am I hesitant to accept things from him? The question swirls in my mind. I have no problems accepting money. Child support *I* insisted on when I was 12. A five-minute lift that was all of one turn and two sets of street lights wasn't that much to ask for, but it made me uncomfortable. I want to compartmentalize him from the rest of my life.

I'm afraid. I've given this one person—a very important person, yes, but just a *person*—, the power to scare me, to throw me off balance.

"You're owed it," my mother reminds me when I confide in her, referring to Islamic law. Fathers are duty-bound to support their daughters until marriage, says the religion. Children have certain rights over their parents just as those parents have certain rights over their children.

But I don't want to be a duty, fulfilled out of obligation instead of any real care. I'd rather absolve him of the obligation and grant myself peace. Perhaps I will, if I find myself being reached out to again.

But for now, I'll put it out of my mind again.

***

Another meeting tomorrow. If it didn't continue to frustrate me, I'd laugh at the irony. I'm getting exactly what I wanted when I was a girl and it's driving me mad. All I wanted then was to know who and what I was linked to. I wanted roots. Well, more roots. My mother's giant family with its 70-plus first cousins per generation wasn't enough; I still felt incomplete. I can fill in a great deal more of my sprawling family tree now. Ancestors, rich and poor. Uncles and aunts. Cousins. So many people that it makes my head spin.

Now, with the wisdom that leaving childhood behind brings, I realize that it would be a struggle to make myself known to these people who I share nothing more than a faint blood connection with. Durban is tiny—tiny enough that I meet my father even when neither of us intend to open that door into the past. They know who I am. They know that I'm part of the family. It makes no difference, is all.

Maintaining ties might be a central part of the faith, one that causes us to welcome near-strangers into our homes just as long as they're *somehow* related to us, but the rules for divorced families are different. It's not worth inviting *that* particular drama in to earn points with God.

Tomorrow's meeting will be unlike any of the ones I've had previously with my father. I'm determined to take back ownership of myself.

I'm tired now. Tired, and deprived enough to not be in full control of my senses. Chances are high that I'm going to offend him if I say something carelessly cutting—and while that's not my intention, I'm not going to let myself use it as an excuse anymore. I'm tired of begging for scraps. Either I'm part of the family, or not... And if not, then I see no need to keep jumping when I get these calls. I want a father. An acquaintance with a blood tie just isn't enough to satisfy me anymore.

We meet at the same little café as last time, sit at the same table as last time. Speak about nothing in particular, and then he gets a phone call which eats nicely into the time I have left.

Now's my chance, and when I let it slip by, there's another lull in the conversation. Here's that chance again. I say nothing. The words are there, hovering in the air as I look at him, but I don't voice them. I can't muster the energy for this fight.

As he always does, my father tells me to keep in touch. This time, when I agree, I can feel the lie coating the inside of my mouth. I don't want to pour in the effort anymore. These meetings take from me, and I'm not in a position to give this way.

I make a decision, all for myself, and it feels like freedom.

IT MADE US MERRY

Set in a violent 1980s Beirut, Mona Merhi writes a striking portrait of the resiliency of youth and the endless search for adventure and mischief, even in the darkest of times.

MONA MERHI

MONA MERHI is a Lebanese creative writer, theater maker, producer and researcher. She has published three books in Arabic, *A Feast UnderWater/Tabula Rasa* (2006, short plays), *Out of Order* (2009, short stories/stop-motion artbook), and *Domino's Devils* (2022). This story is part of the latter collection. She moved to the US in 2019 to complete her doctoral studies in Theater History and Performance Studies at the University of Washington. She is currently serving as a lecturer in the school of Theater and Dance at James Madison University.

This story was translated by **AMIKA ELFENDI**, whose bio appears on page 563.

Gisèle passed the crimson velvet collection pouch to us children, who sat on wooden pews. We put our qurush into the pouch, and Mary played the piano while we clamored loudly, singing our hallelujahs.

We were sitting in the second row, holding booklets of the Psalms, tracing the words with our fingers. "Praise the Lord in his sanctuary... Praise him in the heavens for his power... Praise him... Praise him for his might... Praise him." Mary would tap the piano keys swiftly until she reached the refrain. At this point we would get excited, and repeat it over and over, in quickening tempo. "Hallelujaaah...hallelujaaah...hallelujah hallelujah hallelujaaaaah."

Then the song and the offering would come to a halt. The back doors of the church would fly open, and like dominoes we would push ourselves out to the playground facing our apartment building.

We would elbow one another, racing all the way there.

Between the rear church exit and the sand playground we had to pass by two big sports fields. The first field had a rooftop where we would buy zaatar manakeesh and Bonjus drinks. The juice came in pyramid-shaped cartons. We would stomp on them to make them pop.

To the right of the first field, there was a basketball court where you could find up to three decent hoops. At one side of that court, there was a small staircase leading up to the sand playground, which stood higher than the court by at least two meters.

We would race one another to the wrought-iron gate, about 20 of us kids, or more. The oldest among us had not yet completed his 10th year. We were known as "the kids from Asmar's building," the ones who attended Sunday school.

Not many of us actually cared about the Sunday school teachings. We had one incentive for coming down to the church: the sand playground. There we fought one another to get onto the red slide. And playing on the swings had a certain etiquette that should be respected at all cost. First, there was the pusher, the one who pushes the sitter. The pusher had to work hard enough to get the sitter's feet to kick the low-lying limbs of the nearest tree. When the tree was kicked three times, they would trade positions. Then, the new pusher would do the same for his or her partner, until some others came along whining for their turn. It wasn't easy to make the sitter's feet hit the tree. Rana was the best at this. And my brother, despite his age and size, insisted on pushing us. He usually ended up having a row with the older kids.

For us kids, Sunday was a long-awaited break, as going near the Baptist school on any other day was forbidden. At the school, we were pampered like nowhere else. Because the space offered something nowhere else could. It was like nothing we could find on the streets or sidewalks, not in the narrow play spaces near our homes, not in our building's corridors either. Sundays gave us wide, open spaces, basketballs, and the scent of the sea with every grain of sand on the playground. We picked up the sand in our little hands and blew it lightly into the air—all this play made us happy, simple though it was, and we did not care that it was meant for much younger kids.

It was the war.

And the war cheered us up on every level. When the electricity went out, our parents, dog-tired from being in such close quarters with us, sent us out to play in the corridors. That's where our scrums were formed and then shifted to and fro, like waves, disrupted only by the bellowing of Um Hassan. She was the woman everyone feared, even the men.

The war would cheer us up again when the blackouts ended. Because then we could keep watching *Jongar, the Mighty Hero*. The videotape would always get stuck in the VCR's jaws, and more often than not, the tape would stay trapped for days before things went back to normal and we got the electricity back. Then, Jongar, the Mighty Hero, became a hero again, muddled though, in sound and picture, as the tape endlessly glitched and rolled.

Then we rejoiced as armed skirmishes returned nearby, not knowing exactly how far away they were, or which factions raised arms against one other. All of it made us merry: schools shutting down and us kids gathering at the edges of the fourth-floor stairway, where it was safest to be. And when we slept, like dominoes crammed back in their box, we did so without pillows, sharing rose and white cotton coverlets. Those things smelled of the war, its days and its nights, when we mostly feigned sleep and tittered at everything. We played cards. We became experts at card playing, excelling at all from Fourteen to Four Hundred to Likha.

Then the war days grew too long. Our dads had seeped up the despair, and they took on coaching us in Likha. We began to see our dads getting carried away, outrunning us to the cards, scuffling with their partners, even falling out with them over it.

They became like us, and we became like them. The smallest things now gave them joy too. They drew the war blankets over themselves when they felt cold, and were subsumed by that same scent. Only our mums stayed glued to the radio news reports. From those broadcasts, we children wouldn't recall anything but ricochets and echoes carrying place names.

With every battle, we uncovered a whole new story. The fourth one was no longer the safest. We explored all the other ones and got to know the tenants. Thirty-seven flats housing 37 families, each with several visitors: either those who had fled here from another war-ravished territory (brothers, sisters and their dependents), or those who were forcibly confined. Like this, our domino batches grew in size as battles carried on all around Beirut.

The skirmishes multiplied and so did, with them, our empty, joyless moments. We had to be inventive. We started following the radio more intently. Unavoidably, we came to know the districts that were closest to home by name. And by their distinctive sounds, we learned to discern the origin of the mortar projectiles dropped every midnight. It became a favorite hobby. We also joined in cheerfully in making gypsum sacks to reinforce the entrance of our building. The battles went on as our numbers shot up, and moving through the corridors proved a difficult pastime. We now had to content ourselves with counting square tiles.

We counted almost everything: light bulbs dangling high up from ceilings; bomb shells that plummeted before the eight o'clock news broadcast (such reports which Um Ibrahim listened to into the dead of night); coffee rakwas while the power was out; and candles in wax-covered bottles accumulating in the corners. Wax. Lots of wax. We fooled about with it and burnt our fingers. We sculpted, on top of beer and Mirinda cans, statues out of the melted wax. And we vied over who could pass her finger more often through that blue speck of fire rising from the candlewick.

We were overjoyed with hearing Alec give his wife a good beating, and we heard her shrieking. Alec and Sonya never took shelter in the corridors, except on some rare occasions: like when once they were pissed as newts after a rowdy shelling "party." We were pleased that neighboring residents could run to our building for refuge, since ours was the safest around, even though it had no shelter at all. Through the chinks in the jalousie windows, we observed the hurtling bombs—we were happy to witness this, and this temerity of ours somehow went unnoticed by our mothers.

That was war. It filled us with happiness above anything.

Happiness over the word *armistice*, before we even knew what that meant.

Happiness about school ending without having to sit the exams.

Happiness because we could capably imitate Um Abbas shouting to her son from the fourth floor, in that southern accent of hers: "Hasin, you want kadadeish?" We echoed her words as much as our voice could stretch, and we'd laugh.

Happiness. The dominoes in a state of happiness. As in the happiness over empty pails. As in the happiness over shrapnel. As in the happiness over bullets strewn about on the streets. As in the happiness over bread shortage. As in the happiness over not snitching on the burglar who robbed Elias's supermarket.

This is how we were.

A lump of wicked happiness.

Even when the armistice returned and an acceptable dose of tolerance, love and safety ruled over the place (as suggested by the UNICEF pamphlets that were handed out gratis to kids)—even then, our penchant for coming up with devilish ways of having fun snowballed. We set fire to a number of ant nests at Matar's house, and we erected—boys and girls—barricades in his house's atrium. We baptized it "our square." We waged wars against the kids from Msaytbeh, the upper quarter, and our victories and losses against them amounted to nothing more than the fallouts of soccer matches here or "shelling" someone's noggin with a stone there. We played the game of "War took place in..." till war came nearer to us than our own breath, and we encountered the gunmen face to face. They entered our buildings. They kidded with us. Our building came to accommodate the Progressive Socialist Party's kitchen, and soon after, a hub for the Communist Party opened its doors inside there too. They set up their barriers along our stretch of the street, and our play spaces dovetailed with theirs.

We realized that they too were playing from time to time.

Most of the time.

They often asked us to pass the football to them so they could score one against the adversarial barrier ahead.

They kicked the ball among themselves with skill and perfection. And we stood and waited for the ball to be kicked back to us.

Luckily, Yakoub's scrap metal shop lay on this street, which sometimes allowed for a protracted display of improvised acrobatics. In his shop, Yakoub bartered, mended bicycles and rented out roller skates. He had all types of balls: footballs, basketballs, handballs, and his three sons, Fadi, Joy and Roy, were the sovereigns over all young roller skaters. We tried, my brother and I, to learn as much as we could of their acrobatics. But none could exceed their originality of style. Even the gunmen of the neighborhood, who occupied more playground than we did, started allotting time to watch Fadi and Joy roller skate from where the first barricade stood all the way up the street.

Both camps, ours and the gunmen's, had far too much time to kill, and moments of anticipation—waiting for skirmishes to begin again—outshined actual moments of battle. All summer long, the street was blocked either for a football match between the gunmen or a performance by Fadi and Joy. Both events usually took place on late afternoons as the sun began to retreat.

On one of those busy evenings, a gunman, who was stationed at the lower barricade, decided to put Fadi's gymnastic talents to the test. The gunman installed hurdles, along the street, for Fadi to hop over. As we got used to common obstacles, like bottles and wooden crates, the armed man added a human hurdle. I do not know how or why the Syrian worker at Yusef's grocery store turned into a prop. He was only a few years our senior, and they placed him in a muck pit: I could never forget the smell the boy and we reeked of. And his screams. They clasped him from his unkempt hair and dragged him on as they vied to whack him. Then they transfixed him on top of two iron blocks. And cuffed him.

I do not recall anything but that smell. Fetid.

At the time, the Syrian lad had yet to celebrate his 13th birthday; Fadi and I were just eight years old, and nearly half his size. His yelling filled the space. I recall nothing. Fadi failed to jump. Or maybe he did jump. It doesn't matter. The lad's hoarse voice disappeared then came back, choked, ripped apart. He lay there. In the middle of the street. A sacrifice. A sacrifice among a horde of armed men, children and shopkeepers. This is all I recall. Nothing else. I cannot remember his name, his eye color, or the difference in height between us. I remember his complexion was quite swarthy, and there was a scar linking his upper lip to the bottom of his nose, and many teeny hairs marking the shadow of a burgeoning mustache. That is how close to him we stood. Close enough to see the details. So close as to be engrossed in all the boots and blows he received. Close enough to feel the hot breath of the gunmen as they tortured him, egging us on to smack him too. And we were right there: dominoes, devastated with each kick, with each blow. Then *we* kicked. Just as they did. We melted into one clique of boots. And we kicked. We kicked. Like that. We kicked *him*. That laborer, whose name and eye color I don't recall. As if he were a sandbag, we kicked him. Our shoes got smeared with his blood. We smelt it too. His smell and ours.

We went back home. The smell stayed with us.

When he retired to his home, Yakoub—who had witnessed it all—kept quiet about what had happened. For two hours straight or more, he stayed silent. He asked Silva to make him coffee, ahweh bayda. Just as he liked it, in a small rakwa.

He held a candle plate and swiped his finger back and forth through that blue speck rising from the candlewick. I imagine his eyes blurred, as he went back to that moment, when he attempted to prevent what was underway, and failed. He had seen his own son kicking a laborer he worked with every day. He knew the lad's name and the color of his eyes well. He cursed the unfinished cup of coffee.

And then he exploded at his wife in a succession of Syriac swears.

He then went into the bedroom to get changed. His three sons slept in there. Or they *pretended* to sleep.

He would not beat them.

He wouldn't do that.

Yakoub never hit any of his kids, ever. It was one of his deepest convictions. "I never lay a hand, not on my own kids, not on other folk's kids either." He was used to leaving that task to Silva, if ever needs must. And she had to do it, for he was away working.

Out of character, Yakoub then broke the rule. He suddenly became generous with his blows. He beat Fadi and Joy when he heard them calling out in the landing window, "Hasin, you want kadadeish?" Then he smacked Roy, his youngest, for throwing the house key out of the balcony, even though he owned a number of copies, something he had to do as a keeper of scraps. And, later, after our last class at Sunday school, he again callously rained blows on his two oldest.

We praised and praised at church. Worshiping God. In his sanctuary. Each time our voices rose, we melted into a single mass... Worshiping and singing. Praising God. In the heavens of his power.

We raced to the sand playground like a single uncollapsed mass, like a rosary yet to be undone into its beads. We remained bound.

Then, the second Ahmed and Muhammed Karnib came along, Wael took them on single-handedly, for no good reason. He tossed sand in Ahmed's face, just like that, in sheer coolness. Provocative coolness. When Ahmed tried to retort in kind, we all assaulted the two brothers. We rubbed their faces in the sand. Showered them in it. And they retaliated no more. Then, they scrambled off home, their hair ruffled and caked with sand.

At home, they were served more. We could hear their father's shrieks through the window. The whole block flocked to the Karnibs' door, which stood unclosed. Abed Karnib made no mention of our misdeed. He refused to speak. For him, his own kids were at fault.

Not so long after, word spread. Half an hour was enough to turn the landing into a listening spot where we could hear each other's yelps. The beating moved, along with the sound of our fathers' threats, from one flat to the other.

That was the last time we went to Sunday school.

THE CAT CONNECTION

Set between California and Karachi, Samina Najmi writes about her conflicted relationship with animals, how she became a vegetarian, and the mix of fear and love—or maybe reverence—that she feels for the cats in her life.

SAMINA NAJMI

SAMINA NAJMI is professor of English at California State University, Fresno. Long a scholar of race, gender and war in US literature, she has now also discovered the rewards of more personal kinds of writing. Her essays have appeared in several literary venues, most recently in *The Massachusetts Review* and *World Literature Today*. Having grown up in Karachi and suburban London, Samina now calls California's San Joaquin Valley home. She believes in everyone's three feet of influence, and in the power of the written word to reach beyond it. Samina's cats challenge her to be brave; from them she learns to curl up in the sun without guilt.

One early winter's morning in Boston, in the last days of 1998, my husband opened the back door of our house to find his gray tabby, MoeMoe, stretched in an arc at the top of the porch steps. MoeMoe's front paws lay within touching distance of our door.

Alex rushed indoors to get a towel, folded MoeMoe in it, and cradled him in his arms. Rigor mortis had already set in.

I grieved for a cat I had never touched in all the years I had known him. I'd pour Meow Mix into his bowl from the big plastic Garfield container, place the bowl on the kitchen floor and back away as soon as he approached. Just as dutifully, I made sure MoeMoe always had clean water to the brim. But if, while I was opening a can of shredded turkey for him, his tail caressed my ankle, I'd jump and move away. MoeMoe was a gentle cat, but I, who had grown up without pets and still had recurring nightmares about cats who clawed me, could appreciate him only from a distance. I was the observer who documented the love between Alex and MoeMoe with my camera.

My relationship with animals has been fraught. I had very little interaction with them growing up, either in our immigrant lives in England, or in Pakistan. Dogs may be marginalized as unsanitary in Muslim cultures, but I don't know that cats fare much better even though Prophet Muhammad is said to have been fond of them. The stray cats in our Karachi neighborhood kept me up some nights with their howlings, which entered my dreams. During the day they trod the low walls that separated our neighbors' patios from our own—scrawny, unkempt and terrifying in their vulnerability.

Perhaps the distance between animals and humans has never been great in my mind. Perhaps as a child I could imagine the desperation if I were cast aside and left to fend for myself. Fear erased pity, upsetting the delicate balance of the two that Aristotle considered vital for catharsis in theater. The growls may have been just brawls or mating calls, but they frightened me. Like a Greek chorus, they haunted and held me accountable. For what, though? For the boys who perfected their aim by hurling stones? Or for the dearth of food and shelter and compassion in the world?

My barely acknowledged ambivalence about animals would crystallize around the big Muslim holiday of Baqr Eid, as we call it in Pakistan—meaning the second Eid, which occurs 10 days after Hajj in Makkah, in accordance with the lunar calendar. For those who didn't grow up celebrating Baqr Eid, I should say that it commemorates Prophet Ibrahim's near-sacrifice of his son (believed to be Ismail rather than Izhak), and so in his honor Muslims sacrifice cows and goats at Baqr Eid as a gesture of unquestioning love and obedience to Allah. The flesh of the sacrificial animal is then divided into three equal parts: for consumption in one's own home and family, for one's neighbors and friends, and for distribution among the poor. You're encouraged to do the slaughtering or qurbani yourself, but most people rely on a professional qasai. My father, who could normally not stand the sight of blood, and whose vasovagal tendencies my son Cyrus and I have inherited, could—amazingly—do the qurbani with his own bare hands at Baqr Eid. It's faith. It's also hard labor to clean up after the sacrifice because you have to separate the edible parts of the carcass from those that must be discarded, and because your veranda is now a mess of blood and entrails. That's why most of our neighbors, like most Karachiites, preferred to slaughter their animals in the street rather than in their own yards.

I had no problem with this when I was a child. In fact, we children of the neighborhood would dress up in our festive new regalia and head out excitedly to watch the entire process: the lovingly fattened cow or goat led by a rope to the qasai's butcher knife; the panic in the animal's eyes; its thrashings as multiple hands hold it down; the red fountain spurting from its throat; its will to live still thrumming in the quiver of a leg. But as I grew older, Baqr Eid had me in a quandary. I didn't want to offend Abbu or spoil the festivities for anyone, but at times under some pretext or other I had to shut myself up in the bedroom I shared with my siblings. I'd raise the volume on my cassette player high enough to drown out the distorted gasps from sliced windpipes, the bleatings and mooings, the sounds of dying in the lane.

The annual spectacle should have immunized me to lesser agonies. Or strengthened my faith. Shown me that the end ennobles the means. That loyalty to principle and purpose trumps the heart's rebellion. Or taught me to privilege the symbolic over the literal. Instead, at 35 I turned vegetarian.

It happened a few days after Alex found MoeMoe dead outside our door. There were no visible marks of violence on him, either by another animal or by a car. Somehow MoeMoe had hauled himself home to die. Somehow he had made it up the red brick steps of the porch and laid down on his side, his front paws extended toward the door in a frozen gesture of belonging that claimed us ever after.

Less than a week later, Alex and I were sitting at the kitchen table. Even as he cut into his steak, he remarked, "It's odd that I'm mourning one animal and eating another." He had uttered the precise thought that had been looming in my consciousness since MoeMoe died. Two years married, we were very different people whose ideas sometimes converged in momentous ways. We stopped eating meat after that.

When I visited Karachi in early 2006 with my children, Maya, who was not quite six years old, and four-year-old Cyrus, I had neglected to check the Muslim lunar calendar beforehand. So I arrived at my father's home in Gulshan where I had grown up and, after all these years, was faced with the prospect of street sacrifices again. I was especially concerned for my tender-hearted, Vegetarian-American children. Luckily, Khalammi (as I call my aunt) lived in richer, more Western, and more sanitized Clifton, so without explaining my motives to Maya and Cyrus, we fled to her seventh-floor apartment for three days while Karachiites emulated Prophet Ibrahim. High up there, we were safe from the sounds and even from most of the sights, but when we ventured outside, the children would see the occasional gut lying by the roadside and wonder. Then in the empty compound at some distance beneath our seventh heaven appeared unmistakable blotches of redness and fleshiness. It was time to level with my kids about this particular holiday in the city they had come to love.

"It's a sacrifice," I say.

"What's that?"

"It's when you give up something valuable to please your Creator."

"Why does that please your Creator?"

"I guess because you've passed the test of love."

"I don't like tests"—this from Maya's experienced kindergartener perspective.

I try a different route. "For many poor people in Pakistan it's the only time of the year that they get to eat meat."

"Why would they want to?" Cyrus asks.

Um. For the protein?

"I don't like petting dead animals," he adds decisively.

"Look, honey, Baqr Eid is a holiday—like Thanksgiving. You know how most people in America celebrate Thanksgiving by eating turkey? Well, in Pakistan you celebrate Baqr Eid by eating beef and mutton." Then, with a deep breath: "The difference is that in America you don't see all the turkeys being killed for the holiday. In Pakistan the animals are killed in the open."

I refrain from adding that in Pakistan children don't come home from school with brightly-coloured artwork and hand-prints depicting cows and goats cheerily anticipating the holiday that will massacre them. Thank goodness for small mercies.

We left Khalammi's Clifton apartment and returned to my father's home in Gulshan when Abbu indicated that the coast was clear. No sign of carnage left, though a toneless voice on a travelling loudspeaker still urged us to donate our hides to the orthodox political party, Jamaat-e-Islami. Otherwise, the neighborhood's cleanup was complete. All but that metallic smell which dallied in the air, haunting our street for days.

Alex buried MoeMoe in our backyard, near the blue Siberian squills he had planted earlier that spring. He had lived to be eight years old. Many well-meaning pet owners suggested that we get another cat, but it offended me that they thought MoeMoe was replaceable. Eight months after he died, we sold the house. I didn't want to live there anymore, and Alex was easily persuaded.

For the next 14 years, during which we moved again—this time across the country to Fresno, California—we had no pets, though my children often asked for them.

Then in the summer of 2012 Winnie found his way to us.

We came home that June day to discover three kittens huddled together in the junipers of our front yard. Someone had left them there in a box. They seemed about three months old. My children, who were ten and 12 at the time, saw their chance.

"Honey, I'm not comfortable with pets in the house," I objected.

"They can be yard cats, Mama! And they can come to the garage for shelter when they need it."

I didn't say that there's enough heartbreak in life without attaching yourself to four-legged beings you will one day have to bury. In the end, I said yes because I didn't want my children to grow up like me—skittish around animals, incapable of experiencing the joy of holding them.

So my children named the three kittens Tigger, Winnie and Piglet. Tigger looked almost exactly like MoeMoe and had his serenity, too. He appeared to be the natural leader, not because he sought the position but because he had a quiet confidence that made the other two cats, and the rest of us, look up to him. Piglet had a beautiful slate-gray coat; she and Tigger would snuggle in their sleep. She didn't much care for any humans except Cyrus. For him she would emerge from her various hiding places and allow herself to be petted. And then there was Winnie, a motley white and black in color—a cow print, as Cyrus calls it. He got along with his siblings but spent much of his time doing his own thing. The three became our yard-and-garage cats.

At about the same time, a feral cat we called Molly discovered our neighborhood on San Jose Avenue. Before we knew it, kittens were birthed in our backyard every few months and it became our job to find homes for them. We did keep one kitten from Molly's first litter, a blue-eyed, fawn-furred beauty with a raccoon tale, whom Maya and Cyrus named Snickers. We would also have kept Millie, who was born later—an affectionate and lively little one with black, white and ginger markings, but she disappeared. We like to think she found a friendly home somewhere else. Alex managed to trap Molly, finally, and get her neutered before releasing her into the neighborhood again. For weeks after, he had the battle scars to show for it. But even after Molly was no longer procreating, cats kept multiplying on San Jose Avenue—apparently, there was the proverbial Cat Lady who didn't neuter her cats. Other kindly neighbors who loved cats fed them, too, so more kept coming for the food that was readily available. By the time we moved out of that home—four years after we became cat owners, and a year after Alex and I divorced—first Tigger and then Piglet had disappeared on us. Only Winnie and Snickers moved with my kids and me into the condo on Calimyrna Avenue.

Tigger was actually the first of our cats to vanish. Maya and Cyrus looked for him everywhere. They made a flyer with Alex that had an image of Tigger on it—a photograph I had taken in the driveway one afternoon when Cyrus came home from school, threw his backpack on the ground, and as usual, before anything else, petted his cats, who had come to greet him the moment they heard him. In the image, you can see my 12-year-old's blue sneakers and his hand on Tigger's back. He and his sister went door to door with the flyers. I posted on Facebook, anxious about how my children would handle this loss just a year after their much-loved grandfather, my Abbu, had died in Karachi. Miracle stories about cats making it home months after they had been given up for lost kept hope alive. By the time my children understood that Tigger wasn't coming back, their sadness had lost its sharpest edge, and, to my relief, they showed no visible signs of grief. Two years later, when Piglet disappeared, it was a few weeks before our move to the condo, and my children were already savvier. Young teens, by now they had had to process death, disappearance and divorce. On my part there was an element of relief because I knew Piglet would have had the hardest time with the move.

Not that moving was easy for Winnie or Snickers either. At first, we tried to keep them in the condo's garage until they had acclimated to their new environment. But knowing that Winnie wasn't good at sharing, I had to get past my phobia and let Snickers into our home. I even moved her litter box inside, though I was still far from being able to pet her. At first she hid behind the bookshelf, but eventually she got comfortable, especially in Maya's room. After a week or two we thought the cats would be ready to venture outside. But while Snickers leapt from one rooftop to another and explored the courtyards and common grounds of all the condos in the cul-de-sac, Winnie refused to leave the garage. In fact, he became so neurotic that he would hide the whole day in a cardboard box half-filled with books, or else behind the water heater when the days got colder. We needed to intervene. Now that Snickers wasn't confined to the indoors, we opened the pet-door between the garage and the kitchen and coaxed Winnie to come in. That's when we discovered that he's a dog-cat, as Cyrus puts it: zealous for human company, and not just for cuddles but for eye contact. If anyone should retire to their bedroom before the others, he'll follow them, meowing outside their door until they re-emerge. A quirky cat, he knocks the marble chess pieces around and chases his own tail until we're helpless with laughter. True, on Thursday mornings when the condo's landscaping crew comes by, I see traces of his post-move neurosis, as he hides behind the bookshelf for fear of the mowers and leaf-blowers. But most of the time Winnie is very much at home in the condo.

So much so that as soon as we had let him indoors, Winnie booted Snickers out completely. That was the price we paid for Winnie's sanity, and it saddens me still. Sweet Snickers hasn't disappeared completely like Tigger, Millie and Piglet before her; she comes inside to have her meals while we keep Winnie at bay. I've had a pet-door installed in our kitchen slider, which opens into the patio, so she can come and go as she pleases (or at least as Winnie will let her). And recently, after much research, I found a little cat-house online that Maya and Cyrus assembled over Thanksgiving break. I was eager for Snickers to have somewhere to go before the winter, which is also the time of year our arid San Joaquin Valley gets whatever rain it's going to get. Once my kids had assembled the handsome white structure with dark brown trim and two doorways, I placed it on the patio close to the kitchen slider. Reviews warned that you might never be able to get your cat to go in, and it seemed that they were right. I tried catnip as suggested, but that didn't work. I relocated the cat-house further away, and that didn't work either, so I brought it back closer to the kitchen and under the eaves, and kept close watch.

A month or so went by. The day Snickers began using her house for shelter from the rain I took photo after photo and sent them to Maya and Cyrus with a jubilant message saying I counted it among the greatest accomplishments of my life. All the more so as this year Fresno has seen more rains and storms than all the past 13 winters that we've lived here.

When people hear that I'm a cat-phobic owner of two cats, they are incredulous. Some are impressed. How far have I come? Some distance, to be sure. I don't jump as easily around cats. Once or twice, I have even touched their coats. I keep them well-fed, and I keep Winnie's litter box clean. But it's Maya, on her visits home from college, who replaces the collars that Snickers loses regularly, and Cyrus who administers the flea meds to both cats. I don't know what I'll do in a year when Cyrus, too, has left for college. What if Winnie or Snickers falls sick and needs to be carried to the vet? I'll have to enlist Alex or other cat-loving friends, or hire help.

Sometimes I think that just as Winnie's irrational fear of the gardeners is mirrored in my irrational fear of cats, he and I will experience the empty nest as a shared loss. Maybe then, when it's just the two of us at home, our greater dependence on each other will give me access to a normal kind of love between pet and human. It's something I remain wistful about. Surely, I've been inching towards such a moment these 20 years?

In the meantime, I remain vegetarian. Through all the flux of the two decades since MoeMoe died, that has remained a constant.

And another thing. I don't know when it happened, but I became aware of it only recently: I no longer have nightmares about being clawed by cats.

FROM SULU, A FAREWELL TO DAD

Criselda Yabes chases her connection to wartorn Sulu in the southern Philippines, her childhood home, through her newspaper reporting as an adult. Over time, this work to understand the land her father loved so much becomes an inextricable link between them.

CRISELDA YABES

CRISELDA YABES takes any opportunity to travel anywhere. Before her recent move to France, she was mostly attached to Mindanao in the southern Philippines where she spent her childhood, the subject of some of her books. *Crying Mountain* has been nominated for the Man Asian Literary Prize and re-published by Penguin Southeast Asia. Her second novel *Broken Islands*, set on the backdrop of the super typhoon that ravaged the Visayas, was shortlisted by the German Litprom at the Frankfurt Book Fair.

At Dad's funeral, there was only one picture of him—a young man, around 30, already a father of three girls, me being the eldest. He was standing on a wooden outrigger, posing with his catch of a barracuda, the snakish figure of the fish like a trophy in his hands. It was his smile that made my father who he was in those days, back in Sulu, when the magnificent sea was his friend. His smile didn't show triumph as much as contentment, and it was this phase of his life that I wished to remember him by.

He was 77 when he died, a broken man, dejected about life taking many wrong turns after he'd had to leave the island of Sulu. His home since the early 1970s, he had been sent to the island from Manila to open a branch of a private national bank he worked for.

After a couple of years of living in Sulu and putting the branch in order, we moved to the Christian city of Zamboanga, the hub of the southern islands, just before the Muslim uprising in Sulu in 1974—an uprising that would trigger the separatist rebellion for decades to come. Located at the bottom tip of the mainland, Zamboanga wasn't too far away; it could be reached in a day by a slow boat from Sulu. It was also close enough that we felt the fallout from the conflict, the fighting between soldiers and rebels. Dad stayed on in the city and lived within the atmosphere of provincial comfort and the uncertainty of political order. He stayed for as long as he could, until he was summoned to the headquarters, back in Manila, about a decade later. It was then that I began to see him lose confidence in his work. I urged him to leave the big city when he retired, to start a farm somewhere, but he once said he felt like he was in a Jack Nicholson movie: a man in the doldrums after his retirement.

Today, when people ask me why I spent part of my childhood in Sulu—that dangerous island in the furthest south part of the Philippines—I tell them it's because of my father. They assume he was an officer in the military, because for more than four decades after the uprising, the island practically became a garrison in the wild. Guns ruled. Soldiers came and went in battalions, warlords took control, and rebels flourished in the jungle. But I had believed that Sulu (or the people of Sulu) could fight against the odds and prove everyone wrong—that the Muslims had the tenacity to survive.

Islam wasn't an ideology peddled before insurgency; it blended into a community also made up of Christians. Locals didn't care about their differences, and the island was their home. They went to the same schools and joined the same clubs, as if they were one big family. But there were unspoken rules among the Muslims, which Dad soon discovered. Shortly after our arrival, he made the mistake of inviting the Muslim mayor's second wife to the bank opening's ribbon-cutting ceremony. The first wife threatened to have him taken away from the island, an empty threat as it turned out. Still, it was Dad's baptism of fire. He was quick to feel the island's pulse, and though he was an outsider, it didn't take long for him to become part of the community.

It was amazing that Dad, a northerner, was able to charm the people of Sulu. It was as if he had found his place, basking in the company of the Muslim elite. He loved the parties, the singing and dancing, the food, the sun and the sea, and we went to the beach every weekend. The waters of the Sulu Archipelago were so clear you could almost see another world beneath the surface, so intoxicating you'd want to jump off the boat to be in it, to meld with the blue-green silk of the sea.

Now I wonder, did Dad know something was going to happen that would shatter the fragility of the islands? Was that why he left the island and took us to Zamboanga before the uprising? As a child, even I could sense that something was wrong. We got stuck in the Notre Dame school once, where all families—Muslims and Christians—sent their children. There was gunfire. I was in the first grade and my instinct was to hide in the alcove by the staircase with my sister. In my adult life as a journalist, it's no wonder I am drawn to armed conflict: the news that I follow is about wars and displacement, guns and power, the immeasurable divides of cultures. These were the elements of my childhood.

In the February 7, 1974 uprising led by the Moro National Liberation Front, the island was razed to the ground by the armed forces in order to save it. Nearly all the population fled to Zamboanga, where we had by then settled. I was nine years old, and I couldn't understand why the roaring noise of planes and choppers filled our daily lives, or why Muslims landed as refugees looking for safety, forced to rebuild their lives from scratch. The news that trickled in were mostly rumors. The government had censored the press from writing about the turn of events in Sulu, which was too far away from Manila in any case, the disparity of cultures too great for northerners to understand. The Air Force base across the street from the bungalow where we lived saw daily sorties of C-130s carrying soldiers and refugees and I overheard patches of their stories in the café next door. Sulu was falling apart.

Years later, when I thought my childhood was behind me, I felt compelled to seek out the story. I was partly driven by anger for history withheld—that the island that had anchored my father in inexplicable ways had been significant to the making of our nation. Sulu had been a sultanate to be reckoned with before the colonizers lumped all the islands together and made it the Philippines. We were deprived of that knowledge in school, and I wanted to seek out the truth. I also felt a need to make my father happy once more, so perhaps there was also the subconscious duty of a daughter to fill substance into her father's later years. He didn't talk much anymore and was prone to anger. He hid his thoughts in the dark. If I were to write about Sulu, I asked myself, would it take him out of his lingering depression? Would it take him back to the feeling he had in that picture with his catch, the picture that I have kept with me all these years?

The island's capital, Jolo, is a city so tiny you could easily stroll from the wharf to the colonial-era city hall, to the plaza, the cathedral and mosque that were virtually neighbors. Just outside there is a hill that overlooks the city and the silver expanse of sea beyond it. When I stood on top of that hill, the Bud Datu, something magical would always come over me. I no longer felt the violence or the poverty. I felt that if I stared long enough at the water, the world would be kind again.

In reality, the fighting went on and off over periods of time, and I was obliged to be accompanied by soldiers. Since the start of the rebellion, Bud Datu had become a military outpost. It was a park when I was a child, and I used to tell myself—my head filled with love stories from the komiks Mommy brought home and the movies she took me to—that my own wedding would take place on this very spot. I returned to Sulu roughly 20 years after the failed uprising. The wedding idea was out of the question, for "security risk" reasons for one.

Before I stayed in the military camps, before the kidnappings and beheadings, I spent a summer season in the city, renting a room in a bungalow that belonged to one of Dad's friends. Many families had already left, except for a few who couldn't part from the island. The children of Dad's friends became my friends too, and they took me swimming to beaches in other parts of the island, reviving what I had felt so intensely about my love for Sulu. I was back and the island was going to be mine again. It felt like a continuation of my childhood, and it was as if the burning had never happened. After some time, I couldn't stay with my friends anymore; they couldn't protect me if something were to happen. I had to stay in military camps. It was the only way I could keep coming back to the island.

I often stayed in the camp at Bud Datu; a marine commander who was also a friend accommodated my stay because it wasn't safe to be in any of the inns in town. As if it were my favorite holiday destination, I would find reasons to keep coming back whenever I could, to watch the sun rise over breakfast, and the mist shrouding the green forest late in the day when the rain poured. One fine day the marine commander sprang a surprise by taking me south of Jolo, in a historical port town that had been neglected. We traveled in a convoy of trucks and armored vehicles loaded with marines. One would think we were going to war. As it turned out his men had discovered the remains of the last sultan's palace, the Astana, in the cover of the forest. There was not much of it save an arch and a tomb, the rest obliterated by the elements of time in the same way people forget about history. I thought Dad would have wanted to see it when I told him about the disintegrated Astana, but he was like some of the old-timers who didn't have the heart to return because they knew it was not going to be the same—the Sulu they knew was gone.

I had a barometer for Sulu's snail-paced progress and common decline. It is a place about which news was usually bad, some of which wasn't always true. In the 1990s, when I returned for the first time since childhood, the barracks on Bud Datu was a dilapidated house with peeling white paint. It had the best panorama of the city, the sun peeping out from the east corner, spreading cool light over a landscape beautiful enough to fool anyone about the violence that could potentially strike at any time. The soldiers were trying to win the fight but couldn't for various reasons, systemic but mostly political, and there would be random breaks for peace when a commander was also a promising leader, attempting to make friends with the local people. He could coax them to his side against the rebels breeding the semi-ragtag but radical forces of the Abu Sayyaf Group in the jungle.

Over time Bud Datu was spruced up, transformed into some strange kind of tourist attraction where school children went on excursions. The rundown white barracks house was renovated and built as the headquarters for senior commanders, with an extra room for visitors equipped with a proper toilet. And right by the entrance was a copycat of the Starbucks logo, inviting guests to the balcony-cum-café overlooking the surreal view of the mosque in the town center, by the port. Visitors paid tribute to the shrine of an Islamic missionary that made Sulu a kingdom before Magellan came to the Philippines in the 16th century. They were amazed to see monkeys here, and horses and birds that were endemic to the island—but the people of Sulu didn't even know that. Every day was about survival; things of such nature were trivial. It could get cold in the forest, yet it was the only place where you could breathe some fresh air. Up on this hill you were safe. It was another story down in the city below.

Dad never saw Sulu again. As if pushed by filial duty, I went looking for stories from the past for him as those from the present were so exhausting. Somewhere on this island were people struggling for a way out of the fighting, and Dad would ask me to tell him the latest news when I returned from a trip. Is so-and-so still around? Did you go up to Bud Datu? How about the beaches? What happened to the old mosque? So I tried to piece Sulu back whole in stories I told my father about my trips. It took such a hold on me that I would weep when it was time to leave. Over those years, from the mid-1990s into the 2000s, Sulu was my emotional imperative, the seat of my soul, until Dad died.

The Muslim rebels resorted to banditry and terrorism. This drew worldwide news in 2000, when the Abu Sayyaf, breaking away from the dominant rebel group, kidnapped foreigners from a dive resort in neighboring Malaysia. The rebels had their jungle base in the municipality nearest to the capital, and the town's name, Patikul, became synonymous with terror. A military convoy had to be certain of road security when driving through a barren road into the hinterland. The smaller marine units would set up camp by the coast and, to my delight, there was one by the beach where Dad took us when we were children. It was a long stretch of white sand, and when the marines were out on patrol leaving just a handful on guard, I'd put on my swimsuit and wade into the softness of the water.

I had little contact with the villagers. I stayed in the camp, shared meals with the men, talked to the officers, and spent my spare time daydreaming from the porch of my cottage. The commander had made an unbelievable showcase of turning the camp into a "resort," where some of their guests could come for a Sunday picnic. Mostly they had karaoke nights and gun shoot fests, with the mayor and his young wife among the shooters. Months later, the tide washed ashore and the cottage that was my "vacation home" fell apart. When I saw it gone, I felt the sea had taken it away from me, as if it was telling more about the destructive nature of the island. Little by little the water was eating away at the shore and the bamboo cottages were disappearing one by one. Where was the terrace I used to sit on watching the fishermen paddle in their bancas, where I used to write and draw, where the days lengthened on the horizon? I felt that I was losing something, my hopes and dreams, my aspirations for a wasted island, the happiness it gave my father. I couldn't stop this feeling of foreboding, no matter what I wrote about the silver lining for Sulu. Dad was upset with the article I had written about the camp, and said I was boasting of my company with the marines. But without any story to tell him, I was afraid that he would slip out of my life, depart from my imagined tableau of Sulu.

Where was I to go? If I wanted to keep writing about Sulu, I had to keep going back. And if I was looking for peace in Sulu, I had to follow the men with guns. I had to find out if they were serious about changing their strategy, from one that was purely combat and artillery to what they started calling a "holistic" approach, of helping the communities in the basics of good governance.

In 2012, I went to another camp further up the coast of Patikul where there was another historic community, the bailiwick of a family rival to the throne of the sultanate, on the opposite coast from which I had seen a few years before with my friend the marine commander. There was no sign of grandeur. The wooden house where the sultan had supposedly lived was barely erect, a typical Malay home that might disintegrate anytime, holding onto few family belongings and relics, faded newspaper photographs, some wooden furniture. The caretaker was a woman who said she was a descendant, and she often visited me at the camp, telling me about her crush on one officer who was now gone, his tour of duty over.

Every morning, I'd walk out to the jetty to watch the sunrise over the sea. I made myself useful teaching children from the nearby villages, who went to the camp in droves to learn the alphabet and numbers. At last I could be with the people who lived in makeshift wooden houses on stilts arrayed by the shore. They had little to eat, and if there were no fish and rice, they'd collect cassava crops and turn them into paste with a little taste of salt. Every morning while I watched the glint of the yellow-orange sun, an old woman would paddle in her small banca past the rocks, from where she collected spring water from a source above the hills. The camp had no running water and no power, and ran on a generator inherited from the American soldiers who had been there before and had repaired the mosque. At night, after an early dinner in the wardroom, we would make our way to the basketball court, dubbed the call center, where we could get signal on our cell phones. And in the morning, the island's rare sunflowers were at their best, forming a bright yellow line by the basketball court near the shore.

Life at some intervals couldn't have been simpler. Were the marines succeeding in their new campaign to bring peace? More mothers were bringing their children to school, and farmers wanted to start farming again. A woman who said she was a Muslim princess long ago had returned to help her people harvest coffee beans, sold at the market in Manila. Soon there were little coffee shops in town. Despite it being the rebels' lair, officers were toying with the idea of building a port in this part of Patikul, which would allow commerce to flourish in this undeveloped part of the island.

But in the months that followed, when I thought there was a chance for progress no matter how small, a storm came—which was unusual in this part of the country—and wiped away the jetty and the gazebo built for the villagers' celebrations. I was in Manila when I heard the news, and the photos of the devastation on Facebook said it all. Just as things were starting to look good, achieving a certain equilibrium that makes each day bearable, hopes were dashed again. It was nature's fault, I said to myself, but I took that as a sign: it wasn't going to be as easy as we thought it might be. Just like the cottages that were a part of my vacation home in the previous camp, this camp too was obliterated. I was losing Sulu, piece by piece.

I took Dad to the hospital in early 2014. He was being treated for his heart and kidneys, and had so little money he had to rent out his garage to pay for his medical bills. But this time, his blood pressure suddenly dropped. We had a trifling argument in the emergency room, where he had to wait for about six hours before he could be confined. He was a difficult patient and I was tempted to run out on him. What's become of him? I asked myself. Why have we talked less? The Dad I loved was turning inward and I couldn't follow him there. I saw in his eyes a kind of plea I could not fathom.

Later that year I was out of the country when he was taken back to the hospital. My sisters wouldn't tell me the truth, that Dad was dying. It was too much to digest and they went about caring for him in any way they could. I flew home and had two weeks with him before he passed away. I wanted him to go because I couldn't bear to see him suffer each time he had to undergo dialysis. He was awake during the night and I couldn't sleep. He knew he was dying, but he didn't want to go just yet. I prayed that he would go, as he couldn't find peace in his life. In the evenings, in his state of helplessness and grogginess, he mumbled to people invisible in the hospital cubicle. And then he turned to me and asked, "Why is this happening to me? What wrong have I done?" In whichever way he measured his life, his fate spelled death. I had no answers to his questions and I felt that I had failed him.

I can't narrow down his happiness to a photograph in Sulu. But it was there, in those final days in the hospital, when I could hold his hand without talking about the past. Since my last visit to Sulu not long before Dad fell ill, a new commander, one younger than the previous, was building a replica of the Astana in his camp on a mountaintop, in the center of the island. He didn't want to rebuild the original one in the forest; he wanted it to be new for the people of Sulu to see. I hadn't told Dad about this. He was too ill, he roamed in his own memories and my stories of Sulu didn't matter anymore. The commander had built the Astana replica from private donations for the people of the island, so they could reclaim the pride of their past. He lodged me in what was supposed to be the royal room and took me birdwatching in the forest. I told him about my father and what Sulu meant to him. But I didn't tell Dad about that conversation either, as he lay there, suffering. There was nothing else to say about Sulu.

Three years after Dad's passing in October 2014, I requested a visit to the Astana, to see if the military had kept its presence. I was terrified of what I might find there—that the symbol, though a replica, had been neglected or ruined—, but I felt an obligation to finish my last story on Sulu. I first stayed in Bud Datu, but couldn't move around without my escort, a young female first lieutenant who enjoyed taking selfies and said I should dye some of the gray in my hair. I walked around the trails aimlessly and waited for night to fall, seeing the kerosene lamps of the fishermen out by the wharf. There were more of them now.

And there it was, the Astana copied from the old days of the sultanate that many of the people of Sulu had forgotten. From Bud Datu, I was taken there by the troops to answer my wish. Still it stood on the hill, quiet in its solace, surrounded by grass grown tall and wild. From there, I was able to bid farewell to my grief. Seeing the replica of the wooden palace intact after three years, I could begin to somehow believe in a future that speaks of humanity. If only I could have buried my father on the grounds there, on this island that drew in the best of his life, surrounded by the mountains, looking out to the sea in the distance.

MEETING IN A MINARET

On a mission to uncover Islamic history in Romania, Tharik Hussain shares a witty, factually-rich account of his visit to Mahmudiye Mosque, where he makes a new friend with a refreshing perspective.

THARIK HUSSAIN

THARIK HUSSAIN is a travel writer and journalist specializing in Muslim travel and Islamic heritage. He has co-authored several *Lonely Planet* titles including Oman, UAE, the Arabian Peninsula and Thailand, and recently developed the UK's very first Muslim heritage walking trail. Tharik lives in London with his wife and children, and when he's not traveling the world in search of obscure and interesting Muslim narratives, he can be found turning his nose up at below-par coffee and rummaging the shelves of secondhand bookshops (usually looking for obscure and interesting Muslim narratives). tharikhussain.co.uk, @_tharikhussain.

Casting a large shadow in the early afternoon sunshine, Ovid stood elegantly dressed in a toga, his left arm across his chest and the other under his chin. It was a pose that said "one is thinking," and if the history books are right, Ovid was most likely thinking, "God! What a shithole this is!" Something Italian Sculptor Ettore Ferrari had captured rather aptly.

Romanians love the fact that this great Roman poet of antiquity once resided in Constanta—they've even named the town's university after him. But what they often forget is that he didn't *choose* to live here. The Black Sea coastal town's most celebrated ancient resident was actually exiled in what was then Tomis, back in 8 AD, after royally pissing off Emperor Augustus. What Ovid did or said will never be known, but it is almost certain his widely-read and rather morally lax writings, in particular those offering housewives tips on how to get themselves a nice, rich, adulterous lover, played a huge part. Augustus is said to have blamed Ovid for Rome's "moral decline" and more specifically, the royal "shagathon" that took place in his own family.

Ovid was never allowed back to Rome and ended up dying here in Constanta, a place he described as a "cultural wasteland," and not somewhere he looked upon with much fondness. Yet here he was, being honored with great fanfare.

Ovid's statue was built in 1887, just as Romania was putting the "Rome" into its cultural heritage and reinventing itself as "Roman". The timing is important. The statue was built at the end of a period of almost 500 years of Muslim Ottoman sovereignty, which Romania now wanted to erase. Ovid, despite his aversion to a place he viewed as much a prison as anything else, was therefore a convenient resident and found himself propelled to the very forefront of this cultural reimagining.

I, on the other hand, was looking for those that had been pushed to the very back.

The Mahmudiye Mosque's guardian was a frail old woman with a green headscarf that matched the color of the iron gates at the front. She looked like the hundreds of Romanian nanas we had passed on the train down from Bucharest, and could just as easily have sat beside her husband on a horse-drawn cart.

The small courtyard was shaded and felt several degrees cooler than the streets outside, where the blazing August sun was merciless. A notice read "5 lei". Normally, I wouldn't pay to enter a mosque as it was the right of every Muslim to pray in any one of them, but I wasn't sure if this was a mosque or just a tourist attraction now, so I began rummaging through my rucksack for my wallet. The woman, who had been watching carefully, stepped out from her little hut.

"Musulman?" she asked, using the classical phrase for Muslim.

I nodded and lifted my hands to either side of my head in a mock takbir to indicate I wished to pray. The effect was electric and the old woman's face lit up, revealing a gappy smile and a gold tooth. She wagged her finger from side to side at the entry fee. Was she Muslim? I wondered.

"Free?" I asked.

The old woman's squinting eyes told me she didn't understand. Worried I might offend her by not paying, I tried to put 5 lei into her tiny little hands and promptly *did* offend her. Pushing the money away and muttering something stern under her breath, which probably translated to either "stupid foreigner" or "stupid Muslim foreigner," she grabbed me by the arm and began leading me in.

The old woman also knew I would probably need to perform wudu before I prayed, as she stopped near the entrance to point out three silver taps—each with a stone seat and beautiful Ottoman tiles at eye level. The water was delightfully cool against my skin, and as I rinsed my face, I noticed a crumpled heap behind me for the first time. It was a young man wrapped up in a dark chador leaning against a low wall. In his hand was a copy of the Quran. He was so engrossed in the holy book that he didn't even look up.

Any doubts I had had earlier about the existence of Muslims in Constanta or whether the mosque was being used for its intended purpose were now diminished. It was clear this was a functioning mosque, despite the entrance fee for non-Muslims.

To assist visitors who were not familiar with mosque protocol, a low red rope stood in front of the main hall. Unfortunately there was no signage to explain its exact purpose and so one by one the tourists that came through the large wooden doors stopped suddenly at the rope, assuming what lay beyond was a no-go zone. From here they would stare nervously inside, craning their necks to admire as much as possible, but not daring to step beyond the red rope. Finally, looking slightly bemused, they headed off up the stairs of the minaret.

It was a shame, as all that was needed was a helpful sign asking them to remove their shoes and respect worshippers. I doubt anyone would've ignored this; tourists are very polite like that. I've always felt these tiny little details are important. A lot of damage caused by colonial and post-colonial representations of Muslims and Muslim lands remains undone, and situations like this can often reinforce some of the outlandish claims made in those earlier texts. Take this extract from Mark Twain's *The Innocents Abroad*, where during his time in Tangier, Morocco, an English gentleman describes to Twain the apparent fate of any non-Muslim trying to enter a mosque:

> A loud *Halt*! From an English gentleman in the party checked the adventurer; and then we were informed that so dire a profanation is it for a Christian dog to set foot upon the sacred threshold of a mosque that no amount of purification can ever make it fit for the faithful to pray in again. Had Blucher succeeded in entering the place, he would no doubt have been chased through the town and stoned.

In all my years of traveling across Muslim lands, including vast expanses of Morocco, I have never heard anything as remotely preposterous as this. If mosques presented an open house image, as Islamic tradition suggests they should, it would go a long way to dispelling many of these wild myths.

After several minutes of having the interior of the Mahmudiye all to myself, I was surprised to see a man step confidently over the rope. But before I could begin my game of "Is he Muslim or is he not?" his hijab-wearing wife followed him in. She was the first non-gipsy woman I had seen in Romania wearing a headscarf. The couple were clearly tourists; the man was middle-aged and looked North African, and he wore the kind of sensible clothes middle-aged men go for: navy chinos and pastel-coloured checked shirts, clothes I confess have become increasingly appealing to me of late. His wife was pushing a black buggy, inside which sat their extremely bored-looking son who leapt to his feet as soon as his mother unbuckled him. Released from his plastic shackles, he stood for a moment surveying his new environment, his stance that of a superhero. All the little man was missing was a cape.

The little superhero then embarked on the kind of activity every child loves when they are inside a nice, carpeted mosque: an activity I like to call "Mosque-Olympics". This always begins with several laps of sprinting around the central hall, followed by an attempt to climb every step, banister, bookshelf or pulpit left accidentally open by the Imam. Like any well-organized sporting event, there are of course some rules to Mosque-Olympics. These rules are innate knowledge for every young Muslim child, and one of the most important ones is that you only start the Mosque-Olympics once you are absolutely certain your parents have begun their salah, for this virtually guarantees they will not interfere in your games.

Muslim parents, on the other hand, have come up with a strategy that allows them to keep things from descending into total chaos, without having to break their salah. To deploy this strategy, they have had to evolve as humans and develop Peter Parker-style "Spidey-sense." This allows them to know instantly when the Mosque-Olympics have begun, but even more amazingly, it tells them the very instant young Abdullah is about to enter their orbit on one of his Olympic laps of the mosque hall. As soon as their Spidey-sense alerts them to this, regardless of their salah position, instinctively an arm appears in front of Abdullah, like the tape at the finishing line of a race, only this one is immovable and slams straight into his midriff, bringing the relay session to an abrupt end. What is most impressive about this particular skill is that it also dispels the myth that men cannot multitask. I have personally witnessed Muslim fathers clothesline their sons whilst simultaneously continuing to recite tashahud without flinching.

The parents inside the Mahmudiye today didn't need to employ such tactics. With no segregation between men and women in this tiny mosque, they were able to function as a tag team. First as dad performed his traveler's prayer, mum shadowed the boy around, and when her husband was finished, she simply tagged him in to take over. I was half expecting them to tap each other's hands like wrestlers as they switched roles.

Pinned to the tiles of the Mahmudiye's mehrab were two huge sheets of white paper with the Arabic alphabet inscribed in large black letters—the way you might see the English alphabet hung on the walls of a primary school classroom. It was further evidence the mosque belonged to an active Muslim community. The mehrab was one of several features that were distinctly Ottoman in design. Elaborate stuccos painted red and blue hung above the Imam's prayer mat, framed neatly by a simple floral pattern. To the right was a tall dark-brown, wooden mimbar, where the Imam stood every Friday to deliver his weekly sermon. How many people in total sat listening? I wondered. Was this a large community?

The mimbar was essentially a small flight of steps topped by a tall majestic hat-like cone. It was the kind of thing seen in Turkish mosques all over the world. Beneath the stairs, in a small space designed for hanging the Imam's formal attire, were a number of elegant black cloaks and a flat white turban, like the ones worn by Muslim clerics from Turkic lands.

The mosque floor was covered with a large hand-woven Persian carpet—reportedly a gift from one of the last Ottoman Caliphs, after it was built in 1910 by the Romanian monarch, King Carol I. The most striking feature of the mosque however, was high up on the four walls that supported the modest dome.

Thin and gothic in shape, the Mahmudiye's windows looked a lot like they had been taken from a church either in Prague or Budapest—this was the Byzantine aspect of the design, and it worked surprisingly well. In truth, this blurring of religious design and architecture in Muslim and Christian places of worship was nothing new in Eastern Europe. In Greece, for example, every single church boasts a dome, just like the ones you will see on its mosques, built during the country's Ottoman phase; and in Turkey, a mosque isn't a mosque without the stained glass windows that were originally on all the churches, when the most important city in Christendom was Constantinople, today's Istanbul.

This cross-pollination was not only restricted to architecture. When the 18th-century French traveler Count D'Autrive was traveling through what was then Ottoman territories just a few hundred kilometers southwest of here, this is what he observed in the Bulgarian town of Shumen:

> Now these are half Turkish, half Bulgarian; Muslims and Christians live side by side without detesting each other, marry between themselves, drink together bad wine, and violate both the ramazan and the Christian fast. They know, as their clerics do, only the sign of the cross or Allah; but that does not make them less honest people. Both the imams and the priests treat with equal tolerance the marriages between those belonging to the different religions. It is not a rare occurrence to see under the same roof both Muslim turbans and icons, the Qur'an and the Gospels right on top of one another. Two religions at such a great variance with one another are being preached with equal ease, and children are left to decide for themselves which one to subscribe to.

The view from the Mahmudiya's 164-foot minaret was spectacular; I found myself staring out over a very different Constanta to the one I had walked through earlier. No longer did it look like a city of hideous gray constructions. Before me lay old Constanta, one where beautifully ornate buildings with wrought-iron balconies stood in neat rows like mini Parisian streets, at the end of which were little piazzas where locals sat sipping coffee. Close to the city's huge port—the largest on the Black Sea—, there was a bell tower that displayed very Andalusian features and beside it, a Greek Orthodox Church, complete with a beautiful white dome. But the most stunning building was in between. Yet another church, featuring a large dazzling gold dome flanked by two smaller, equally dazzling golden domes. The scene was not what I had expected at all.

As I stood there, holding my hair back against the wind with one hand, admiring this unexpectedly charming view, I heard the familiar sound of a middle-aged man making his way to the top. Deep wheezing accompanied by the odd forced cough to clear the airways was preceded by a heavily-set, tall fellow who almost fell onto the platform as he negotiated the final steps. He was closely followed by a woman wearing dark aviator sunglasses. I politely stepped aside, so they too could appreciate the wonderful views.

The woman headed off around the back and the man, caring less about the view than his respiratory issues, leaned against the wall beside me. After a while, when I was absolutely certain he was not having a cardiac arrest, I offered, "Tall, isn't it?"

This only brought about an awkward smile. Maybe the poor fellow doesn't speak English, I told myself.

Cristian eventually confessed that the reason for the smile was because, although he had stopped wheezing, he still wasn't seeing straight at that point. He then told me that the last time he had climbed the minaret was aged 10, and naturally he had completely underestimated it this time.

"So why climb it today?" I asked.

"I dunno, I just felt the urge to come up here again after all these years and went and dragged my girlfriend to join me."

"Why the mosque and not one of the churches?"

"Well, I know my girlfriend likes it, because she is Muslim, and so I thought it would be something nice to do together..." Cristian's voice began to trail off as I started looking around for his girlfriend. When I had briefly glimpsed her earlier there had been no indication she was Muslim. I tell Cristian that I am a Muslim too, and at that very moment, his girlfriend makes her way over to us.

"This is Sibel, my girlfriend," introduces Cristian. "She's Muslim, like you."

I am momentarily stuck in that awkward 'should I shake hands or not' situation one finds themselves in when meeting a Muslim woman for the first time. Sibel looked liberal enough; she had short, styled hair, wore trendy sunglasses and was wrapped in a colorful dress that said this was not someone prone to conservatism. But that's just it, you can never be too sure, and so I waited. It's always safer to wait.

Maybe sensing my hesitancy, Sibel put her right hand forward and with her other hand took off her sunglasses to reveal a pair of beautiful south east Asian eyes. This was not what I had expected a Romanian Muslim to look like at all. In fact, Sibel was not what I had even expected a Romanian to look like! Maybe, I thought, she was part of some migrant community I knew nothing about. And for once I was right, but this was no recent migration. Sibel was a sixth generation Muslim Tartar whose family had been in Romania longer than the minaret we stood in had been erect.

Romania's Islamic heritage stretches as far back as the 11th century, when Muslims first arrived with the semi-nomadic Pecheneg Turks, who briefly ruled parts of what was then known as Wallachia. Later, the major Islamic influence in the country was Tatar and Ottoman as Romania first became a part of the Mongol and Tatar Golden Horde Khanate, and then the Ottoman Empire during the Middle Ages. It was in this period of shifting populations that Sibel's ancestors first made their way to this part of the world. As a result, today Romania is home to over 65,000 Muslims, most of whom, like Sibel, are ethnically Tatar, or Turkish. The community even has their own Grand Mufti, whose official base was in fact the Mahmudiye Mosque.

Sibel was a warm and interesting woman, and as we stood atop the minaret, she told me more about herself. She had a 22-year-old son from a previous marriage to a Hindu-Christian man. This man's mother, she revealed with much amusement, had kidnapped their son and had him baptized as a baby.

"She had been terrified I might make him a Muslim!" Sibel laughed. It seemed her mother-in-law didn't realize that Sibel and her then husband had a very open take on religion as parents, one that sounded a lot like that held by the parents Count D'Autrive came upon in 18th-century Bulgaria. Sibel and her son's father decided from the beginning they would let their son choose in his own time what, if any, faith he wished to follow.

As I listened, I found myself again astonished to have met a Muslim like her living here in Romania. Sibel, it seemed, subscribed to the Islamic position that there is no compulsion in religion, which stems from the famous verse in the second chapter of the Qu'ran, Surah Al Baqarah, often cited to argue that Islam cannot be forced upon a person. She didn't believe in imposing her faith on anyone, not even her own son. Born into a Muslim family, Sibel had *chosen* to stay Muslim and she wanted to give that same choice to her son. Interestingly, a strong tradition cited in the hadith collection Sunan Abu Dawud says the Quranic verse was originally revealed to warn Muslim parents in Medina not to impose Islam on their children. Scholars like Jonathan Andrew Cleveland Brown also believe this is the verse's context, adding that it has since been understood as a general command that people cannot be forced to convert to Islam.

I have to confess, Sibel's position was very refreshing as it was one I almost never came across when discussing such matters with Muslims. This level of tolerance and religious cross-pollination was a feature of Constanta, explained Sibel, with Cristian also chipping in. As I listened to their descriptions of the historically multicultural and tolerant community that had flourished here, I found the parallels with what Count D'Autrive had come upon in Ottoman Bulgaria uncanny.

To emphasize this, Sibel pointed out that we were standing in a mosque, and across the way the churches I had spotted earlier were all of different denominations. She then showed me a building I hadn't noticed earlier, close to the churches.

"That used to be the local synagogue," she said. It was a square mile dedicated to all three Abrahamic faiths. One I would never have expected to find in Romania. As I stared out across Constanta's own mini Jerusalem, I imagined it filled with people from all three faiths, living as harmoniously as Sibel and Cristian had just described it, long before communism and the horrors of World War II. This coexistence and religious pluralism, like the example in Bulgaria, I later learned, was an Ottoman legacy. The Turkish Muslim Empire's approach to governance meant religion was separated from state and, in the main, Islam was not imposed onto non-Muslim subjects, especially those that were Christian or Jewish. This was achieved using an approach popularly known as the "millet system," which allowed each faith group to self-govern within the wider state framework and thereby flourish, virtually side by side.

The direction of the vista we were admiring meant our backs were now turned on the statue of the Roman poet Ovid. He had been chosen as the symbol of modern Constanta, and yet as I stood imagining the community that had once flourished in the shade of the mosque, synagogue and churches before me, I couldn't help but feel *that* was the real legacy of this historic little-known town on the very edge of Europe.

BLOOD HABITS

Paying particular attention to the traits she shares with her mother, Marina Reza tries to make sense of her own identity by combing through the details of her family and her Bengali heritage.

MARINA REZA

MARINA REZA, Dhaka-born, NYC-raised and now based in Berlin, is a freelance writer, performer and organizer of Berlin Spoken Word. Featured in places like *New Moons: Contemporary Writing by North American Muslims* (Red Hen Press) and *SAND Journal*, her works explore the nonlinear nature of recovery—oscillating between indulgence and absence, the divine and the devilish—all while honoring dailiness in incisive, hilarious and surprising ways. Past stints at mental health nonprofits and major book publishers provided financial stability but left her creatively parched. Her current wage labor includes freelance odd-gigs and juggling technical words for SEO purposes. She hopes to find more fulfilling work, insha'Allah. marinareza.com.

A few blocks away from my family's canary-yellow house near the 61st-Woodside train stop, I recalled a piece of gossip. One summer, a Bengali girl about my age was sent back to Bangladesh because her mother was informed that she had been seen holding hands with a boy. While remembering this, I kept an eye out to make sure that my mother, whom I call Mimi, could not see me and Jamie, my then-boyfriend, sitting there through the café window. If someone from the Bengali community saw us, would my parents be informed? Would that inform how my life unfolded? Do the stories Mimi tells others inform how my life unfolds? What do we remember about a life, and who controls the narrative?

***

Mimi is economical. She doesn't like to throw out food, even when it has soured or rotted, because she'll find a way to use it. She learned home remedies from my grandmother, from beauty shows on the Indian television channel, and from the beauty section in the weekly Bengali newspaper. She saves orange peels and freezes them so she can blend them with a turmeric paste to apply to her face and wash off later. She says honey, milk and lemon have similar beneficial properties for the skin. When the milk in our fridge turns sour, she coagulates it with lemon juice or vinegar and drains off the whey to produce paneer. She then cuts it into little cubes for me and my sister, Sharina.

If the number of habits Mimi and I share is any indication, my habits may become similar to hers as I grow older. I might even become a sort of second-rate Mimi. Our collective habits include clipping coupons, clipping articles, picking scabs, feeling slightly nauseous after sipping a cup of tea (hers with milk, mine with lemon and, eventually, milk), staying home unless it's absolutely necessary to leave, consolidating food, bending the edge of a page and pushing it back out to see the edge curve up (by which point we start crinkling another edge, and by the time we finish a book, realize we have ruined it in its entirety), crinkling our hair from braids, crinkling our hair from damp buns, sliding our fingers inside jars to swipe out what's left, eating spoonfuls of powdered coffee creamer when the other one is not looking. We easily accumulate dark rings under our eyes. We have a poor ability to delay gratification.

***

Born in 1958 in Bangladesh (East Pakistan at that time), Papa, pronounced Pup-paw, not Paw-paw, does not say much about his childhood. He never mentions how he felt about his sister, Afroza Sultana "Ratna," who quickly rose to fame in the sixties as the Bengali actress "Shabana"—a name suggested by a talent director. In Bangladesh's film industry, Dhallywood, or Dollywood (not to be confused with Dolly Parton's family amusement park), Shabana acted in nearly 300 movies, the first being the successful Pakistani Urdu film *Chakori* in 1967. On a fan site, she is described as a "beauty queen" having been employed in a variety of roles, including the lover, wife, servant, mother, bandit and bhabi, with her "typically rural Bengali look."

***

When Papa and Mimi got married in 1985, Mimi was just out of high school. Sharina, my sister, was born four years later, and I arrived in April of 1991. Papa was not around very often in the first year of my life. He was a photographer and took on temporary jobs in Kuwait and Iran as Mimi continued catering to her in-laws, feeding me mashed rice and lentils through a bottle and mixing Horlicks and milk from plastic packets for Sharina.

Last year, an older cousin informed me that while my dad was away in my first year, Mimi would go to the movie theater with my father's brother and bring along my cousin, who was five at the time. Here, Mimi and my father's brother would make out thinking my cousin wouldn't notice. Years later, my father's brother married my mother's sister.

***

Born in 1965 in Bangladesh (East Pakistan at that time), Mimi has a nose tbat would bleed when studying before a test and she feared swimming after an incident in which she almost drowned. She was an inactive girl who preferred studying and admiring Bollywood actor Aamir Khan from afar, while her sister, Nasima, was more active, the reason for why, according to Mimi, Nasima reached a height of 5'5" while Mimi grew no taller than 4'10".

In 2013, Mimi's father, whom I called Nanajaan, died while I was detoxing at the psychiatric ward in Bellevue Hospital. My stay was instigated from a typical episode of blackout drinking. It was routine at that point—waking up in emergency rooms not knowing how or who got me there. I missed Nanajaan's funeral and Mimi lied about my absence. She once mentioned

Nanajaan was said to have liked his drink, too.

***

"When did your family first settle here?" I asked Jamie.

"1846," he said, chewing on his banana and hot fudge crepe.

He spoke of the men in the Lawrence lineage like Henry Miller, the German-American rancher who, at one point in the late 1800s, was one of the biggest land-owners in the United States (from California), and the American physicist and Nobel Laureate Ernest Lawrence, who helped invent the cyclotron atom-smasher in 1929 (where from, I don't know).

Sitting across from him, I felt inexplicably weepy eating my crepe. I couldn't have a conversation about my own family history because I didn't know much about it. I had never had the curiosity to ask them.

***

Mimi, what do you remember about delivering me?
What was your first impression of Papa?
Did you know he was in love with another woman?
When did you first have sex?
Use a tampon?
And why do you seem to equate the two?
Tell me about your experience with large bodies of water.
And why do my large, brown glasses bother you?

To which she responded, *Akta gay er motho dakha jai*. Or, *They make you look gay*.

***

Mimi likes morals, seeing every moment she has with me as an opportunity to impart morsels of wisdom. As the winner of the first season of *American Idol* was announced and confetti rained down, Kelly Clarkson took the stage, and Mimi, with tears in her eyes, told us that we, too, could do anything we wanted if we tried hard enough. Then she pointed out Clarkson's mother crying in the audience, and swiftly went back to cooking. When I suggested we watch *Precious*, Mimi said she would only do it if she could also tailor some of my pants with her sewing machine as we watched. At the end, she shook her head and said I was lucky I did not have a mother like Precious' vicious one, and that Precious' delivery scene was painful to watch.

Mimi and Papa are unthinkably talented and yet it can be easy to focus on what they do not know. Mimi is learning how to send text messages. One of her first messages was sent by accident using the preset text messages, "I'm sorry" and "I love you." One of them asked if I had heard about "one eye baby," a story that, I am certain, she read about on Facebook. Papa speaks about eight languages, can multiply three-digit numbers in his head and pronounces bear as "beer," and fluffy as "floppy."

***

Many of my peers in high school are the descendants of prominent Americans like Sir Harold Evans, Tina Brown, Estée Lauder, Andrew Carnegie and, perhaps regrettably, Harvey Weinstein.

My family's history is not written in books and cannot be found on traditional genealogical websites, so I've discovered alternative forms of documentation.

A Facebook artist page and a few fan sites are dedicated to Shabana. I vaguely remember this incident regarding Shabana's daughter:

GUTTENBERG, N.J. – Hudson County authorities are investigating the disappearance of a 16-year-old girl... She may have been spirited away by someone she met on the Internet.

And weeks later:

GUTTENBERG, N.J. – Police have found the daughter of a Bangladesh movie starlet, in the New York City apartment of a man she met on the Internet... N.J. police spokesman told United Press International that there was no preferential treatment for the family.

I remember the nightly news crew interviewing Shabana as the search began. My younger cousins and I huddled in the bedroom and were shushed as the news went on air. Mimi never mentioned this disappearance after Shabana's daughter was found, nor while the search was going on. This is an incident we do not talk about.

Here is another story I will not forget.

Upon my family's return from doing Umrah in Saudi Arabia, my father was taken aside to an isolated room in the airport for questioning.

Here is our list of terrorist suspects.

Here is your name.

Are you acquainted with Osama bin Laden?

I razzed Papa as soon as they let him out of the room. He did not seem bothered, but rather amused in response to the hyperbolic suggestions these men were putting forth at the airport.

***

How is the past constructed? Why are certain forms of ancestral documentation such as letters and articles of possession privileged over oral histories? What do you do with what you do not know?

Most of what I know about my family is what I have witnessed myself, and I have not witnessed very much so I cannot say much about the history that is not mine. Though one's impulse might be to justify how or why that is, I like to think Mimi and I are more likely to share our habits than our histories.

It's been nearly five years since we've spoken to each other. I never told Mimi that I moved to Berlin, Germany from New York City over four years ago. Upon googling my name, this is something she may find out.

ALL FOR A WORTHLESS MAN

In this unabashed, politically candid story set in Baghdad just before the US invasion, a recently drafted Ali Bader falls for an American journalist and finds himself bitterly jealous over a man who has deceivingly won her attentions.

ALI BADER

ALI BADER was born in Baghdad, where he studied western philosophy and foreign literature, and is now living in Brussels. He has written 18 novels, several works of non-fiction, scripts, plays and two poetry collections. He has also worked as a war correspondent covering the Middle East. His best-known novels include *Papa Sartre*, *The Tobacco Keeper*, *Running after the Wolves*, and *The Sinful Woman*, many of which have won awards. Elements in his novels include character study, social criticism, philosophical reflection and explicit language. He has written about art, politics and philosophy for many Arab newspapers and magazines.

This story was translated by **AMIKA ELFENDI**, whose bio appears on page 563.

I became acquainted with the American journalist Sandra in 2003, a few days before the war.

At the time, I was a drafted soldier, had completed a three-month course in desert combat, and was given a week's leave to visit family. After that, I had to join the frontier south of Basra, where the war would break out less than a week from then. On my last day home, I received a phone call from Aida, an Iraqi friend and freelance artist. Aida had tight connections with expats in Baghdad and invited me to a soirée at an Iraqi businessman's house. He was called Nizar and was a well-to-do, handsome bloke, though suspected of working with the Mukhabarat, the Iraqi Intelligence, as well as other clandestine political and financial organizations. It was Nizar who used to receive the American anti-war activist Susan Lindauer, who later in 2004 was accused of espionage for the Iraqis.

First I declined Aida's invitation, because I descend from a well-known family of Trotskyists, most of whom were professors who expired either by execution, in exile, or while interned during the Baath reign. So, I had qualms with those who had even the weakest ties to the government.

Aida told me then that there was an American journalist called Sandra, and that Sandra was keen to meet an Iraqi soldier, one that was not introduced to her by local officials. Still I provided my deepest regrets.

Then, when the military vehicle assigned to deploy me never showed up, I reconsidered. Another car would pick me up, but not for another five hours. It would be a mistake to return home, for my farewell with my relatives had been gravely emotional, full of tears, especially on my mother's part. I did not want my mother to sob twice on the same day. And I had no wish either to spend those hours in the streets of Baghdad, which after years of sanctions had no good cafés or bars left. Not to mention that Aida, who knew me well, had remarked that there would be lots of good red wine and many women with fetishes for military uniforms.

I beelined to the closest phone booth and called her back. She passed me over to Nizar, who chatted with me cordially and inquired about my whereabouts. After a quarter of an hour, a black Mercedes, curtained from within in black too, pulled up where I stood on the curb. The car was a very recent model, similar to those driven by Iraqi ministers, Saddam's guards, men of the Mukhabarat, and mysterious persons brandishing black mustaches and spiteful glares.

This was the first time I climbed into such a glamorous vehicle. I was driven to a sizable house in the rarefied neighborhood of Al Mansour, where many officials resided. We descended into the cellar garage that resembled a cave. I followed the chauffeur to the lift and we flew up to the second floor, where Zaki greeted us. I had expected a mustached, scowling chap like Saddam's men, but to my astonishment I saw before me a neat and slender person, with clever eyes and an attractive voice like that of Peter O'Toole. Zaki shook my hand firmly and led me into a hall where a table, covered lavishly with flasks and dishes, centered the room with eight people ringing it.

I recognized my friend Aida, who welcomed me warmly. Directly next to her sat Sandra. She looked American. No one could mistake that. With her strong build, wide blue eyes and outstanding smile, her beauty was real, primordial and ephemeral all at once.

There was also a French journalist present, two Russian businessmen and a Lebanese-American lady, one of their wives.

Two other men from Iraq were there too. I don't know what their professions were, but their English was lousy.

Sandra held sway over the conversation, and even though she did not direct her words to me, I felt she wanted to hear my stand. She was against the war, but still, ideologically, she was, let's say, of the Hegelian sort, believing in the Western mind's, particularly the American's, superiority over the world.

As she fell silent, all eyes riveted to me. Then, Nizar poured me a glass of wine. Everyone was looking at me; I was clad in commando uniform, heading to the frontier later that day, with shaved head and a sun-beaten, athletic physique. My muscles must have bulged under my clothes. I realized how the other men differed from me: they had long drowned in a sedentary lifestyle.

Everyone wanted me to speak up, especially Sandra, because the words of someone going to war were like those of a dying man—he gets full attention since he may never speak again.

But I kept my mouth shut, enjoying the wine after so many years without it.

"The wine's good?"

"Oh, very," I replied.

Wine makes you feel powerful, unlike smokes, which only offer a sort of misguided sentimentality. Maybe that's why the people of Iraq are suffocated by sentimental decisions. They consume seven billion cigarettes yearly.

Those sitting in front of me were peace advocates, wanting me to blather on as they did. True, I was not joining the war of my own accord, but to ask a soldier to talk of peace is like asking a pastor to feature in a porno. I wished to act differently, however. Not to be a raving nationalist, but not to talk like a goat either.

Many Westerners imagine that public opinion *can* stop wars, and that exposing wars' atrocities *can* make politicians budge. That's outright wrong. I told them that simply, nobody could stop the war as long as the rat race for money, resources, animosity and supremacy went on.

How many books have been written on the monstrosities of wars? Millions of people read them. To no avail. Decision-makers who wage wars read volumes on war. To no use. Perhaps on his break the very officer who will launch missiles on us will peruse a great book, like Erskine Caldwell's *Tobacco Road*. While, on the other side, a soldier smeared with mud holds his helmet in trembling hands as he falls, terrified.

"Are you going to fight?" Sandra asked me.

"We're Iraqis. We'll only fight because that's what we are," I explained. "We fight because we're vindictive and obsequious. Nothing in us has changed since the dawn of history, not our forebears nor our ideas, that is if we indeed have any. That's all we are. We'll live in poverty and terror as pawns. The Muslim Arabs subjugated us and made us their pawns. Then came the Communists and with them also we were pawns. And now here we are, having to croak by the bullets and shit of America. Because we *are* pawns."

Sandra asked to sit by my side, and then I felt two flames glowing inside me: the wine and her eyes.

"Don't you believe a spark of humanity might change the course of war?"

"I don't...I don't trust man." Man hates man. Man is a destructive, ruttish gorilla. That's all he is.

Ours was a chance meeting between two dissimilar things, like a sewing machine and an umbrella on one table.

"You Iraqis are in general religious, no?"

"No, not religious. This earth is ruled by a sad and lustful god. In the morning, he counts his coins, and, in the evening, he counts the dead."

It was a beautiful discussion, and since she too was beautiful, I tried to entice her with all my power. I was versed in American literature. The Americans, unlike Europeans, have no sense for music, spirituality or metaphysics, but they have great literature. That kind of literature produced by nations that endure civil wars, famines and poverty. I was perhaps trying to ensnare her in a certain discourse. I had to drag her somewhere we could despise each other. She, in her turn, was like a sorcerer attempting to spellbind me. And her outbursts were many. A portrait artist would have toiled hard to catch one of her expressions. She was a whole cathedral of tizzies.

And so, I was sucked into a heated argument with her, by an overbearing need to talk aloud, to make my thoughts thunder and explode. Maybe it was my feeling that death was near. Maybe it was that I felt these were my last happy moments. For with my own eyes I was witnessing an unnameable insolence. A terrible destiny was on the march, with the war and after it, and not only would it ravage us, but it would claim trees, cats, and even the rain as well. I was macabre and celebratory at the same time.

I could no longer hear what she said; I was daydreaming, glass in hand, admiring her face, drowning in her blue eyes. I felt my understanding of humans deepen, like I was myself being renewed. I realized this better later when I joined the forces, and pondering it more closely, in those settings and under the blazing sun, gave me an immense feeling. It gave me creative inspiration and a connection with the supernatural.

Yes, these moments, pre-war and pre-death, endowed me with the ability to see the world more clearly. On that day, I came to know my truth and shed off all conventions, those which had previously held me back from emerging into a broader, merrier universe.

I left the soirée feeling conflicted. Had it been up to me, I would have stayed until morning, forever. But I left. The Mercedes drove me back, and I boarded the military bus. It charged us to the frontier. Sandra's image, however, did not leave my mind. I thought of her every minute, every second. I did not want anyone to disrupt my reveries, so I spoke to no one about her. I dare say I hadn't grasped love before that day, love as a force of nature, constantly moving.

Since love is driven by desire for the other, that feeling reaches its peak in wartime. I realized then that love would take me along with it to places I did not expect.

***

The war fledged its wings a week after my meeting Sandra. The first onslaught fell out at Um Qasr. We had arrived at that little town's port 72 hours earlier with Infantry Brigade 45.

After midnight, we were ambushed by an American-British coalition and we fended them off valiantly. We managed to prevent any breach into the area and stopped their headway. As the first light of dawn appeared, the US bombers fell to shelling us mercilessly, and cruise missiles came down on us like sheets of hail. But we did not surrender, we did not retreat one foot. Most of the men in our brigade were killed, but we kept going strong.

I soon lost sense of days and hours from fatigue and the fight, and the pain of losing friends, killed without mercy, their body parts and blood covering the battlefield. Then another ruthless skirmish blew up between us and an American unit that ambushed us from the right flank. I got critically wounded and was captured by them. They transported me on a stretcher to a field hospital.

Between life and death, I opened my eyes, conscious for the first time, and found myself in a vast yard. The yard was all that was left of this mobile hospital, with many men sprawling about. To my right lay an American soldier by the name of David. He looked at me and I at him. We both smiled.

A light breeze blew about and the tree leaves danced. I don't know why I was moved by the spectacle of leaves rustling harmoniously in that great silence, right after my waking up from warranted death. It must have been life, in all its beauty and mystery. Something mesmerized me at that moment, and I wanted to see Sandra. A blond female soldier approached me, and my heart almost halted when I thought it was her. When she saw my confusion, she smiled and pressed my hand gently.

"How are you doing?"

"Like someone sitting on nails. Haven't eaten in four days. Feels like my stomach is glued to my back."

"Oh, you didn't eat?"

"How could we, while you bombed us?! All the great sciences, all the greatest human inventions were being used to hunt down a few Iraqis like rats."

"You were brave..."

"What's the use if you could mince us like you could a mountain peak from so far away? Everyone knows that the Americans who set off missiles sit in air-conditioned cubicles, with pretty, rosy women, listening to great American hits."

"Hah, you're envious because these dudes have pretty women, and not because they won the battle. Up and confess, you spiteful Iraqi."

"Believe me, all your victories are for me like my lost and forgotten shoe..." But victory, *all* victory, is if I could spend a few minutes chatting with a striking woman.

***

Upon my release, I joined a team of journalists in Baghdad. I never forgot Sandra, though. The only issue was that I did not know her surname. I had perhaps heard it when they presented her, but I forgot it. Aida had left Iraq, I do not know where. Nizar vanished, pursued by the Americans.

I tried to Google her name: Sandra journalist. Sandra anti-war activist. Sandra Baghdad.

All these searches returned nothing, and, for years, I waited for a miracle.

After finishing my novel, *The Tobacco Keeper*, Islamist groups threatened me. There was nothing else to do but leave. I had to wait because of my cat, Sphinx, who was quite old at the time. This put me in danger, but after he passed away, I left, and out of sheer coincidence, met Aida at Books Café on Rainbow Street in Amman. There was my miracle! Even before I mentioned Sandra, Aida asked me about her.

"Remember that American journalist Sandra, the one you met right before the war?"

My god, my heart almost stopped beating.

"Of course, I do. What's going on with her?"

"She's always asking about you!"

"Seriously?" I nearly fainted.

"I swear..."

"Is she in Iraq now?"

"No, actually she left before the war. A year ago, she returned to Baghdad, and something terrible happened with her."

"Oh, what?!"

"She hired a guide called Basim, a cab driver in Baghdad. But the militias tracked him down, considering him a traitor conspiring with the Americans. They killed his wife, mother and two daughters. He escaped, returned to Sandra and told her the story, saying he didn't know where to go. She managed to smuggle him out to Syria. She rented a house there and put up some Iraqi artists fleeing that Hell. If you wish, you too can go and live there."

The idea elated me. I got Sandra's number and phoned her. I had imagined that her relationship with that taxi driver had only one dimension: sympathy. I had not thought that it had become complicated, strained and dangerous to boot.

"Sandra, you remember me?"

"I do, very well. I asked about you last time I was in Baghdad. I feared for you in that war and wanted to know what had become of you."

"Listen, I never forgot you. Thought about you all the time."

"..."

"Did you hear me?"

"Yes, yes, I did. I was there to find you. Then something horrible happened..."

"Aida told me. Were you really there to find me?"

"I was there for many reasons. What's important, this incident changed my life..."

"What are you saying?"

"My conscience is torturing me. I feel a moral responsibility toward this guy. And I need you, need your help."

"Sure, of course."

"Can you come to Damascus? I have a house in Bab Toma, several rooms. You'll have your own. Some people you know live there now. You will have a blast. Things here are much better than down in Jordan."

On October 11, 2008, I arrived in Damascus. The taxi pulled up to a big house in Bab Toma. This Christian quarter was built by those fleeing the carnage in Mount Lebanon right after the insurrection of Tanyos Shahin against Druze feudalists. Later it turned into a most gorgeous neighborhood, evoking the colonial ones of Baghdad. Loads of foreigners inhabited Bab Toma: Italians, Frenchmen, Russians, Brits, Eastern Europeans and a small number of Americans. What distinguished these Europeans from the rest was that they were not wealthy or diplomats, but mere students. Because Bab Toma was a quarter of the common people, rents were markedly cheaper. With time, and especially after 2003, the neighborhood turned into a place heavily populated by Iraqi artists.

Sandra greeted me with Basim. He was about 30 years old, lean and swarthy, far from handsome, ordinary, uneducated. But he had bright eyes and was courteous. He left me with Sandra in the hall. He was anxious and looked in on us from time to time.

My second meeting with Sandra was much better. She had not lost her beauty, but I caught a change in her eyes. They were sharper now, probably due to the incident in Iraq. From the first hour listening to her, I realized this secretly delicate woman had decided to dedicate her life to one definite mission: a grand resignation, sacrificing herself for this Basim.

"Holy! What? Are you saying you're involved with him?"

"Yes..."

She was almost coercing herself, choosing resolutely to squander herself by caring for this man, physically and mentally. Her resolution looked more like an ethically-rooted obligation, with her deep belief that she had brought it all on him. This Basim was extorting from her all she offered him, by crying before her or reminding her of his daughters or mother. She threw parties for him in her house, inviting everyone she knew, with tables of food and drink, music and dance, so that he could forget his misfortune.

Their conversations tasted of cruelty that day, and many a time, it bordered on worrisome callousness. I sensed there must be a destructive tendency in her, a creative talent to forge the facts. I sometimes felt an absolute joy as she sat opposite me, the same joy I draw from the violent forgeries of impressionists.

Anyhow, a few days later, I found myself part of this game, also partaking in the food, drink and dance, while he glared at me unkindly. He felt a constant threat on my part, and so we misliked each other. Not only was he uneducated, but also cruel, seeming comforted by his hate for me.

During these days, gradually, my love for Sandra turned into a bomb stowed inside a store of earthenware.

***

I stayed at Sandra's house for two months, but I never felt things change. My enmity with Basim became clearer. She asked me to take it easy. She said his goal was to get to Europe for trauma treatment.

"Why do you keep mocking him?" she asked.

"Don't know. He makes me laugh until I'm blue in the face. It's not wicked laughter, though...Mockery, yes, but it's innocent, instinctive, not least when he does something comical and self-contradictory."

"I beg you, respect him for my sake."

Here I lost my temper. "Do you mean that?"

She gestured "yes," with conviction.

"I don't know whether I believe you."

She looked at me as if hurt. "Ah, that's how it is then..." She refilled our glasses.

"Tell me a little about after I left for the frontier. Did you think of me?"

"Can't say."

"My god!"

Then, she crossed her legs, disclosing a black knot in her leggings at knee level and a bit of thigh.

"Funny that you investigate a thing that's years old."

"Years, yeah...Feels to me more like one day."

"And you, did *you* think of me?" she finally asked.

I came closer, knelt, and fixed my eyes upon hers and put a hand on her thigh. She quivered as if shaken by my hot, lustful energy. Maybe she noticed me readying my lips to devour hers, but she heaved forward and drank from her glass, then stood up, thwarting my attempt.

"Listen, he's sleeping...But he can feel everything."

I hadn't yet stood up from my kneeling position when Basim entered on tiptoe.

"What's the matter, why haven't you come to bed?" He addressed her, horrified.

He shifted his eyes between me and her as I rose from the ground. She flew to him, placed her hand on his forehead and wiped it.

"What's wrong?" she asked him.

"Nightmare... my wife and children again."

"Oh, jeez," she exclaimed.

She placed her glass on the table, took his hands and led him upstairs as she comforted him with kisses and rubbed his chest.

I felt despair that day. I went back to my room but couldn't sleep at all. I was attacked by the dilemma: my jealousy on the one hand, and, on the other, my inability to commiserate with him, who had lost his wife, children, mother, and to recognize his need for Sandra.

My god, was I right or wrong? I could no longer tell. My hatred and jealousy made me lose faith in everything. Next morning, not able to stand breakfast with the others, I left early and walked the Damascene streets. I traversed the distance from Bab Toma to Bab Sharqi, and then to Al Hamidiya and the Omayyad Mosque. There I sat at Al Nofara café and sipped coffee, listening to Fairuz.

In the evening, I returned, climbed the stairs and resolved to see her. I headed directly to where she usually sat, but didn't find her. *He* was there, though, sitting. When he saw me, he rose and stretched out an arm towards me as he spoke. His hand looked mutilated and scary like those in Scandinavian myths. He talked to me with that hand while I could see

Sandra's face through the crack in the door: the face of a sleeping, innocent child. I retired to my bedroom and slept feverishly. In a dream, his hand came to me, and his teeth showed in his mouth, which resembled a urinal. She hid behind me, but he managed to snatch her away. I was chained, couldn't take her back. I woke up in a cold sweat, possessed wholly by a dumb silence.

***

Some days later, I was in the hall with Ziad Turkey, director of the 2007 flick *Under the Ashes*, which I had scripted. I was drunk. Sandra entered and looked quite distressed. She put her hand on my shoulder, and that annoyed me. Then she asked me, her eyes tearful, to be kind to Basim.

"Look, don't talk to me like that," I told her. "I'm in ruins. I am one of the war's invalids. Love in me turns to war. And you know that I was in combat with the Americans and that I fought like the heroes of Greek tragedies. I was shot, imprisoned. Had Hollywood heard of me, I would've become a Gary Cooper. I can't understand how you can prefer him, who looks like a mop!"

"Oh, Ali, you're so bigoted. Your selfishness has changed you into a bigot!"

"You're relenting to a sacrificial obsession. Pure masochism. If you hadn't given up, your life would've been glorious. But now look at you! Have I become a scapegoat for revulsion? I hate him because he's a yokel? Big joke. Maybe I inherited my hatred for peasants from Flaubert, and my mistrust of them from Marx. But 80 percent of my people *are* country people."

"They murdered his family in front of his eyes, what do you want him to do? If you were in his shoes, what would *you* do?"

"If I were him, I wouldn't have let the terrorists get away with that. I would've hunted them down, each one of them, like rats. And I would've most certainly not moved to Europe to live like an ewe."

"Please, he wants to talk to you. All you do is ignore and taunt him."

"I don't wish to talk with him. I hate his voice. He should be shot dead just because of his voice."

"Ugh, I can't bear this anymore..."

"Believe me, Iraqis are foolhardy and cruel. I don't like when they speak. I once had a friend, a poet, who spoke the most beautiful of languages, but he died in the war. His marvelous voice, silenced under the sand, will forever ring in my ears, but others'? No!"

"Fine. Don't listen to him, Ali. Only don't treat him cruelly!"

"In my teens, I envied deaf people their deafness, but I got used to sitting among them, deaf and dumb. Hardly could I remember what they said. Their voices vexed me, and I based my first novel on the restlessness they caused me."

"I don't know what to say to you."

"I don't *need* you to say a thing. There's no love in the hearts of American women. Not even in the hearts of all the world's women. Only cats know love—and even then not all of them do. It's known only by the neglected, dismal, banished, thrown and degraded ones. This category alone knows love. Leave me be. I don't want to see your face."

She left, looking dejected.

***

A few days after that, Ziad Turkey wanted to say two words to me. We went out to the enclosed courtyard and sat facing each other. He said that Sandra was through with this life with Basim and wanted to get him to Europe by any means possible, so that he could get his asylum and she, her peace of mind. I was delighted to hear this. Her plan was to smuggle him there with the pretense of joining a cinema festival in Stockholm.

"But how is he to participate and in what capacity?"

"It's simple. We exchange his name for yours in the movie's roster and then he can be granted a visa and leave."

I outright refused, but when Ziad insisted, I accepted. The cover was tweaked so that Basim's name appeared instead of mine. My only hope was for Basim to stay in Sweden while Sandra could come back to Damascus or some place else where I could join her. I wanted this nightmarish chapter of our life to end.

Despite that, I later told Sandra that I felt pessimistic about all of it. "I feel it will all end dreadfully."

But she assured me that once his life stabilized, all of it would be over for her, that she couldn't handle it anymore, and that she couldn't afford his expenses any longer.

Then, she, Ziad and Basim flew to Sweden, and I started gathering my stuff, hoping to move elsewhere.

Ziad returned to Damascus a week later. Sandra had finally gotten the monkey off her back and left for the US. Before I abandoned the house, someone from Baghdad came by asking for Basim, saying he was family.

"Basim's in Sweden."

"Huh, when did that happen? He didn't say so to his mother."

"Mother? Wasn't she killed in Baghdad a year or so ago?"

"No...killed?! His mother asked me to swing by and see about him. He calls her weekly. Only this week he hasn't phoned."

"Man, what are you saying? His mother, wife, daughters weren't killed in Baghdad by terrorists?"

"You must have someone else in mind... Basim's not married."

I hurried to Ziad. He had pictures of the parties. We showed them to the visitor.

"Is this him?"

"Yes, him. Basim, my cousin. Here, his mother's number. If you will, you can call her up."

And we did. She corroborated the news and it shocked us terribly. Basim had lied to Sandra! He had flipped her life upside down, made her come from Baghdad to Damascus so he could sponge off her! What should we do, call Sandra and let her know? If we did that, the woman would really collapse, particularly if I were to be the messenger. And I, too, would be erased from her life, Ziad maintained.

"Best to keep it as is. Till she moves past this role she has created for herself."

***

Two weeks went by, and my life got complicated. I had to run away from the Middle East altogether because of my book, *The Tobacco Keeper*, and articles I had written. I set off to Turkey, then to Europe, hoping, with the help of smugglers, to go all the way to Belgium.

On my first day in Brussels, I found an email from Sandra in my inbox.

Hello,

How are you doing?

I would like for you to join us on this. Basim is facing a vehement amount of xenophobia in Sweden. We're forming an association called Basim's Friends. A lot of artists and authors from Iraq, the Middle East and other countries are in, and we want you to be a part of this.

Please, let me know what you think.

I don't know why this didn't anger me, why I didn't lift my hands to the heavens in one grip of rage.

I had waited two months for a letter from her and I didn't receive any. She also had promised that she would phone me and didn't. She knew that my life in Syria had become complicated and it had gotten worse. She knew that I could no longer stay but she didn't even ask about me.

"I think Westerners love the victim," I said to Ziad.

"Why do you say that?"

"Because I am not a victim. I am not weak. I do not cry because of the terrorists. Instead, I dance, drink, write and that's why she doesn't tend to me. Westerners love victims; they want people to save. This gives them a sense of superiority. Because I'm not a victim, I am out of the equation."

So when I read her email I only smiled, a pale smile, and shut the phone off. I leaned back and reeled through the years since 2003 when Iraq was invaded, until my coming to Belgium as a refugee. If, in fact, I had any feelings toward Sandra, it was not conscious. Maybe this need for love had welled up due to the miserable state of war, and intense infatuation and passion.

All in all, the reaction was forced, entirely unmeant. I never actually loved her.

Let it all be over now. I won't answer her messages after today.

I rose to my feet, feeling myself freed from a huge part of my past that had been bringing me down. And I braced myself for another life, a refugee's life, in a cold country, completely alien to me.

FORK IN THE ROAD

Leila Aboulela describes a revived connection with her native Sudan, and how she dismisses her peers' judgment upon returning to Khartoum after so long.

LEILA ABOULELA

LEILA ABOULELA grew up in Sudan and now lives in Scotland in awe of Sudan's youth, their revolutionary energy and sharp consciousness. She is the author of five novels: *Bird Summons*, *The Translator*, a New York Times 100 Notable Books of the Year, *The Kindness of Enemies*, *Minaret* and *Lyrics Alley*, Fiction Winner of the Scottish Book Awards. She was the first winner of the Caine Prize for African Writing and her latest story collection, *Elsewhere, Home* won the Saltire Fiction Book of the Year Award. Leila's work has been translated into 15 languages. leila-aboulela.com

I left Sudan in 1987—I was 23 years old and the idea of writing was the furthest thing from my mind. I was a statistics graduate and literature had not been one of my university subjects. Instead I read fiction for pleasure, freely, without guidance or recommendation, entering fulfilling secret worlds that left me with no urge to write.

The move changed all that. It made me pause and reflect. I was in awe of the sharp contrast between Khartoum and London, compelled to comment on the differences in weather and colors, and on Islam compared to a secular Christian democracy. Like many of our generation, my husband and I were not sure whether we would return or remain as immigrants in the UK, or move on to a third location. This uncertainty created in me a sense of dislocation. There was homesickness to deal with, cultural confusion and the awkwardness of being Arab in the Europe of the 1990s; the vulnerability of being a practicing Muslim and wearing hijab. It was a situation charged with conflict and tension—an atmosphere conducive to writing fiction.

In 2006, I traveled back to Khartoum after 17 years of absence. I walked down the steps of the airplane and waited with the other passengers for the bus to the terminal. It was sunset but the familiar flat landscape was clear, the sky more spacious than anywhere else, cloudless with a bottom layer of sandy yellow then blue and darker blue. The low buildings, the dust in the air, the slowness with which everyone moved...this was the start of everything I had missed.

What did I want after being away for so long? Forgiveness or a heroine's return? Evidence to justify my reasons for leaving? Or incentives to launch an abrupt U-turn, a moving-back-home to pick up where I had left off? Years ago I had nonchalantly swung my baby son on my hip, boarded a British Airway plane and enrolled him at the LSE nursery. So confident I was of returning after my degree, that I had washed his last nappy and hung it to dry in the bathroom. After 17 years the cotton was stiff and beige with dust. It almost crunched in my hands. Time to dust off his baby toys and give them away: his tub, his plastic bib, but I kept the congratulations cards with their blue design and the signatures of my old friends.

They said, "We know what you look like now, we've seen your photo in the papers!" They laughed with surprise at my three books. "Oh you were always the dreamy type. But seriously, Leila, you must get yourself a job!" They disapproved of the image of me sitting at home. They remembered the only girl in the Statistics Honors class, the one who had annoyed the boys by getting higher grades than them. It was a disappointment that I had let my degree lie fallow; it was embarrassing that all I wanted to do was write.

So I sought out new friends. I met a woman who sold her gold bangles to self-publish her first novel. I met a publisher who despite sanctions and restrictions was keeping his business afloat, and despite political repression was keeping himself out of prison. In a reading event at the University of Khartoum, I signed a pirate copy of my collection of stories. It had been blown up to the size of a coffee-table book! Then I signed a stained, worn out copy of *The Translator*, dog-eared and with notes on the margins. It had been passed around and poured over. Everything in Sudan was scarce and everything had value.

I found the city changed in predictable and interesting ways. More built up areas, more congestion, a higher visibility of women in public. Social life seemed to have moved indoors because of the widespread use of air conditioners. My wedding in 1985 had been in my parents' garden, with a tent for the men pitched on the road. Now large halls were booked and couples didn't have to wait for the cooler months in order to get married. People no longer slept on their verandas or received guests on their porch. Khartoum was hotter, everyone explained, with more mosquitoes and flies; less privacy because of the higher buildings next door. The Sudanese were changing their habits. But that particular beauty I had ached for while I was away was still there, still potent, still able to stir me. The same smells of sweat and sandalwood; a dust storm surging through eucalyptus trees. At twilight I looked across the Nile and saw the ferry dock at the island of Tuti. Sky, river, green fields, men in white jellabias, women in colored tobes and it was like a painting. I had been right to cry over this. I was right to miss this.

This story was first published by Granta.

A MARRIAGE REINVENTED

In this family love story, Naazish YarKhan allows writing to open her heart, as she seeks to find the kind of intimacy she and her husband have never known before.

NAAZISH YARKHAN

NAAZISH YARKHAN is a college application essay consultant and owner of WritersStudio.us. She has contributed to numerous media outlets in the US and internationally, including NPR's *All Things Considered*, Public Radio International, Common Ground News, and Chicago Public Radio. Her writing has been translated into Arabic, French, Hebrew, Urdu, Malay and Tagalog. Her latest story was published in Red Hen Press's *American Muslims: An Anthology of Contemporary Writing*.

April 13, 2020

My husband has always been a man of few words. Despite his unstinting support of my aspirations and goals, he wasn't one to ask about what's on my heart. Consequently, I've often felt like I didn't exist for him during these 25 years of our marriage. I once clung to the idea that books on self-help and marriage advice worked. These therapists and experts could so accurately pinpoint the culprits souring a marriage, surely they knew how to resuscitate it better than anyone else, I'd reasoned. Consequently, I religiously devoured relationship advice whether it was online or pouring out of a book. But this fourth week of being walled off from the world thanks to COVID-19, I actually feel my jaw clench when relationship advice floats across my social media channels or my browser feed. Not only do I unfollow these relationship gurus—I physically trash (not donate) copies of their books. Tigers do not change their stripes and people do not change either, I want to rant.

"It is a desi thing. Do you recall your parents ever asking you about your feelings?" My best friend rolls her eyes at me via Zoom, slurping into the ice cubes at the bottom of her glass of lemonade. "So why would the generation that followed, aka our husbands, ask us about our feelings? Who would have role-modeled that for these men?"

It is clearly a rhetorical question but still I nod in agreement. "Yes," I scowl, "but," I raise my hands in the air, "it does not take away from the fact that I have emotional needs that remain unmet. And if we are to stay married, let alone aim for happily married, something's gotta change." I am rehashing a conversation she and I often have, but once I get started on it, it's like I can't find the stop button. "When he and I speak, it's usually about something functional like whether a bill has been paid or if the laundry has been done."

"Some days I can count the words we share," I growl. I concede that my husband and I may talk about something he's heard in the news on NPR or an article he's read. Or something that happened at his work. Or something related to the kids. "But," I make it a point to clarify, "each of these topics are addressed on a different day." Or so it feels like. Worse, it feels like superficial chit chat. Not like the meaningful, necessary, healing, often hilarious, conversations my girlfriends and I have.

Yes, she's heard this before too, but we never tire of being each other's therapist. "The more hostile you feel, the more hostility you express and the less he's inclined to want to share your space," she says. "The more passive-aggressive you perceive his comments to be, the more unpleasant you grow. Vicious cycle, yes?" she asks.

I tell you—I love this woman. She helps me make sense of my world, even if I feel like nothing will change this marriage. She should definitely consider a career as a couples' counselor, I respond. At least she'd get paid for her insights.

If I were to recall an actual recent conversation with my husband, it would look something like this:

Me: "I don't feel like you know me. Why can't we do more together, as a couple?"

Him: "I don't know. What do you want me to say?"

Me: "I don't feel heard. Or seen." Except when we are having sex, I think to myself.

Him: "I don't know what you want me to do."

Me: "I feel it takes away from everything when I have to tell you to put your arm around me when I'm upset. Why can't you do it instinctively when you see I'm sad or unhappy?"

At that point he usually gives up, turns around in bed and faces the other way.

Another pea under my mattress? His paucity of interest in my words. I, a writer! Someone for whom words are like water to fish! And I see this total disinterest in my words reaffirmed as we sequester ourselves from the world during the pandemic. He saunters downstairs after a day of working from home. Promptly, I lose him to the couch and TV. This single act brings me face-to-face with the stark reality that it is not his two-hour commute (round trip) that leaves him too tired for words. A man of few words is just who he is.

My gripes aside, during this period of sheltering in place, there is no denying it, we are the fortunate ones. We are blessed. My husband and I are able to work from home. My young adult kids are contently e-learning not just in separate rooms but on different floors. Our wi-fi doesn't disappoint despite a lag here and a lag there. There is food on the table.

It is not lost on me that so many weeks into quarantine, all four of us continue to enjoy being in each other's company, Alhamdulillah. Praise be to God. Before we were homebound, none of us did breakfast. We often skipped lunch together even on weekends. Homebound, we now coalesce for lunch and dinner, the latter revived after, what? Maybe a 15-year lapse? As a result, I am cooking more than ever. To my shock, I'm also getting so much better at it. My daughter has taken to baking relentlessly. Thanks to her, our kitchen smells divine. Sweet potato pie, lemon bars, cookies, brownies. And there are even better days, days when her treats don't get burned in our aging, temperamental oven. No longer away on campus, she's even begun helping me make dinner. My son handles the clean-up.

Each evening sees the four of us piling into our big comfy couch, snuggling under a single plush blankie, prepared to binge watch our favorite shows. Or we watch the news, horrified at the heartbreak the virus has unleashed.

Just as this time of being sequestered has given me the space to, ironically, breathe, it has also given me room to read my year-old copy of a book applying ideas from quantum physics to understanding relationships. Brand new, it had previously escaped the rubbish pile. From its pages, I learn of emotional contagion and entrainment, and their impact on relationships. Of energy, whether positive or negative, being palpable. Of energy being channeled to create your reality through your thoughts and words. The ideas really resonate with me. I read with interest the author's example of a client who came complaining about her stepson. For "homework", this client is assigned to write something nice that she notices about him each day, for 30 days. This woman, a skeptic, had nothing to lose and gave it a shot. Thirty days later, she had reinvented her relationship with her son. The idea captures my interest.

Should I try this? I wonder. Should I write down all the nice things I notice about my spouse? Maybe I can go a step further and hand him the list at each day's end.

And so it begins.

Throughout our marriage, I have been grateful that my husband has always helped with the housework. Now, too, he has taken responsibility for the grocery shopping entirely unprompted. I make a note of this on my gratitude list. He tracks what's whittling down, makes an order online with my daughter and the duo pick it up curbside. As a team, we sponge down, wipe or wash each and every grocery item that can be treated the moment it crosses our threshold. Canned food sits in our mud room for three days before we venture to stock our shelves with them. We immediately separate the cardboard boxes from the plastic cereal bags within, tossing the former. The counters are wiped clean as soon as we have put everything away.

And so, with fingers crossed, I also began handing my husband these notes. Soon, I began reading them aloud to him, for good measure. I had to ensure he was getting the message.

The notes have said:

1. I love that you rally the kids and me to eat lunch and dinner as a family, checking in each day to see what time our schedules allow us all to gather.
2. Thank you for making room for my "me time". I like that you encourage me to make the space in my day for my interests, whether meditation, reading or catching up with friends on Zoom.
3. I like the funny quips you make, even making my friends laugh during our Zoom chats. It makes me very happy that you like all my friends.
4. I feel happy that we, as a family, like each other's company and, rather than disappear into our own rooms, hang out together often.
5. I like your soft skin. There isn't a wrinkle or a blemish on your face. You are still quite handsome at almost 50.
6. I like us entwining like a pretzel when we are in bed.
7. Thank you for taking the initiative to fix the washing machine the very same day that it broke.

8. I feel so grateful you're taking the time, despite a long day at work, to teach our girl driving every day.
9. Thank you for heating the food and setting the table, even when you were fasting and hungry, rather than delegating it to me, though you are as tired as I am.
10. Thank you for your ever persistent equanimity and ready humor.

As I fill my gratitude list with these observations, I realize that it is the pandemic that has given me the space and time to slow down enough to actually appreciate my spouse's positives. As I write these notes to him, pressing ink to paper, I literally feel my heart soften. The writing, it works on my heart. It makes me feel happy and loved. It makes me want to be nice to him. It shifts the energy in our relationship from frustration to kindness and smiles. It makes me want to write more nice things about him. As I read my notes to him, I think he is listening though I can't really tell. That annoys me but I must be positive, I coax myself. I must assume my words are leaving a mark.

I notice that the more intentional I am about focusing on his positive attributes, the more I feel this shift in my heart. I see clearly how I've fixated on the random black dots on a white page. His stinginess with words has been the black dot. His muted interest in what I am thinking, what I have to say, is also a black dot. The white page is all the good stuff, the majority of our life. The white page is this loving family we have created together, despite our daily arguments.

As I pay attention to the good things he does, I can see how well I've fed my dissatisfactions. Fattened them up like a lamb before slaughter but here there is no end in sight. The black dots, consequently, have grown monstrous, overshadowing what I know to be good about my husband. I have to be very diligent about writing the good things or I fall off the wagon and find old patterns and new reasons to be disgruntled.

Mine may not be the marriage that's based on things like revealing our deepest, darkest fears, sharing my favorite childhood memory, or having him reassuringly pull me closer when I'm feeling anxious. I am just not married to a guy who communicates like that, or who thinks about things as deeply as I do. But, for the first time, I've begun to feel that acknowledging the good in him consistently will definitely enrich our relationship. I do have legitimate needs, but it is also my responsibility to decide what to focus on, what to appreciate. To ferret out the most effective approach to feeling, and giving, love consistently.

April 23, 2020

We have completed our fifth week of self-quarantine. The mosques have been forced to close their doors to the public. As Ramadan unfolds, our local mosques have gone online to deliver daily sermons and our family religiously unites, toggling between different speakers and sermons, listening devoutly. I love being able to tune into Omar Suleiman, Dr. Miraj Mohiuddin, Celebrate Mercy, our local imams at Darus Salam masjid, Uthman masjid, Islamic Foundation mosque, all in one day. They are innovators who want to reach their flock, come what may. We are spoiled for choice. In real life, we'd have to cherry pick and stick to one mosque, one speaker. We aren't feeling strapped for time between iftar and isha, nor rushing to the mosque for isha and taraweeh, to make it before the parking lot fills up. Instead, now we assemble in our living room, as a family. Some days my son leads the prayer, other days my husband does the honors. This is the most peaceful, the most spiritual Ramadan I've experienced. Just the four of us, praying into the night on our own. No hustling to get anywhere. I have never felt so connected to my prayers, or to my kids. I have never read so much of the Quran as I did this Ramadan. While I missed seeing familiar faces at the mosque, I cherished being the family that prays together, rather than splintering off to the men and women's sections in our mosques, or going to separate mosques altogether. I have never felt more content spending time with Allah as I now do.

December 21, 2021

Vaccinated and boostered, we have now completed one year and nine months of living with COVID-19, with the Delta variant, with Omicron. President Biden warned today of an outbreak over the winter holidays if more people didn't get vaccinated here in America. My husband and I are still working remotely, and are more attuned to one another than before. I believe the hurry-scurry, the waiting in traffic, the tiring commute, the waiting in grocery lines, the many obligatory places to be, the endless things to do having been stripped away through the pandemic has given us a chance to be our better, less harried, less hurried, less impatient, more considerate selves. Once we were more considerate, we became just nicer overall. Not more romantic nor more lovey-dovey, just more decent to each other as human beings. We had more room to pause to choose a response versus a reaction when triggered.

The loving notes facilitated the paradigm shift, but doing less in life turned out to be our saving grace. I want to stay married to this guy. I feel he gets me more than ever before.

What we have fostered through quarantine and beyond, dare I say, is what happily married feels like.

When I learned that gratitude vibrates at the frequency of 540 MHz I didn't register what that really meant. I didn't put two-and-two together at the time, but what that gratitude list was doing was opening the door to better vibes in my life as a whole. My best friend and I, we still don't tire of being there for each other but, somehow, along the way we've learned to say, "shit or get off the pot," albeit in less crude terms. When we need to vent, we only give it 10 minutes, and that's all. We don't let our resentments and disappointments rule the roost.

March 3, 2023

Three years later, we still aren't asking one another the *36 Questions to Fall in Love*. A bout of C. diff that left me bed-ridden, and the months it took to recover fully, however, did draw us closer than anything else before it. Taking care of my every need, his commitment to my recovery made me see and appreciate the kind of man my husband truly is. MashaAllah, he has also grown into my sounding board. I have found he now hears me when I'm sharing my deepest, darkest fears or feeling hopelessly sad. He has learned to reassuringly pull me closer when I'm feeling anxious. I am still not married to a guy who wants to hear every word that comes to my mind, but, Alhamdullilah, I have found he listens and responds when it's most important to me. And vice versa. Despite our daily squabbles, we have found our way to lasting love. Inshallah.

FORTY DAYS

Homebound in Baghdad, Wasan Qasim recounts her family's day-to-day life in vivid detail at the start of the Iraq war. She reveals a surprising calmness and the fortitude required as the bombs drop around them, and they celebrate her 18th birthday.

WASAN QASIM

WASAN QASIM is a translator who writes narrative and poetry. She grew up in Iraq then moved to UAE then Canada, where she currently lives. She has a BA in translation from Mustansiriyah University, a BA in writing from MacEwan University, an MFA in creative writing from Lindenwood University and a Masters degree in education from UBC, for which she wrote her thesis using poetic inquiry research methodology. She has published poetry and translations in both Arabic and English.

The first thing that hit me when I entered Al Yassamin Middle Eastern Food store on Vancouver's Main Street was the voice of Fairuz singing Gibran's poem. *Give me the flute and sing, for singing is the secret of existence.* The zesty melody and familiar Arabic lyrics took me back to that period during the war in Iraq. My other senses soon started to awaken from their slumber, and the smell of spices, ground coffee, dry dates and henna instantly transported me across continents to the old souk in Baghdad.

I took a few steps further inside, into Ali Baba's treasure. I ran my hand on the shiny silver samovar. Delicate istikans (miniature glass tea cups) stood on one shelf, a line of hookahs of different sizes and colors on the other. But right there, in front of me, my whole childhood was packed in the upright freezer of this store on Main Street. I spotted bags of sammoon, the local Iraqi stone bread, shaped like a tailless fish.

I smiled, remembering how my father used to pick me up from school after he had made a trip to the stone bakery to buy a load of sammoon. He would spread them on a sheet of paper on the back seat to air them and keep them crispy. From where I sat in the front seat of the car, I would turn back, grab one and gobble it all in seconds, ignoring my father's warnings that I would not be able to eat dinner if I stuffed my stomach with bread.

My smile turned into a sigh when I remembered my father, who was buried in foreign lands. Will this be my end? Frozen and in exile, like an Iraqi sammoon, crammed among the other flavors of my wounded country?

***

The despicable air raid alarm sounded. You can't mistake the sound, not if you have lived all your life in Iraq. We knew the signals from previous wars: short, interrupted howls for the start of the raid and long, moaning cries at the end. This sound is not like any other, a mixture of the wail of anguished mothers and the cry of an injured animal calling for mercy.

The night before the war began, my mom baked kleicha, a famous pastry we usually made during the Eid. It wasn't a random act, my mother told me. She wanted to make something that would be handy for us to eat when the war started and the shops would be closed. We had heard in the news that Iraq was given an ultimatum. We knew what was coming, but we hoped against the inevitable.

As soon as the war started we knew we were having a feast. It wasn't a celebration of the war, but rather a forced feast. We had to consume the entire contents of our fridge and freezer before the electricity went out and everything had to be thrown away. We basically turned into human garbage cans.

There was no gas for vehicles, so our car stood silent in the garage, a worthless machine. Without gas it was a mere bundle of steel and leather, fit for nothing, gone into premature retirement along with the fridge and the freezer.

At first, we kept sleeping in our bedrooms upstairs, pretending there was nothing going on. But soon the bombs fell nearer and it became foolish, even dangerous, to sleep there. My father decided to move his bed downstairs in the hall. We huddled up in his double bed whenever the raid sounded.

There was a surprisingly calm attitude in our house, despite the unavoidable fear. I think it was mostly a defense mechanism, where I didn't want to believe that we are actually going to be attacked. So I shielded my emotions, and so did my father and brother. My mom was the only one who was vocal about her feelings. She cursed Saddam. She cursed the war. She cursed us for not being as hysterical as she was. I was numb. I just wanted to ignore the whole thing.

My father, quiet by nature, was just being himself. He spent most of the time reading, and I did the same thing. I read my father's entire library and wanted more books. Books kept me alive, kept me sane. They were my true companions in my exile. Books took me far away, to places where there was no war, no horrible air raid alarms, no bombs. I read and read and I burned through dozens of candles. I even learned how to make new candles from the melted ones using a garden hose as a cast.

We lived as people had lived in past centuries. With no water, no electricity, no telephone. It was hard without water or television, but it was even harder without a telephone to make sure all our family members and friends were safe. We were suddenly cut off from the world, forced to live in the dark. Blind people facing blind bombs.

We knew that the first target of the bombing would be electricity and water, as these are people's lifelines. We couldn't do anything about electricity. There was no way to store it before we lost it. But we could store water. So right from the beginning, when the news about the war loomed ahead, we started storing water in every container available. We filled the tub, the buckets, the tanks on the roof, the jars, the jugs, our bellies. We looked at the last drop of water from the tap with yearning eyes. Taking a "shower" was not an easy task during these days. We had abandoned the bathtub; without electricity we couldn't get water upstairs anymore, and now used the guest washroom downstairs as a shower stand, scooping water over our heads. It didn't help that it was winter, as winter in Baghdad can be really cold. It is the damp kind of cold, the one that penetrates your bones like thousands of knives.

The war turned us into stopgap interior designers. We shifted beds, we moved mattresses around the house, we used my father's huge bookcase to cover our big ceiling-to-floor window to protect it from shattering. We put candles on end tables when we wanted to read. Our furniture soon bore the effects of war, with bumpy surfaces from melted-down candles, and black spots on shelves under which candles stood with their fire-licking tongues. Suddenly, material possessions had no value. We cherished nothing but us. Plants dried up, floors suffocated with dust, and once-precious china plates turned into candle trays.

It was January, two weeks from my 18th birthday and almost 10 days into the war. I didn't realize how resilient we Iraqis could be until my mom decided to bake me a birthday cake. She had, somehow, calmed down and surrendered her fear. We were out of cocoa, and going out to buy some was out of the question. Some shops stayed open during the war, but we limited our shopping to buying the essentials. The local dates were our only option.

My mother and I mixed the birthday cake and baked it on Aladdin, the traditional stand oil heater, named after the *Arabian Nights* character. It is a piece of Iraqi genius, a cylinder heater with a removable top. You can take off the top and make tea or cook your food or, in this case, bake your cake. Ironically, the candles on my birthday were not in the cake, but all around it, everywhere. Yet they were not candles of celebration. They were candles of fear, of uncertainty, of unknown future.

Wars don't care if it is your birthday. They don't have emotions. They don't care that you just turned 18, that this birthday should have been the happiest of all your birthdays. I had to pretend there were guests. Who would come at such a time? The candles and the books were my guests. My present was that I was still alive.

We realized we were not very safe where we were. Our house was close to one of Saddam's farms, and we knew that it would be a target for bombs. And it was. Yet as days passed, my mother calmed down and started to shift her attention to other things. We tried to keep ourselves busy by playing cards, even though we were still afraid for our lives. We used to play card games in the afternoon before the dark. It seems as if every time we dealt a hand, a bomb would explode close enough to shake the crystal chandelier in our living room. I would look up, willing it not to fall on our heads.

In all the eight years of the war with Iran I hadn't gone once to the shelter. This time I wanted to go. It was the curiosity of checking it out that drove me down, not the desire to hide. I found women and children lying down on mattresses playing card games or talking. Nobody looked truly terrified. I met people on their way to the shelter, carrying pillows under their arms, and I couldn't help smiling at the sight. Here they were running to safety, in fear of their lives, but that didn't stop them from thinking of comfort.

Shelters gave people a sense of security. We were told that nothing could possibly happen to us when we were down there, and we believed what we were told. Until that fateful day when two American missiles hit Al-Ameriya shelter. We heard that people were barbecued underground. Some of them melted to the doors they had tried so desperately to open. The pressure of the missiles shut the doors forever, entombing them. My family and I never went to a shelter. It was more out of convenience than out of anything else. There simply was no shelter beside our house.

During the 40 days of this war, we did everything mechanically. We slept, we woke up, we ate, we lit candles, blew out candles. As if stranded on a deserted island, we lost count of the days. We had watches and clocks, but we didn't care about time.

The plants in our garden dried up in front of our eyes. We couldn't spare them a drop. Would you bother to water your jasmine when you didn't know if the little water you had left would sustain you? Our garden was lifeless. A few days into the war, the cats disappeared. After enjoying their own feast in the first days of the war, they couldn't find any food. The neighbors fled their homes. We resisted the idea of leaving. "Where to?" We would ask each other. Then, out of despair, we used the last drop of gas in our car to go to my uncle's house just to be together with the family.

So many things happened during these 40 days, but more happened after. People survived, people went back home after a self-imposed exile, people walked in the streets after spending a long time underground, finally taking their pillows back home. Plants had water, cats roamed the garden, neighbors visited each other, fridges and freezers went back to work, cars were woken up from their slumber. Saddam counted his losses, licked his wounds, and prepared for the next war.

***

Standing on Main Street, in front of the upright freezer in that Middle Eastern food store, I thought about how much we went through during those days of war. I also thought about the other subsequent wars in Iraq that I was fortunate enough to escape. I came to realize that even if I were to die in another country, away from my fertile soil, in a foreign land, the notion of me is something I would have the power to create. I am not the sammoon I see today wrapped in plastic, I am the memory evoked when I see it in the freezer—of being in my father's car, ignoring his sensible warning, stealing just one more last bite.

HUMAN, KIND

In this tender story based in Saudi Arabia, Shiraza Ibrahim shares the experience of her road trip from Madinah to Makkah, escorted by a driver whose generosity and warmth dissolves her misconceptions.

SHIRAZA IBRAHIM

SHIRAZA IBRAHIM was born in Colombo, Sri Lanka. She currently resides in Connecticut, USA, and is a banker by profession. She is also a lover of art, a storyteller, a lifelong reader and an occasional poet. Her heart belongs to her family; her smile often belongs to her son.

I rose with the sun that day, like every other day, except I was no longer in small-town America. I was in the city of Madinah. I looked at my son, wrapped in white cotton hotel sheets, sleeping in the bed across from my own. My gaze fell lovingly on the undisturbed face of this boy on the cusp of becoming a young man. I felt reluctant, like always, to break his sleep.

Instead, I leaned towards my boy, pushed away his wavy black hair, and gently kissed his forehead then his cheek. Cheeks, once round as apples, now turning more angular, more like his father. His father had risen hours before me to make the early morning prayer at Masjid an-Nabawī, the mosque of the cool white marble floors, the mosque of the intricately carved statuesque minarets guarding the lone green dome, home to the final resting place of our Prophet. Muhammad (Peace be upon him)—the last prophet, the namesake for my son, for his father, and for a million other men of my faith. And for the new friend that I would make today.

It was my last day in this city, the prophet's favorite city, a place of love. Each time I visit I fall more in love with its peace. I placed my feet on the soft carpet and heated water for coffee. I walked to the window and let in the morning light. The large windows were the best part of this hotel room. They allowed me to watch the city like a foreign language movie without the subtitles, a silent movie, moving; this early morning gathering of hundreds of thousands of people of all ethnicities and every skin tone imaginable, all in one place; the street vendors and store owners closing shop five times a day to answer the call to prayer; the Arabian girls with endless dark lashes fringing mesmeric kohl-lined eyes, phones in hands, getting their selfie-game on, not much different than girls in any other part of the world except for the piece of jewel-like, bead-embroidered (often black) cloth covering their hair. The commonality we shared was being in the same place, mostly for the same reasons, walking to this centuries-old mosque to go down on our knees, to ask God to forgive us, to beg to be forgiven. For being human.

This journey to a place propelled by a shared faith, alongside people with whom you only shared one universality, that of humanity, has a special feeling to it. The essence of this place, Madinah, could be bottled like perfume, to be dabbed on the wrist for days when you need it. I captured the feeling of this sacred place in the only way I knew how, by lending my words to it:

I closed my eyes
and on bended knee
aligned forehead to earth,
in prostration
in metaphor,
to kiss the ground, where
a beloved
once walked upon, where
now
he rests.

– a prayer for Muhammad of Madinah. (May peace ever be upon him.)

I allowed myself the luxury of time as I wrapped the hot cup of coffee with my hands, as my tongue woke up to the bitterness of the strong Arabic brew, its sweetness warming me. How I would miss the taste of this city, this coffee.

I kept any reservations I had about traveling to Makkah to myself. First was the fear I shared with my husband, of becoming separated from our young son in the crowds of that city. The second, apprehensions formed from a mostly buried memory of being a young woman in a swarm of people moving in a circle of prayer. The proximity to strangers, of the occasional unwelcomed hand that would seek and touch parts of a woman not meant for them, to the smell of sweat on men—and me, bobbing along trying to keep my head above the sea of humans. The first time I experienced this I'd been holding on to my sisters and mother, plowing through for a moment to kiss the face of this sacred building of black stone. Pulled along by my sisters, jostled by the throng of people; the strangeness of a nameless, faceless hand feeling me is a distinct memory, like a bad taste in my mouth. It's a memory that is rapidly suppressed, as one does with a bad taste by overpowering it with a tall glass of water, by drowning the bad thoughts with the good ones. This is not my story to tell here today.

Instead I recall my father's words, and the small solace they bring, that not all men come to this city for spirituality alone. Each visited it with an agenda that was entirely their own. I am grateful for my father, and his words, still guiding me today.

Then, with reluctance, I shook my boy out of his sleep and together we said our morning Fajr prayer. In silence. He and I.

When we were ready to leave, we met the man engaged to drive us from Madinah to Makkah. He was seated in the lobby beside the exquisite wooden kiosk, which displayed the medjool dates in individual paper flutes alongside coffee served from an ornate gold jug, poured into small glasses edged with more gold. He was handing a date to a young child beside him.

I started to extend my hand to greet the man, a habit from years of living in the West. I was unsure it would work as fluidly in this world, so mid-way I retracted and instead said, "As-salāmu ʿalaykum." This simple greeting translating to *may peace be upon you* allowed me to easily find common ground with another person of my faith. Hearing my words, he returned my greeting, his eyes not quite meeting my own, and offered me a smile that stretched across his bearded face. I smiled back.

We embarked on our journey in his American-made Ford, a model that was a good decade old but impeccably maintained. We stumbled past the initial awkward moments—we were strangers riding together after all, feeling the kind of unease on a blind date where conversation was searched for and sometimes found, stilted, before flowing. The boys settled in the last row of seats to watch videos, play games and communicate with minimal use of language, since his son didn't speak much English and mine wasn't conversant in Arabic. I settled to read and watch the moving landscape. My husband, usually prone to falling asleep if he wasn't behind the wheel, made some feeble attempts to talk to our driver, but soon succumbed to his habit.

Muhammad, our driver, must have noticed me fishing out my headphones because he asked me if he could play some music.

"I have American music," he added in his accented English, which placed emphasis on certain letters and sounds that were formed in his throat, adding depth to his words, making my own sound feel flat and one-dimensional. The sound of his voice was low, the kind of soft speech that could draw the listener in. "Yes, what do you have?" I inquired with some curiosity. He handed me a stack of jewel cases from his glove compartment and asked me to pick a CD. When I saw the faded image of two wild-haired men on the cover, I smiled.

"Simon & Garfunkel? Really?! You listen to these guys?" I said as he chuckled in response.

I told him of my fondness for songs by this duo; the words of men I hadn't imagined would travel beyond the shores of my America, crossing an arid desert only to be the music in a young Arab man's life. Two men who were only poets with guitars, nomads who crossed oceans and time, erased boundaries, on their words alone.

Muhammad had a curiosity about my adopted home country, much of which he had gathered from movies, books and music. He was eager to know about my own experiences. Yet, it was my own misconceptions that revealed themselves to me, my assumption that he would not know or love my music. He asked me about being Muslim in America and this was where our conversation first met on our common faith. He asked me if it was a safe place to live, reminding me of all my American friends who had asked the same question of traveling to Muhammad's home country—is it safe? How little we knew of each other. Still, he was unabashed in acknowledging his love of most things American, including American fast food, of the halal variety. This common thread of love for American things was similar to the one our sons seated behind us had found. Soon we were engaged in easy conversation that I hadn't quite expected to have with an Arab man. I asked him about raising a son at his age. He was a young man with a young son. He spoke of his challenges, and I of mine. We spoke of dreams we had misplaced along the way and replaced with responsibility and aspirations for our sons instead. I told him of this poet hiding in the closet of my mind. He spoke of his own love for words, and we spoke of our favorite Persian poets. I told him that the only thing I collected was knowledge that came from reading books. And like a rich person building a trust fund for future generations, I gathered the words I read, words written by masters, words that carried wisdom, and lovingly passed them onto my son. The only gift I was rich enough to give him.

I told him my story, one of longing for things I was not. Of being a solitary writer, a shy poet, feverishly gathering words by the handful, giving life to my feelings, and then keeping the words captive in notebooks, too ashamed to allow them to meet other eyes. I told him my story because he gently drew it out of me like an expert sartor untangles a knot and pulls out a long thin strand from a twisted ball of thread. I was the tangled mess of thread, he, the soft, skilled untangler.

When we stopped for fuel, Muhammad went into the store and insisted that my husband not pay for anything. He returned laden with pastries filled with apricots, a variety of dried fruits, and an assortment of nuts, including pistachios. He had nectars made of apricots, carrots and mango. Large bottles of dew-covered cold water. He handed these to each of us. My husband and I exchanged glances, filled with gratitude, surprised at such generosity, a hospitality that made us feel like family.

We broke journey many times that day, once to catch the sun sinking into the distant sand dunes. Muhammad took pictures of my family alongside his boy, drenched in the ochre light of the desert sun, which colored the sand, the sky, the occasional tree, framing the four of us both squinting and beaming at him through the tiny square of my camera. In my mind, I captured Muhammad's smiling face taking happy images of photographs he would never see. I placed that image in the darkroom of my memory. To restore, to flip through when I needed to find moments that couldn't be contained in a photograph.

The final stop before arriving in the holy city of Makkah was at a mosque to prepare ourselves for the pilgrimage. Muhammad walked us through the prayer; he placed a hand on my son's shoulder and gestured to my son to follow his direction. He smiled when their eyes met, my boy smiled back. In that fleeting exchange I sensed my son's comfort around this man. I felt the same. Then, softly, he began to lead us in the prayer—the same prayer my father would read aloud to me—reciting it patiently, kindly, with love, like we were children, like he would teach his own. In supplication, for the second time that day, my mind drifted to my own father, yet another Mohamed, with kind eyes, bushy eyebrows, infinite generosity and wisdom which he imparted with his words, and even more so with his deeds. My father, who lived in my country of birth, a great distance from my adopted country—both homes far from here. And it was at this moment that our young friend, Muhammad, our trusted guide and traveling companion, effortlessly stepped in to play the role my own father had played in the past for me. He became our teacher. Our elder.

It was dark when we reached Makkah, and I felt the redness of my husband's eyes, the whine in my boy's voice, and the quiet of Muhammad's child. Muhammad, on the other hand, simply remained himself; a smile never quite leaving his topaz-brown eyes. He made sure we had all the guidance we needed to complete this part of our journey. Then, without much fanfare, without exchanging formal goodbyes, he placed his young boy on his shoulders, and walked from our hotel to the main mosque to perform tawaf, where he would walk seven times around the Holy Ka'ba.

My husband, my son and I watched the disappearing figure of father and son, as they walked away from our lives as simply as they had walked in.

he was an old man,
trapped in his youth,
an elemental creature—
a gentle man—from
another time,
when our days
crossed paths, and
in the briefest of moments
I found a story, untold
of a
human,
kind.

BLACK MARKET TICKETS

On a coast-to-coast train journey in the south of India, Fatima Muhammed recalls the anxieties of being a young woman traveling solo, navigating relationships with strangers and the tensions alive in even the most mundane of moments.

FATIMA MUHAMMED

FATIMA MUHAMMED writes about living in many places including India, Ireland and now, Arizona. Her work has appeared in the anthology *Of Dry Tongues and Brave Hearts: Khushk Zubaan, Bebaak Jigar* (Red River, New Delhi) and in *Autonomy* (New Binary Press, Ireland). She has written online about tea for Kaitley, an organization that provides work skills for disadvantaged individuals in India. In 2021, she won the The Prof. Barbra Naidu Memorial Personal Essay Contest for her story *Woman, Driving Away*. Her writing tries to untangle her views on holding onto her roots, children, faith and a migratory life. lifemoonlighter.wordpress.com

"Chechi, Chechi? Can you get us a seat?"

I turned back to see two college boys calling out to me. I did not know them. Why were they talking to me?

A Malayalee woman is often called Chechi (elder sister) by her younger siblings, but also by strangers if she looks a little older than them. I was at the Chennai Central Railway Station in Tamil Nadu, trying to board the train to my grandparents' home in Ernakulam, about a 10-hour train ride into neighboring Kerala. This station is where the masses throng from the metropolis back to wherever they came from. There are multiple platforms at this terminus, all parallel to each other. It's a classic setting often portrayed in Indian movies. Two characters will notice each other from across different platforms before a train passes through, making one character disappear while leaving the other with a fine mystery to solve.

Each platform has its own little tea shop selling snacks and magazines, and this is where passengers come once they have figured out where their reserved bogie is to arrive. You can purchase tickets to pretty much any corner of the country and very hot egg biryani meal parcels—it's always a good idea to take one with you on the train. There are also toilets and showers, resting rooms, railway restaurants, and concrete benches overloaded with people and their numerous suitcases and cardboard boxes of things to be transported across state borders. It can be hard to get your bearings if you do not know what to do. I had come prepared with my ticket and my bags hitched up on my shoulders, and since I was standing at the platform where the train to Ernakulam was expected any minute, I couldn't fault the boys for calling me Chechi. This platform was teeming with Malayalees, and I was carrying the air of a woman who knew what she was doing.

The list of passengers is printed and pasted on the outside of the train right next to the doors. It includes the name, gender, age, and a seat or waitlist number for each of the passengers who have bought a ticket. I read through the list carefully a couple of times, but my name had only a waitlist number next to it. It seemed unlikely that I would get a seat on this train. I didn't have much time to figure out what to do, so I tried to ignore the boys, but they came closer through the crowd to stand in front of me.

"Chechi, can we travel with you on your seat?"

"Huh?"

One of them started to explain. "This is my friend. He has to travel to Ernakulam as well, and he doesn't have a confirmed seat. Can you share your seat with him?"

In Indian trains, the majority of passengers travel in the sleeper class compartments. These are coaches with three berths across the width and two lengthwise. During the day, the lengthwise window seats are like regular chairs and at night, the two seats slide back to make a bed. One of the passengers sleeps here and the other one climbs up a little ladder to sleep in the upper berth. Yet more often than not, passengers share their seats. Perhaps it's a mother with her young children sleeping in a single seat, like we did when I was a kid. Or it could be two adults who have only one reserved seat between them.

There are also times when people resort to sitting on the floor if the reservable tickets are too few and children far too many. I recall at least one such journey when my mother spread out a large bed sheet on the ground between two of the bigger seats in the aisle, and all three of us kids had slept cozily there on the floor. My parents had always taken care of everything related to our trips—I simply had to sit down where they asked me to and stare out the window.

I tried to make the boys go away. "I don't have a confirmed seat for myself so I can't really help you. Sorry."

They were persistent. "Chechi, both you and my friend have waitlisted tickets, so in case yours gets confirmed, you can both travel together on that same seat."

There was no logic to what he was saying. I had no seat for myself. How could I share a non-existent seat?

I left them standing and continued to pace the platform. I phoned my father for advice, and his suggestion was to get on the train anyway and sit anywhere. He had traveled plenty of times sitting on unreserved seats, on three-day journeys even, so his advice was perfectly sensible for him. But he was a man. Young women could not just sit in random seats when they didn't know what sort of men they might have to bargain with for a proper seat. Trying to be an independent woman made for a difficult life. I paced some more before getting in a line with other hopeful travelers who wanted to board the train with similar tickets. When I had almost reached the ticket conductor, I heard him tell the man in the front, "There are no more seats available on this train to assign to waitlisted tickets, so no point in asking me. Try another day."

I abandoned the queue without consulting him.

Pacing, I tried to call my father again, but he didn't answer. I realized that I was sweating profusely. Chennai is always hot and humid, no matter what time of year. I didn't care much about that, though, as I was too worried about the train. My suitcase and handbag felt much heavier than when I had first reached the station, and I was exhausted.

To add to my consternation, the two boys were still hanging around me. They had probably overheard me talking on the phone. The train to Ernakulam was now slowly moving away, leaving the station without me. I had stalled getting on the train, and now I felt stranded. Maybe if I had at least gotten on the train like my father had suggested...

I finally looked at them. The same boy spoke again. "Chechi, we have a plan. We will get two tickets in black."

"What?"

I thought back to the day I had gone to the railway station to get this cursed ticket. The long queue forming outside the upstairs reservation room started right at the bottom of the stairs. When I finally made it up the staircase, I entered a room with multiple rows and began playing musical chairs, each person in the queue moving up, one by one. It was painstakingly slow. I reached the ticketing window after almost an hour, my entire lunch time taken up by this business. I bought one of the only available tickets—a waitlisted one—and hoped that it would be transformed into a reserved seat in the week leading up to my travels.

I looked at the boys. One of them had a backpack slung across his shoulder, the type usually carried by college students here, and he hadn't said a word since I came across them this evening. The other boy was grinning widely, almost as if he could read my state of mind. Perhaps they were delighted with their clever solution for the journey, and maybe they thought I would agree to their plan since I was stuck at the station with no other recourse.

I would never travel on a ticket bought on the black market—that was illegal. But my train, the one I had a valid ticket for, was gone now. I had to either give up my plans to travel tonight or try to purchase a new ticket for the next train. It was impossible to purchase tickets last-minute and also be guaranteed a seat.

"Chechi, there is another train scheduled in 30 minutes that also goes to Ernakulam. We have inquired. We can get the ticket. It's just that we don't have the money for it."

"Hmm. Okay. I will give you the money." I must have lost my mind by then.

The boys went to get those tickets while I stood on the platform. Waiting. I had stopped my frenzied pacing. They came back and the three of us rushed across an overbridge, to another platform where this train was already stationed. The boys told me to board one of the train compartments, and the boy who was going to travel with me handed me his backpack through the rails on the train window.

The boys were still standing out on the platform when the friend said, "Chechi, we tricked you! We did not get the ticket. Sorry, you are traveling ticketless. Can we get our bag back please?"

I sat there, without a ticket in my hand, on a seat that was probably somebody else's, clutching the boy's bag in my lap. Given how badly the night was turning out to be, I had to give myself credit for the placid way in which I was reacting.

I imagined that they had done this as some sort of revenge against me for not helping them out earlier. Then the friend burst out laughing, and the boy who was supposed to travel with me was also faintly smiling. The train started moving out of the station. I had not even checked the destination to see where it was going! Somewhere in the back of my overwrought mind I had a thought to hold onto the bag, but then what would they do, try to reach in and grab it?

After a few terrible seconds, the friend relented. "It's okay, we have a ticket for you," he yelled through the window.

The other boy swiftly got into the train and sat down. His friend on the platform waved goodbye as the train picked up pace. I didn't say anything when the boy showed me two tickets. I squinted at them, trying to decipher what it was that differentiated a ticket sold in black. Were there any markers on them? I hoped that the ticket conductor would not detect anything dubious when he made his rounds.

The boy and I shared a single side berth and spent the night journey alternating between sitting or lying down to sleep. I sat trying very carefully not to touch my co-passenger, and he seemed to be doing the same. I spent half of my wakeful time thinking back to another journey when my mother and us kids shared a seat with another man, and how the man had mentioned that he had two wives. I wondered how a single train seat could have held three children and two adults comfortably. Maybe one of my siblings had been on some other seat with our father.

The train only took us till Palakkad, the first big town after crossing the state border, and so we got off there to walk to the bus terminus. I handed the boy some money and he went to purchase tickets. Bus tickets are simple enough to procure, and there is no hassle about reserved tickets like for trains—if there are no more seats, people simply stand for the length of their trips. It was still very early in the morning when we embarked on a bus to Ernakulam. The street lights had already been turned off but the sun hadn't risen enough yet to light the way. I could only see the dull silhouettes of houses and trees by the road, and an occasional vendor who was setting up his wares on a cart by the light of a couple of oil lamps.

We were sharing another seat, and after a while my partner in crime pointed and said, "That lady probably thinks I am your boyfriend." I looked over at the middle-aged woman gazing at us and shrugged. She could also be thinking that he was my brother.

He asked, "Are you taking a holiday?"

"Yes. How about you?"

"It is my college vacation. It is December, right?"

"Ah, yes." Everyone has holidays this time of year.

"Going to see your parents?"

I thought back on weeks of frenetic matchmaking that had happened in my family and replied, "Yes, and I'm also going to see a guy for a marriage proposal. He is coming to my grandparents' home."

"I see."

After a while he added, "You smell terrible."

"What?"

"You smell of sweat."

"Oh! It's all that pacing I was doing at the station in Chennai."

"You got really scared when we told you that we had no ticket, right?" I tried not to give my feelings away so instead of responding, I stared at the passing greenery. I never got bored looking out at the many homes tucked into plantations, backwaters, and even the roadside antics of small towns where, judging from all the banners plastered onto walls, it looked like there was always an election campaign going on.

He was less loquacious than his friend. Throughout our interactions at the Chennai station, the friend had initiated all negotiations, whilst he had stood quietly observing. In a South

Indian movie, the talkative friend would be the sidekick and the boy squeezed in beside me, the hero.

The views from the bus moving into Alappuzha and then Ernakulam would turn eyes green from the coconut trees and blue from all the water. It is a sight like nowhere else in my memory. As children, we would travel to Kerala to spend a few weeks in the summer holidays and, invariably, the moment we crossed the border into the state, regardless of where we were coming from, the scenery would switch like magic. Even the food that the Indian railways served on board would be transformed from a bowl of unrecognizable vegetable curry accompanying a few dry flatbreads to a lavish plate of rice, multiple vegetable dishes, buttermilk, mango pickle and a pappadam. We would try to savor this meal slowly while our mother told us to hurry up and finish the plate before the train pulled into our station. Perhaps the food tasted so good because it represented home for us, where the people loved our mother so much that they were eager for us to come, year after year.

Nearing my grandparents' home, the bus seemed to slow down imperceptibly as we passed an abandoned apartment building next to the highway. It was the very first one to be constructed in that town, and no one had wanted to buy or rent the units so the builder had committed suicide due to his losses. Now, it was a crumbling structure that nobody wanted to do anything about. Many years on, plants and small trees had started growing out of its empty terraces. I was not sure if the boy knew this story. We both dozed off again, bumping shoulders, in the solace of companionship.

We were reaching his stop now, and he would get off before me. I found it strange when he wrote down a phone number on a piece of paper.

"This is my mother's number. Can you call her and tell her that you have reached your home? Whenever that is?"

"Don't you have a phone for yourself?"

"No."

"Okay then."

I got off at the next stop. My mother and uncle came to pick me up. I looked at the billboards, at all the sumptuous golden jewelry and silk sarees displaying the eternal goal of the people here: to make a prosperous match and celebrate an even grander wedding. These advertisements have been there for ages, always updated with fresh faces and brighter jewels. The very sight of these billboards evokes the joyous drums of a wedding band, with the bride about to walk daintily up to the stage, decked out in the latest fashions dictated by the stores that peddle these luxuries.

The prospective groom did come to my grandmother's home. I wore a blue salwar kameez and was both exhilarated and annoyed by the proceedings. It was gratifying to find someone for my happily-ever-after and to put an end to the ordeal of our families' matchmaking, but these useless ceremonies were also very uncomfortable. I refused to serve him tea on a tray when my uncle asked me to. It was all too clichéd for me. I had grown up with many tea parties where, similarly, I had refused to bring the tray out for visiting uncles and aunties. It was not because I bore an ill-will towards people who visited my home—I just could not trust that my hands would not shake and spill tea onto an unsuspecting guest.

I didn't end up calling that boy's mother's number. I did plan an elaborate dialogue in my head though, about how I would introduce myself, how I would explain that I had reached my destination. I kept that paper with the phone number in my wallet for many months, neatly folded into two, wondering what might have happened if I had made that call.

THE CONSEQUENCES OF TELLING A STORY

Traveling to Damascus by bus in 2013 for university, Amika Elfendi is taken hostage by the Syrian Army in a story that depicts the paradoxes of war and the vulnerability of all those involved.

AMIKA ELFENDI

AMIKA ELFENDI, Syrian-born and Oslo-based, writes in Arabic, English and Norwegian. His work has appeared in *The Best Asian Short Stories 2019*, *New Reader Magazine*, *Sukoon*, and more. His first poetry manifest *The Anunnaki Season: the Green Booklet* was launched in 2023 together with Tamil transdisciplinary artist Ilavenil Vasuky Jayapalan. He also double-agents as DJ unnaki and filmmaker, and suffers from an itching obsession with Ramallahian rap, Clarice Lispector, and Felis Concolor.

Every time a Syrian writes something honest and defiant, he is knowingly putting his life and those of his family on the line. This I write for myself and for those others who do the same, realizing that if ever there will be consequences, these are ultimately unforeseeable, in the hands of mysterious powers, dealt out with incomprehensible motives.

It was the day they found the pictures on my laptop—

It happened on my birthday, although this chance fact would be insignificant to me then—that day I turned 20. The year was 2013, and like most young people, I made a great mistake. It was the peak of dry winter in Hawran, that lovely and fragrant ancient volcanic region of my forefathers and rural childhood. And I still recall how groggy I was that morning, seated there as an innocent passenger near the folding door of the bus. When they seized me and dragged me outside, I told them I hardly had anything but my music and anatomy programs on the device. But still they stared at it as if it were some dangerous curiosity. A sensation that could be called shame spread over my wind-beaten face, which had started tingling. There were people waiting in the minibus that I had boarded, bound for Damascus, city of jasmine and epiphanies. They were laborers that would go hungry for a whole day if hindered, questioned, delayed. And so, they had begun to get restless and perhaps even anxious for their own safety, afraid maybe that my incarceration would lead to theirs.

I wasn't entirely unlucky that day, though; I hadn't yet paid the fare for my trip to the city. This was nearly five months after I had had to switch universities. I had moved back home, a medical student with little mental capacity for that line of study. My original place of learning was in Aleppo, but as things had deteriorated with the escalating conflicts there and in other towns along the motorway, Damascus was the securest, most stable and closest to my modest hometown, Mothbeen. Mothbeen borrows its name from one of the gods in the Semitic pantheon: Mot, god of death.

Soon after, the minibus was trembling to start; it was an amnesiac déjà vu. People inside were ogling the goings-on outside. A surly soldier ushered the vehicle to move on faster with a swat to the right hind edge of its robust frame. It was a shuttle propelled into a predestined, yet unpredictable trajectory in that deep land of calamities.

The metal sounded like metal, and so, as I watched the minibus drive away, my mouth went dry in trepidation.

The recollection of this unpleasant happening came to me at a class discussion of Tim O'Brien's "How to Tell a True War Story," but this time I was a refugee in a safe country far off and far removed. In a small town in ever-green, tortuous, always-clean Norway, that's where I live now.

O'Brien argues that a true war story is never moral, and if it is, it is then unworthy of being told or believed. He recounts the too-awful-to-be-true incident of his combat buddies, Rat Kiley and Curt Lemon. Those two are, or were, young—children, actually—soldiers in the Vietnam war. They are playing a dangerous though war-appropriate game of catch with a smoke grenade. For a minute they are having the most exhilarating type of fun, and the next minute, Lemon steps into the sun. Just before he's killed, it shines on his body, like Helios, like Shamash, who shines also on the bloating carcasses of my own countrymen as he rides his chariot among the clouds. And what kills me is that it's not their game that puts an end to Lemon's life, but a provoked booby trap, stepped on at a moment of grand illumination. Just as he moves from shade into light, everything blows up.

And this same thing incidentally happened at the same time as we were reading the story, in an unnamed place in Deir Ezzour, Syria, except the grenade was not a smoke grenade like in O'Brien's piece, and the casualties were more than one. Three enlisted blokes perished in that characteristically Syrian accident: an adolescent soldier in his barracks pulled the pin and his allegedly uninformed act ended his and the lives of two other comrades. Another one ended up being sent to the intensive care unit.

How a story is told changes its meaning. Who tells it and who listens to it. The medium and language used to convey an event contribute markedly to the perception of this event. No one, in my opinion, can ever tell a completely factual war story, as most of those involved in it would not have survived long enough to validate its truth, as details in such accounts are almost always grubby and gory. You only relay an impression of an impression, repainting over the picture with even thinner blood every time you tell it, every time *anyone* tells it, neglecting the abject hiss that precedes the explosion, foregrounding nothing near the larger-than-life horror in the eyes of those solicited by the unnegotiable handshake of death.

A war story never amounts to the truth of death because with death all truths are neither longer existent nor intact. They become shriveled, mangled, splintered and prosthetic. With death, all is nothing, and the one and only truth can *only then* blossom forth: the truth that everyone is bound to be touched by death.

My sister tells me the story about these four Syrian soldiers. Used to death tolls from the current Syrian tragedy being broadcast in numbers, and not used to hearing about the victims as individuals, I ask her their names. Surprisingly, she knows each of them: Jalal, Nawras, Mahmoud, Alaa'. Out of habit, I associate each name with someone related to me, or someone I have known before. In my head, Jalal is an Arabic script calligrapher and friend of one of my uncles, Nawras is a school friend's father, Mahmoud is a cousin, and Alaa' is a maternal uncle whom I love deeply.

In reality, the first three, Jalal, Nawras, Mahmoud, are the dead ones; Mahmoud was the one whose naivety brought on the demise of them all. The last, Alaa', lies in a hospital bed, cared for and kept alive by strangers' hands, not yet visited by his family who fear the road's menaces and, possibly and most importantly, the costliness of the 500 km trip.

Since all four victims shared the same hometown, the whole of Deir El Bukht was devastated. Mothers woke up to the desolate scene of tombstone slabs, funerary processions and ineffable grief. And orphaned fathers, their eyes wet with tears, chokingly commanded the bawling be over with.

In class, I am sitting in the first row as usual and struggling to pay attention. I can feel myself drifting back to that day in January of 2013, to that small brick lumber room where I was locked up.

I know fully well that I'm trapped. Four or five of them had grabbed me by my elbows and shoulders and escorted me to that pen-like room, dark and dank as it was. They ordered me, with the Syrian army's well-known repulsion for anomaly, to *stay there like an ass would*. And I did.

I must have squatted in there for about 25 minutes—still owning my ears, if nothing else. And, hearing the jostling cars on the old interstate, my existence was still faintly palpable.

Yet I was stripped of all means of interaction with anything material but walls, stripped of all means of time telling but my arrhythmic galloping blood. It was not a heart any longer. It was not anything I owned anymore. It was theirs, those who spit on me out of their tobacco-smelling mouths, those who would later take me out into the main building to stand me in the center of the hall, as a sort of unseemly dejected clown laughing nervously at his own stupidity. *You motherfucker!* I chastise myself silently as they taunt me by throwing little stones at me from behind. My eyes are tightly blindfolded, and except for through lower corners of my vision, I see nothing but sheer darkness. Someone approaches from behind or from either side to say, after lifting the blinkers slightly off my eyes, that I am to sit with my anus square on the sun-scalded green traffic cone in his hands. Not necessarily out of his own drive to insult me, he bares his darkened warlord-like fangs, cursing at me with a fake coastal accent, breathing too close to my face, something he would not have done had he not been the omnipotent soldier and I not *al-mundass*—the infiltrator, *al-mudannass*—the defiled—, the blinkered ass in the center of the room.

You motherfucker, this is your second time! I thought to myself repeatedly. And it was indeed my second time, being captured by those "homeland protectors" (as the national anthem calls them) a year and a half before. It was my second time on the edge of the cliff, again on the brink of being liquidated without a trace, without dignity.

Shame, shame, shame. It captured me. I was ashamed of what my family would think of this life-threatening blunder of mine; ashamed of what my friends would think of my missing out on the bacteriology exam; ashamed of the outcome of this captivity; ashamed of the destiny I had managed to force upon my pendulous existence, which seemed for all of those die-hard jingoists ready to be reaped. Ashamed of everyone's efforts in my now threadbare life, all the letters, friendships, doctor visits, holiday candies and ma'moul and bitter coffee in all the houses I'd been to, the smells of orchards, of smashed olives underfoot, of manure, pesticide and sun-worn hoses, of all the minutes I thought I possessed my own free will.

Those photos, those long-forgotten photos lurking on my hard disk, those *bloody* photos that were the first (the first!) files that unfolded under the sergeant's weary yet lustful eyes—while the other soldiers were frisking me diligently for other contraband. Those pictures were bright, colorful, meaningful. They were bright pictures, promoting a bright future, which the dictatorship, those ignorant eyes, failed to comprehend. Those pictures and those dark eyes. One might be tempted to wonder: can't those dark eyes see themselves reflected in the screen showing those bright pictures on this wintry day, this day or any other day?

I will simply never know.

NUMBER FOUR

Asma Elbadawi recollects her past in Sudan, which she has left for England, where she suffers racist abuse in school until she hits her stride and finds her strength in basketball.

ASMA ELBADAWI

ASMA ELBADAWI was born in Sudan and raised in England. She is a basketball player and a global Adidas brand ambassador. She holds a BA Hons in photography, video and digital Imaging, and a Masters' in visual arts. She is best known for her involvement in the globally successful FIBA Allow Hijab Campaign. She won the 2015 Words First Leeds award, and has performed at TEDx Bradford, The British Museum, The Bradford Literature Festival, Liverpool Acoustic Festival, Women of the World (WOW) Festival, and Word of Mouth London with international performances in Sudan, Brussels and Malaysia. asmaelbadawi.com @asmaelbadawi

Bismillah rolled softly off my tongue like wind escaping from my lungs. I fixed my shoelaces as my coach announced the starting five. Standing tall, I marched onto the court, greeting my opponents with a firm hand and wishing them a good game. My mind raced to past games where I warmed the bench, when the smell of fear clouded my vision. Shaking those thoughts from my mind I reminded myself that I am a different player now. I tasted success as the whistle blew and the game started, blood pumping through my fingertips. I believed that I deserved this moment and cherished every footstep of my stride. I adjusted my number four jersey, unaware of the eyes following me. I made the basket and high-fived my teammate on the way back to defend.

My family is the reason I play. Number four because I was born on the fourth of January. Number four because there are four members in my nuclear family and I am the fourth to arrive in this world.

I wasn't always this confident in my own skin. My high school days were filled with teachers telling me I would fail, mainly because I wasn't the kind of student they could mold into their version of what a "good Muslim girl" should be. I was in the top sets, but I spent lunch breaks and evenings at the art and sports clubs. I talked to the girls next to me after salah, and defended myself when I was told off for ridiculous reasons. I never forgot the look my science teacher gave me while telling me I wasn't worth the fee they would spend on me to repeat an exam paper, or that of my English teacher saying maybe I should sit a lower grade exam because I wouldn't be able to get a passing mark. I acted out in retaliation then played it cool when put in detention, but below the surface I was like a sponge, silently absorbing all the negativity they unloaded onto me. Every negative word chipped away at my confidence. I believed I wasn't worth anything. Believed I didn't belong anywhere.

My family moved to England in the nineties. The sun appeared less often than my mother was used to, so she wrapped me up in mismatching layers to keep the snow from kissing my skin. One evening, my mother, older brother Mohammed and I passed by the butcher's where my father worked after attending university classes. I saw the plaster on his finger and asked him what had happened. He had cut his finger while cutting the meat. My throat tightened. My father was hurt. I wasn't able to help him, but in that moment something profound happened: I realized then how dear my family was to me.

We did everything together. We picnicked in the park and took trips to see family friends around England. Whatever the occasion, there was always some kind of sporting activity going on which involved all of us playing football or cricket. Baba loved sport. He encouraged both my brother Mohammed and me to attend after-school clubs. At home, on our street, we played pitu, rounders, slam and basketball with our East Asian and Arab neighbors.

Throughout my life, each family member influenced me in some way. My mother was caring and compassionate and did everything with purpose. She sat me down to the dining table to do my Arabic school homework and she combed my hair and told me stories of the Sudan of her childhood. She instilled kindness and gratitude in me. My father, quiet but observant, listened attentively as I shared my career and sporting goals. He advised me about which route to take, always inspiring me to go beyond the court or workspace and inspire others.

My brother was calm, competitive and supportive. He taught me how to ride a bike and play game consoles. His ground floor bedroom window was the entrance into the house any time I needed to swiftly disappear after being chased by our neighbor's parents for being naughty on the street.

In the school playground, it didn't take long for some of the children to realize I wasn't like them. One of the boys put me in a headlock and called me blackjack and nigger, telling me to go back to Africa every single day for almost a year. Other boys joined in on this, whilst the girls played "unders and overs," oblivious to the fact that every time the boys came running towards me I dropped the ball and ran to escape their abuse. My pain felt invisible. I didn't understand why I was punished for something I had no control over. On the first day of high school, Simah asked me what I was doing at a Muslim girls' school because she noticed I was a nigger. I started straightening my hair and contoured my nose till my early twenties, in hopes of erasing my blackness.

I knew I had another family in another country that spoke my mother tongue and shared the same skin tone and hair texture as me. I heard stories of Sudan, a Sudan full of hospitality, love and the Nile. My strong and bold mother spoke of her childhood at boarding school, and how she trained to be a teacher. How soldiers used to jump over the university halls' gates and scare them, how the sounds of their laughter echoed into the night as they sat around Nadia's bed. Nadia, the girl who occasionally sleep-talked in the night and exposed conversations other girls had with her during the day.

In many ways I knew this land my mother spoke of. I had visited every year since the age of 11. I sat on bambars around the seeniya eating kisra and mulah, and laughing with my uncles, aunties and grandparents in the evenings. I shared a room with my cousin, where we would confide in each other under the mosquito net about boys we fancied in the village. I felt emotions I couldn't explain when my grandfather held my hand, but even while amongst my own people I counted down the weeks till I came back to England. I felt foreign. The sun came out too often, and I couldn't get used to the heat and bucket showers.

For years I lived in limbo, trying to decide where home was. Some days I felt my tongue sway towards the خs and حs of my mother's tongue, Arabic, and other days to that of the colonizers.

But then I hit 20 and joined the basketball team. On the court, things were different. It didn't matter what color my skin was, or the texture of my hair, as long as I knew how to play. I found a coach that saw potential in me and when I first started playing, my heart would race when the ball was passed to me. I didn't trust my legs to guide me to the hoop, or my fingers to push the ball into the air at the right speed and precision to make the basket, so I unconsciously passed the ball to one of my teammates. Coach Mathew pushed me to find the harmony between my body and mind, and the ball and basket.

After some time, the ball became an extension of myself. I loved the way it glided across my hands and flew into the air, swooshing straight into the net. The way it danced between, behind and in front of my legs to the backdrop of a chaotic audience before I passed it to a teammate. It was the shot fakes, screens and jab steps that would send my opponent to one direction only to be met by the opposite of what they had anticipated. The sweat dripping down my forehead and my heart beating hard all added to the thrill of this game I had come to love so much.

I met women from all over the world, and so many of them I still consider to be my closest friends. I laughed with them, shared court with them. We broke bread together, over different cuisines. I found the space in the world where I belonged, which transcended race, religion, nationality and gender, where the texture of my hair and skin color didn't matter. Where only basketball mattered. The court became the place I go when there is too much noise in the world or when I am consumed by joy. Today, I have played in dozens of courts around the world—sometimes with people who didn't even know my name. They knew me as number four.

IMPASSIONED ELEMENTS

After finishing his studies abroad in 1970, Salahdin Imam returns home to Dhaka in time for local uprisings and natural disaster to strike simultaneously. Stunned by the synchronicity of these events, he ponders the climate's influence on human affairs.

SALAHDIN IMAM

SALAHDIN IMAM is part of a growing English-language literary community in Bangladesh, where many new voices are being heard and inspiring each other. He hopes his own writing, touching on hard realities and the gloriously ornery ways of the human race, will convey reverence for the great drama of life in this universe. Following his book of short stories, *Diana Juxtaposed and Other Unrealities*, his forthcoming memoir covers the momentous sixties when he was at college in the US and active in the counterculture, following which he returned to his homeland just in time to play a role in the Bangladesh Liberation War of 1971. salahdinimam.com

There it was, a huge cargo vessel, lying on its side in the middle of a lime-green rice field, miles from the coast. Eyes round with wonder, my siblings and I gazed upon its rust-colored bottom and its decks high up in the sky. Our guide told us how it had ended up there, abandoned and desolate, like a metal whale. How it had been caught in a cyclone at sea and transported three miles inland by an ocean wave. In our children's imaginations this triggered the frightening but delicious joy of reliving the mighty natural phenomenon which had taken place right here. The raging storm, the terror of the sailors, the size and power of a cyclone that could take a ship and toss it here and there like a leaf...

We had been visiting the home of our uncle in Chittagong, in then East Pakistan, and had been taken on a ride into the countryside to see this local sensation. When we returned home that day, my mind still reeling from what I'd seen, I went to find my aunt, who was always a fount of stimulating stories.

"So how did you like the ship?" she asked, preparing me a plate of the town's specialty, seeded biscuits.

"I can't stop thinking about it," I said, "and I'm trying to understand what is meant by this thing called a "cyclone". How is it different from a storm?"

I was sitting at a large, heavy mahogany dining table. My aunt pointed at it and said, "You know we've been through some cyclones in this house. I've seen this table shake as if it was in the grip of a demon and slide slowly right to the end of the room. Even though all the doors and windows were tightly closed! This gives you an idea of how strong the wind can be. At such times I send your cousins away to a relative's farm deep in the countryside, because this house is at the top of a hill, more exposed than most. Only your uncle and I stay behind, and I sit in my bedroom with my prayer beads, praying for salvation."

"Do you think it could be so strong that it could carry away the house like it did that ship?"

"It certainly seems that way. In the middle of the day the sky is dark as night, and what is most scary is that for hour after hour the cyclone makes a deep humming sound, not loud but persistent, which goes on and on, with no escape. It's enough to drive you mad."

"But that was years ago?"

"It is happening more frequently," she said. The thought of this splendid mansion falling victim to such an assault and ending up in splinters struck fear in my heart.

Then I left for many years, to foreign lands and boarding schools, then college. Wherever I was in the world I would grasp at some whispers of news that arrived from my homeland, news that, oddly enough, almost always concerned some disastrous cyclone or other. Over the 1960s no less than four major cyclones, with wind speeds higher than 200 km/h, pounded the country. Such a concentrated onslaught had not happened in 500 years, and has thankfully not happened since.

Throughout the same decade, along with these natural catastrophes I kept getting news of political storms periodically shaking the nation. The people of East Pakistan, my people, Bengalis, had had enough of the colonial exploitation of their agricultural resources for the benefit of West Pakistan, more than 1000 miles away. Under the leadership of Sheikh Mujibur Rahman, head of a political party called the Awami League, Bengalis mobilized in wave after wave of mass demonstrations. They were met with violent repression each time.

From a distance I started associating the two sets of occurrences in my mind, those of impassioned nature on the one hand, and of impassioned society on the other. I even began to fancy that these were both aspects of the same underlying dynamic.

Situated exactly on the Tropic of Cancer, East Pakistan was a land of rolling rivers, lush fertile soil and rain-laden monsoon clouds. The flip side is that these are the exact climatic conditions which breed monster cyclones. Another geographic quirk is that the Bay of Bengal acts like a funnel, so cyclones build up in intensity over the ocean and are then impelled to set off upwards towards the coast like gigantic bowling balls. In a similar symbolic way, the Bengalis are moderate and peace-loving, with a talent for a multitude of arts from song to cuisine. They are generally tolerant and quick to forgive, but push them too far, for too long, and they will react with unbridled fury.

Both these series of natural and political convulsions came to a head in the same year, 1970. As it happened, I also returned to the country that year, just in time to witness the build-up to the climax. Fresh from four years of college in the USA, bursting with the counterculture's spirit of rebellion, I found I had become something of a misfit in my own country, with my long hair and boisterous attitudes. But the scale of the events I was soon to be plunged into cut me down to size.

I landed up in East Pakistan in June, when the political struggle was in full flow, and I, too, got swept up in it. Because of my social science background, I quickly fell in with a group of distinguished senior professionals who brought out a weekly magazine called *Forum*, which provided the intellectual rationale for our national revolt. Detailed economic analyses were set out showing how the precious export earnings of East

Pakistan were being largely spent in West Pakistan, resulting in a growing gap in living standards between the two wings of the country.

An exceptionally wide-ranging uprising the previous year had seemingly forced the issue, and the military dictatorship had been compelled to announce a general election, to be held on December 7, 1970. However, as the date approached for this handover of power to a civilian government, political and social tensions rose to a fever pitch. The main worry was that the military government would find some excuse to delay or even call off the elections at the last minute, as they had done many times before in Pakistan's history. With a leftist uncle of mine I roamed the streets of Dhaka, talking to tea sellers, rickshaw drivers, agitated students and even some grizzled farmers who had come into the city to mobilize. They shared the same opinions as those I heard in the elites' drawing rooms, namely that it was time for a decisive, uncompromising, stand.

This was remarkable as it is rare that all social strata feel the same way about any issue. An abstract concept, which I had studied in a college course on Political Participation offered by Samuel Huntington, became real for me then. I witnessed that a polity sometimes achieves such complete unity of purpose that it graduates to a state in which it can be termed "politically aware", making it then unstoppable. Because of this theoretical insight it was obvious to me that the politically-aware masses of East Pakistan would hit back strongly against any attempt to dash the cup of freedom from their lips. Our military rulers, however, had not made the same social theory calculations. They continued to believe that any resistance could be easily crushed by armed force, a misconception which led to their ultimate catastrophic defeat.

In this atmosphere of distrust of the military's intentions it was inevitable that, when General Yahya Khan, the President of Pakistan, left on a mysterious trip to China in mid-November 1970, there would be suspicions that he had gone there to plot the cancellation of the general elections with his closest geo-political allies of the time. And it was precisely at this moment of nervous public excitement, charged to the maximum with political, emotional, electrical, and, presumably, cosmic energy that, once again, the natural elements swooped in to play their role. A brute of a cyclone smashed into the coastal regions on the night of November 12, 1970.

Known as Cyclone Bhola 1970, it had formed a few days earlier but had remained stalled in the Bay of Bengal, gathering strength and feinting ominously this way and that. The folklore related that the more erratic their paths, the more dangerous cyclones became. And so it proved. Full of menace, whirling like a mighty djinn, Cyclone Bhola rode in on its final angular charge.

Its wind speed was 222 km/h, one of the highest ever recorded in this part of the world. It tore up the tallest palm trees *by their roots*. As if fated, Cyclone Bhola made landfall exactly at high tide. (On a hunch, I checked the dates tensely when writing this piece and yes, it was a night of full moon too!) This coincidence brought about the most massive tsunami imaginable, one which reared up 50 feet high as it raced forward at tremendous speed over a broad frontage. What chance did the densely packed populations in its path have when this towering, teetering wall of water fell upon them? In one night, one swipe of ocean blow, 500,000 souls perished all along the coast, the deadliest tropical disaster in history. What to make of such a loss? The human mind searches frantically for some mitigation.

The energy borne in a single severe cyclone is equivalent to that of several thousand atom bombs of megaton strength. The rule of physics is that energy is always conserved and can never be destroyed, so where did all those thousands of atom bombs go? A frightful price was paid in terms of lives lost but I believe that, in return, the cyclone's energy was violently transferred into the total system, made up of the land and its people. That is why, when the assassin's dagger was plunged into our nation's back a few months later, in March 1971, it was as if it had been plunged into a lighted ball of buzzing energy—which responded by blazing back with redoubled force.

The day after the cyclone the world awoke to scenes of desolation, the news headlines shouting in every language. Seen from the air, piles of bloated corpses lay strewn in the surf for mile after mile. General Yahya Khan, returning posthaste from China, flew over the coast to see for himself. Global attention, which had hardly ever given a thought to this part of the world, swiveled into focus, and largely stayed there, which had important consequences as the political drama of the next phase unfolded the following year. In the glare of this global searchlight on the cyclone all conspiracies shriveled up and vanished. Any idea of canceling the December 1970 general elections became unthinkable. This turned out to be decisive, a great boon to our eventual independence struggle.

But the final succor of Cyclone Bhola was the spirit that was instilled in the populace. Stunned by the size of the blow, a kind of numbed calmness befell us. The people of East Pakistan, contentious by nature, became, in their millions, completely one. A single consciousness was forged encompassing every man, woman and child. This was a level of "unity of purpose" of which even Huntington could never have conceived.

The Government of Pakistan was blamed for not providing adequate relief or moral compassion but, to be fair, the scale of the challenge was beyond them. It was however the last straw for the relationship between the two Wings. We in East Pakistan understood that we were on our own and that we had to pull together. The first thoughts of becoming an independent country began to stir in our mass-consciousness.

When the elections were finally held in December, less than a month after Cyclone Bhola, the vote in favor of Sheikh Mujibur Rahman was practically unanimous and the Awami League got so many seats in East Pakistan alone that it was in a position to command a majority in the all-Pakistan Assembly, and in effect become the ruler of both West and East Pakistan. This politically explosive outcome was totally unexpected, and I can only understand it as a direct consequence of Cyclone Bhola 1970.

To anticipate what happened next, two days before the newly elected National Assembly was supposed to convene on March 3, 1971, the West Pakistani military canceled the sitting, essentially the same desperate move as the one which they may have been planning in the days just before the cyclone hit. But by this time the people of East Pakistan were fully alert and, legitimized by the results of the election, Sheikh Mujibur Rahman led a huge campaign of civil disobedience which was morphing inevitably into a demand for full independence. The military then played their final card, a surprise genocidal attack by the armed forces on the ordinary people of East Pakistan. It took a further nine months of guerrilla warfare and diplomatic resistance, as well as the intervention of the Indian army, but we finally did emerge as the sovereign nation of Bangladesh, in December 1971.

For me personally, Cyclone Bhola had functioned as a metaphor for the wringing out and remaking of soul that I had endured in the six months after my return. The roller coaster intensity of these times had left me unsure of myself, stripped of facile certainties, humble in the face of the awesome powers which seemed always to be lurking so near.

One tiny but ferociously meaningful incident haunts my memory of those frightful days. Men and women caught in the open the night of the great cyclone were picked up and thrown high into the sky, their eyes blinded by sheets of foaming moisture. In this desperate state one young male encountered a flying solid shape and the two of them held on tightly to each other (in thin air what else was there to hold on to?), so that in the morning they were both found lying dead on the beach, a boy with several coils of python wrapped around him.

Snake and human, habitual enemies joined helplessly in an embrace. Now they lay deposited at one's feet, the debris of an act of authentic performance art, magnificent and terrible. Seeing this photograph in the newspaper it wasn't difficult to imagine myself in the grip of such an implacable fate as this one, or even maybe in the stead of the terrified sailors on the doomed ship that would be abandoned in a rice field. I tried to find reassurance knowing that such extreme outcomes emerge from an inscrutable domain, and that there's nothing to do in the greatest matters but take part with full mind and heart. And so I have done ever since.

THE UNFINISHED REPORT

Living in the north of Iran in 1979, a young Sepideh Zamani recalls the kindness of her Muslim neighbors while she and her family, who belong to a minority faith, find themselves at the mercy of the Islamic regime.

SEPIDEH ZAMANI

SEPIDEH ZAMANI was born in 1973 in the north of Iran and graduated from law school in 1999, moving to the US a year later. Her essays, short stories and novels focus on immigration, gender inequality and the lives of ethnic and religious minorities under cultural cleansing. Her published work in Persian includes short story collections *Barbuda* and *Women Looking at the Sky*, and her first novel *Ouroboros* and the forthcoming *Sleeping in a Dark Cave*. She also translates from and into Persian. She translated *The Divine Kiss* from Carolyn Kleefeld and *Pumpernickel* from Stanley Barkan into Persian. sepideh-zamani.com

The sound of huge raindrops hitting hard against the window had shattered my concentration. I still hadn't finished writing my report on religious persecution for the Iranian journal, but I couldn't resist being drawn into the beautiful melancholy of the falling rain. It had been raining continuously for two days. I got up from behind my desk and filled my cup with the cold, bitter leftover coffee from the morning. I stood by the window and watched the downpour. The sound of the rain took me back to many years ago.

It was 1979 and I was seven years old. We were living in Shahi at the time, a small town in the north of Iran. Most of the youth in our town were members of the Communist party and the target of the new Islamic regime. The sound of gunshots from outside had become constant. The revolutionary guards were now arresting, and executing without proper prosecution, those who opposed the new radical system. The Revolution was wreaking havoc all around Iran, but it had been a quiet morning in our home.

I sat by the window in silence with my sketchbook in my lap and tried to draw the clouds that floated through the blue sky. The birds on the pomegranate tree were singing and the wildflowers in the garden were shimmering in the autumn sun. As soon as the doorbell rang I jumped to my feet and raced past Jahan, who was watching me worriedly, and opened the door to the courtyard. It was the mailman. He gave me a letter and said, "Hey. Don't lose this. Give it to your father."

When the mailman left I went back to my sketchbook, but the clouds were moving too quickly now and the singing birds had started to scatter. Mum told me once that these were the signs of a hurricane coming.

When Mum and Dad came home from work, we gave them the letter. Once he read it, Dad turned pale and looked nervous. "We only have one day," he said. Apparently the letter should have reached us ages ago; it had gotten lost. Dad had been sacked from his work at the textile manufacturing plant due to the new government's religious cleansing policy, and we had to immediately leave the property which belonged to the organization from which he'd been dismissed. We were not Muslim, you see.

"What should we do?" Mum asked.

"We can go to the house in the country." The house was located between Sari and Babol, next to the bridge over the Black River. Dad was referring to the house he was building in the middle of the plot, which was nowhere near ready. There were brick walls and ceilings, but no proper floor or plumbing. There was no electricity and the only access to water was a well on the property. We would use a bucket to collect our water.

That night, Dad gave Jahan and I each a big box to fill with books and toys. I packed all of my baby dolls and story books. Then I looked for my baby dolls' clothes and shoes. And my bicycle. Dad had bought it for me months ago, just before the revolution. It was pink and still shiny and new. In one day, Dad moved most of our belongings from the house in the city to the plot in the country. He took me and Jahan with him early in the morning and left us there. The house was still half-built, windowless; maybe they hadn't had money to put in windows.

On Dad's second trip to the house that morning, Mum came with him. She started unpacking some of the cardboard boxes, with Navid tied to her back to keep him warm. Jahan and I followed her around. As she was shuffling here and there, she had to think about our lunch as well. There was no working stove in the house, so she gave us bread, cheese and walnuts. I hated bread and cheese, so I didn't eat it and threw it in the well.

By lunchtime we were ready to go to school. Mum said, "I'll come with you this one time to show you how to get there. Your father has asked Mustafa to allow you to go through his gardens. This way it is much shorter."

"Who is Mustafa?" I asked.

"He is our neighbor," Mum said. "Mustafa and his family are living in the house behind our garden."

"But there is a river behind our garden," I said.

"What river?" Jahan said. "That's not a river. That's a water canal. Our teacher taught us about water canals in our city." Jahan was three years older than me and everyday since first grade he would tell me about the things he was learning. I knew what every page of his textbook was about. I didn't know it word for word, but I knew all the subjects. It seemed he'd forgotten to tell me about these canals.

"The canal separates our gardens," Mum said. "We need to cross the wooden bridge to get to Mustafa's garden."

"I don't like crossing that wooden bridge," Jahan said. I asked him if he was scared, but he didn't answer me.

There was a desolate, mysterious alley next to our garden. It was quiet and narrow, lined with tall sycamore trees. The only sound that was ever heard was the rustling of the leaves as the wind blew past them. Dad had always asked us to stay away from the alley. Of course I was always curious about what was at the end of it.

On the way to school that day, Mum asked us to follow her as she entered the alley. At the end of it was a water canal and a half-broken wooden bridge. I now understood why Jahan refused to talk about it. He had probably come here before and knew the bridge was old and very fragile. Mum held our hand one by one and passed us over the bridge. On the other side was a half-open wooden door. That door stayed half-open for many years, and I never found out if someone left it open for us to pass through on our way to school, or if it had always been like that. Mum knocked on the door and we entered the garden. It wasn't as big as our garden, and the land was nearly empty, with just a few scattered apple and orange trees. There was a small and run-down hut in the middle of the garden with people crowding around it. Bald, half-naked children were running around with bare feet, while two plainly dressed women were washing clothes in an old muddy pool. Mustafa had two wives and 14 children.

As soon as the women noticed us, they left the clothes in the washtub next to the pool and walked toward us. Two little boys followed them, one holding a long branch between his legs like it was his horse.

The women kindly greeted Mum. "Mustafa told us a couple of hours ago that you are moving in," said the older woman. "He said you and your husband were dismissed from your job. We are so sorry for what is happening these days."

"Yes, we got our letter yesterday," Mum said. "They asked us to leave as soon as we receive the letter."

The older woman continued, "We are so embarrassed of what these radicals are doing. You are our fellow countrywomen and countrymen. God will not forgive them. What they are doing is a sin. It will prevent many blessings from our land."

“They have been very unpredictable,” Mum agreed. “They’re acting as though we are their enemy, or we came from another planet.”

“Oh dear. God help us all. They are a shame on humanity,” said the older woman.

Mum said she was worried they would arrest us. “Most of those who were dismissed from their jobs are being interrogated and some have been arrested.”

“We will not let them harm you and your family,” said the older woman.

I was listening to them, unsure of the meaning of the things they were saying. Why was she talking about harm? And what could happen to us? Why would we need them to protect us? I knew Dad was a brave man. Surely he could protect his family.

“God will help us through this,” Mum said. “We are not worried about ourselves. We are concerned about our children.” The younger woman quietly shook her head. The boy with the wooden stick was trotting around us and neighing loudly, trying to catch our attention. I tried to ignore him and to listen to the conversation. The other little boy was shy, hiding behind the young woman.

“You are our brother and sister,” said the older of the two women. “Your children are our children. We will protect you.”

We said goodbye to them and left. We passed a few more gardens, fences and alleys on the way to school, and I thought about the women’s conversation the whole way.

“Do you know the route home, or do you want to wait to come back with Jahan?” Mum asked.

“I know the way.” I don’t know why I said that, as I didn’t have much clue on how to get back.

After the bell rang, I picked up my bag and quickly left school. The caretaker helped me cross the main road. I hadn't walked more than a few steps when I realized I didn't know which street or alley I should take next. I became anxious and agitated, looking around for someone on the street to whom I could ask how to get to Black River bridge. But there was no one on this side of the street. Cars passed by at high speed and every once in a while one would honk at another for cutting them off.

As I was standing there wondering what to do, the sky was getting darker and darker, threatening rain. Minutes later a tremendous downpour began. I wanted to get back to school and wait for Jahan, but I was afraid to cross the main road. I thought I would take the beltway, but the beltway was at least four times longer than the shortcut. I had no alternative. I couldn't just stand there on the pavement of a busy road on my own. I started to walk. The rain was getting heavier and heavier, and I walked faster and faster. The raindrops were lashing on my face and head. I could hardly see where I was going. I was completely drenched and my shoes made a squishing sound. I was cold, but worse than the cold and the rain was the feeling of uncertainty about the direction I was going. I was completely unsure whether it was the right way or not. I was lost. I could feel a lump in my throat as tears began welling up. I was angry with myself for not having paid attention; with Mum for not coming to get me from school; and with the school caretaker for having returned back into the building so quickly. What if I have come the wrong way? Every few minutes a large truck would pass me by with a loud roar and shake the earth beneath my feet. I felt like I had been walking for hours. I was tired, cold and shivering. My heart began to race as I heard the screech of a car pulling up behind me on the side of the road. I was afraid to look back, and wanted to run. I thought this was it. I was going to die. Finally, a voice from the car shouted, "What are you doing here?"

It was Dad; he looked tired and anxious. "Where have you been? Jahan came home an hour ago. We looked everywhere for you. I went to school and you weren't there. I asked the boys in the alleys, but none of them had seen you. Why did you come this way? How did you walk all this way on foot?"

Wet, exhausted and frozen, I felt embarrassed to have made him worry. I dropped my head and climbed into the cherry-colored Jeep.

When we got home I noticed Dad had used a plastic sheet to stop the rain and cold air from coming through the windows. He had also made an odd makeshift door with scraps of wood and plastic film.

"Where in the world have you been?" asked Mum when she saw me. Her face was red and her hands were shaking. Mum would turn bright red whenever she was angry or anxious, but this time I couldn't say which one she felt. Probably anxious.

"I don't know," I admitted.

"What do you mean you don't know? There were only two alleys there. Your father has been looking for you everywhere."

I didn't have the gumption or energy to answer. She went on and on about how much I had scared her, asking how could I have possibly forgotten the way home. I stayed quiet. I didn't tell her that I'd spent the entire walk to school with her thinking about her conversation with the older woman, distracted. I took off my waterlogged shoes, and Mum immediately took a towel from a box. She took off my wet clothes and wrapped the towel around me. She dried my hair and helped me put on dry clothes. I sat next to Jahan who was sitting by the heater and candles, doing his homework. I took my notebook out of my bag. It was sodden. Mum took a new notebook from one of the boxes and gave it to me. I opened the notebook but still I couldn't stop thinking about what I had heard in Mum and Mustafa's wives' conversation. Dad came in and sat next to us.

He looked at Mum and said, "Mustafa just came to our door to make sure we found her safe and that everything is fine. He said we shouldn't sit in the dark, and that we should get a wire of electricity from their home."

"We shouldn't bother them," Mum said. "That could cause problems for Mustafa and his family"

"He even offered for us to have a doorbell to their home," Dad continued.

"A doorbell? What for?"

"In case they attack our home," Dad said "We could ring the doorbell if we need Mustafa's help. He told me to not worry about anything, and said he and his family would protect us. Our family and our home will be safe, and our children protected anytime on these streets. Mustafa said they'd have to kill him and shed his family's blood before anything happened to us."

I looked at Dad's face. He looked drained, but at peace. On that dark evening in that windowless room without a door, as I sat by the heater on top of which Mum was cooking dinner, I felt I was in the safest place in the world.

A horrific sound of thunder and lightning brought me back to reality and the report I had yet to write. I drew the curtain and stood there with tearful memories, and a bundle of damp papers in my hands.

RADICAL MUSLIM IN LOVE

In this coming-of-age story based in Nigeria, Wardah Abbas remembers her upbringing, when she chooses to abandon parts of her culture in order to deepen her faith, discover herself and find love along the way.

WARDAH ABBAS

WARDAH ABBAS is a lawyer, writer and social justice activist. She's the founder of *The Muslim Women Times*, an independent media platform spotlighting the stories of Muslim women. She has been published in various magazines, online media platforms and anthologies. @wardah_abbas on Twitter, @wardahabbas on Medium, @heywardah on Instagram.

I looked up at the emerging rays of the sun, hands spread out on my folded legs just the way some Arabs would sit to make du'a. While I prayed for him to be the noor of my eyes at first sight, I found myself asking questions. After many phone conversations, I had accepted his marriage proposal. I didn't care much about what he looked like or how much he earned for a living. He had the qualities I was looking for. He was a feminist and a Muslim. So how could I finally not realize that he was truly the one for me? I felt my pulse rise as the time for our meeting grew nearer. My eyes fell on the wallpaper in front of me, a rough blend of perfect strokes transformed into an orderly row of coconut trees swaying in the breeze. Calm, peaceful—it's how I hoped I would look today. I took a deep breath as I walked to the door. Today could be the day.

***

I was born in Ikeja, on the mainland of Lagos in the southwestern region of Nigeria. We lived on the first floor of a story building flanked by sweet-scented tulips and well-nurtured vegetable gardens, enclosed by a high fence and two giant iron gates. I grew up with my father, a professional journalist, and my mother, a chartered accountant, as well as three sisters and two brothers in a multi-ethnic and multi-religious environment. Our street was not tarred. It was a dusty path lined by countless rows of palm trees, and it was beautiful. While everyone had different yardsticks by which they identified themselves, my parents taught me first to be a Muslim, second to be Yoruba, my tribe. For the first 12 years of my life, my parents gave us the best a middle-class family could afford.

I grew up with a fusion of the Yoruba, Arab and western traditions, and my parents instilled a rich blend of ethics from these three cultures. Kneeling before the elders was an integral aspect of the Yoruba tradition, while our table manners were uniquely from the English culture. We grew up knowing right from wrong without anyone having to tell us. We learned not to do to others what we wouldn't want to be done to us. We learned not to cheat or be avaricious. We were content with the little we had.

Just like the majority of southerners in Nigeria, I had a semi-religious upbringing. We only prayed together as a family every morning, except on weekends, when we observed the evening prayers together before going to bed. I hardly ever heard anyone recite the Qur'an except while observing salah. Mum never wore the hijab, so we never wore it either. We were made to believe that the hijab was not a necessary aspect of the deen. "Islam is in the heart, my dear, not in your dressing," my mother would remind us.

Life was chocolates and pancakes until one morning, seeing how much expectation and pressure had been placed on me, I realized that growing up wasn't as fun as I thought. I remember how, out of love, I offered to assist an uncle press out his crumpled kaftan and trousers on a hot sunny afternoon. He handed me the chore while he stood behind me. To my surprise, just as I began pressing the clothes, he grabbed the iron from me, fuming. He said I was "big for nothing" and blamed my mother. "You had better start learning how to do these things. You will soon become a woman. And I'm sure you don't want your husband beating you and sending you packing all the time." I was dumbstruck. I dared not talk back. Too overwhelmed to do or say anything at that moment, I walked away swiftly. I was so angry and sad that I wasn't paying attention. I stubbed my toe on the pavement in the backyard, letting out a loud, liberating cry.

I grew up resenting my culture. I saw women suffer in their marriages. I discovered that the society frowned upon divorced women, and it was a stigma to be a single woman. Such women would never be respected, let alone be given another chance at love. Domestic violence was rampant. I had first-hand experience of parents treating their children as chattels. "God, give me a child that would serve me" was a mantra that most aspiring Yoruba parents would often chant. It was worse if you were a girl: you would serve your parents as a child and grow up to serve your husband and in-laws cooking, cleaning and bearing as many children as your husband pleased. I felt terrified to become that woman. All that time, the thought of leaving my community and running away to an unknown place stuck with me.

Were the thoughts I secretly harbored so strange? Were there others who felt the same? I loved being a girl, and an African too. Being a girl meant flowing floral dresses and beautiful cornrows. Being an African meant dressing up in our traditional iro ati buba with a stylishly wrapped gele to match, delighting in the heavenly taste of my mother's egusi soup and gathering with my siblings to listen to the elders' tales by moonlight. But I despised the reality that came with being both at the same time.

Was it possible to renounce certain aspects of my culture? I never chose to be part of it in the first place. As I continued to think about this, an idea suddenly crept into my mind. That idea changed me, stretched and heated my notions like white cloth dyed into Kampala fabric.

I wasn't only African. I was also a Muslim who was passing through some rigorous stages of western education. So, I thought to myself, if Islam is truly a total way of life, why don't I explore what it means to live the life of Islam? And so I began to separate the religion from the culture. Was I going to abandon one for the other?

The journey was complicated, but I felt liberated. Women were not only equal to men in the sight of God, they also had full rights and an esteemed status. Reading about the lives of the Prophet Muhammad (PBUH) and his companions was unshackling. His relationship with women and children was not ordinary; He was so humble and kind to them, and sometimes women overpowered him. Right before me was an invitation to a beautiful life, a life of freedom. However, living Islam meant sacrificing some elements of me. I could no longer mix freely with the opposite sex, dress sexy in public, attend parties or clubs, listen to just any type of music or dance to the beats. The list seemed endless. I began to wear the hijab not just as an Islamic obligation, but also as a statement: I was no longer the same. People began to consider me a social recluse.

I will never forget my embarrassment one day. I met some of my high school friends as I walked into a computer store on a scorching hot afternoon. For the first time, they were seeing me in a long over-the-head abaya, all sweaty from a hectic day. The shock on their faces. The way they sneered at me, shaking their heads as if I had been struck by misfortune.

"I could have bet my life that it wasn't you," one of them said.

"Is this some kind of costume or have you suddenly joined the Boko Haram Movement?" said another.

I just stood there, looking into their faces, feeling disgraced. The news was definitely going to go round: Wardah had become one of those backward, frumpy Muslims who cover up and isolate themselves from the world. I knew I had made the right choice for myself, but being scoffed at still stings like nothing else.

My parents, who had obviously also noticed the changes, summoned me to a family meeting one morning.

"What's with this extremist garb you have been parading lately?" my dad asked.

"It's not extremist garb," I answered. "It's just the Islamic way of dressing."

"Do you want to teach me about Islam?"

"No sir," I replied, looking into his eyes.

"Go ahead. Tell me more," he said, annoyed. "Who exactly do you think I am?" he continued. "I lived with the Arabs, I schooled with them, wined and dined with them and even speak their language very fluently in different dialects. And I know better than to throw away my identity to embrace their culture."

"I'm not embracing their culture, Dad. The hijab is not from Arab culture. It's from Islam."

"I don't care what garbage you have been learning. Listen and listen well. As long as you remain my daughter and are still under my roof, you are not to wear this frumpy looking dress again."

I didn't say anything. I was sorry but wasn't going to yield. He got the message. I saw it in his eyes—in their eyes, staring at me icily, pain and disappointment all over. I felt the same. They had raised an ambitious little girl and, in their eyes, all that was left was a little walking black cloak—a complete social pariah.

It had become clear that I would never truly get an equal dose of being black, African, Muslim and a woman all at the same time. I had to choose what aspect of my identity to prioritize.

As I continued to learn about Islam, I discovered that the hijab was not a one-size-fits-all kind of dress. The Muslim woman's dress had some minimum requirements: it must be loose, opaque and not showy or ostentatious. It didn't have to be a burqa or an eastern style abaya. I could fulfill the conditions of the hijab in my own unique way. I could create my own signature style or even switch between various styles. I could wear my headscarf in different colors and fabrics. And I did just that.

As the years passed by, the idea of getting married began to appeal to me. I didn't want a man from my community whose practice of Islam was tainted by certain cultural practices. I wanted a true Muslim by my own standards. That meant a man who believed in the equality of men and women, who respected women and their rights, and who saw women as partners in matrimony, not possessions. It definitely wasn't a man who saw women as fitnah or some sort of temptation. I wanted a feminist man, a soulmate who could tap into my spirit and connect with my soul. A man who didn't think that being a woman made me genetically wired to want to clean the dishes and scrub the floors. That man was rare but I was going to do whatever it took to find him. And until I did, I was just going to enjoy being single.

Having prepared a realistic checklist and a number of highly sensitive questions for my potential suitors, I sprawled out and relaxed, awaiting a long line up of prospects. As a little girl, I had naïve ideas about love. I would easily find my handsome North African prince and every day, I would wake up to my lover staring back at my own kohl-rimmed eyes, stroking my black curly hair and loving me forever. Today I can't help but laugh at my childish ideas. The reality would be much more complex.

I met a heart-rending bunch of unsuitable guys. There was Jamil, who met me at a chaperoned date wearing studs and all kinds of bling-bling. He eventually took my money because he didn't have the lower denominations needed to pay the bill. And there was Sahad, who audaciously told me that I met all his criteria except that I wasn't the hip girl he would be proud to show to the world. Or Yunus who, after a series of dates and negotiations, had the nerve to tell me that he had to first get married to his baby mama before considering me. Were there no decent men out there? Or was I the wrong kind of woman? Maybe my true Muslim man didn't exist. Still, I knew what I wanted and no matter how long it took, I was going to wait for it.

Five years down the line, I decided to stop searching and just concentrate more on finding fulfillment on my own. I began doing the things I loved: reading, writing, road trips and photography. I even pushed back my law career to pursue a living writing. I decided to be less bothered about marriage. If he was destined for me, he would find me.

Then one hazy harmattan evening, I received a call. It was from a man from a different culture and environment. He was Fulani, originally from Borno State in the northeastern part of Nigeria. But he grew up in Sokoto, amongst the Hausas. Interestingly his mother was a full-blooded Yoruba woman, like me. He had heard about me from a relative and wanted to meet me. The sound of his voice made my heart skip. It was soft and smoky at first, and then grew husky as the conversation went on. I loved his accent too—it reflected a blend of both western and Fulani civilizations. There were lots of long awkward pauses during our short phone conversation. But I knew he could be the one.

***

We met at a botanical park. I had arrived before him. I hid between a lineup of palm trees so I could have the first look. And when he appeared at the other side of the park, my heart melted. I closed my eyes for a while, filled with so much gratitude. He was tall, but not too tall. And handsome, too, in a way I hadn't imagined. His hair was wavy and dark brown, neatly arranged by a pair of perfect hands. His eyes revealed the innocence of his soul and the gentleness of his character. The color of his kaftan complemented his skin tone and blended perfectly with his head-cap. In his right hand was a small gift bag; the first of so many more. I slowly walked towards him looking straight into his eyes with so much awe. He couldn't look into mine. All he did was smile.

A HEAVY WALK

Residing in London in 2019, Shirazuddin Siddiqi contends with the guilt of moving his mother to the West, while he works through a recurring nightmare about a brutal event he witnessed during the in-fighting of mujahideen factions that laid to waste his Afghan homeland.

SHIRAZUDDIN SIDDIQI

SHIRAZUDDIN SIDDIQI, born in Kabul, has written and directed drama for a range of platforms, including stage, TV and radio. He taught at Kabul University until conflict between militia forces forced it to close in 1992. He moved on to edit Kabul's art magazine, *Honar*, until 1994, when he and his family fled worsening fighting to Pakistan. In Peshawar he joined the BBC and was responsible for editing the educational soap opera, *New Home, New Life*, that continues to be broadcast to Afghans across the country. Creating illustrated storybooks for children in Dari and Pashto, drawing on Afghan folklore, also became a passion in the mid-nineties. He now lives with his family in the UK where, in between his professional work, he enjoys cultivating flowering plants.

“What a clean park! Wish we had parks like this back at home... Our God-damned rascals keep destroying, fighting. That’s normal for them. Why should those war-mongers build anything anyway? They would lose their profit if the country was stable. Oh dear God, what is that? So much, so much human flesh scattered everywhere...dead bodies... Dear God, what the hell has happened here? I thought we would be safe here... But our fate never leaves us... Oh, no, they are moving. They are not dead. But why are they naked? Oh my God, I sinned. Tobah, tobah...Is this what kafirs do? Oh God, forgive me I have sinned. I must keep my eyes to the ground. Why should I open my eyes so, so comfortably in the land of strangers? I should have kept my eyes shut. I wish I had no eyes. My faith must be in flames now, my eternal resting place must be on fire. Dear God, please forgive me. I am weak, I am a sinner, only you can forgive me...”

Did I make up my mother’s internal conversation, did I dream it, or did I experience her shock myself? Whatever the case, I deserved all the scolding.

“Where has he brought me? Why did I agree to come? I should have died there in Peshawar, it was after all a Muslim land even if it wasn’t my home. I could have had a chance of a peaceful afterlife there; it is all gone now. God, you should have cut my legs so I couldn’t move. The decadence here is sickening.”

***

My oldest was the first to notice that Mother had pulled her chador forward to create a small tunnel big enough to see only the front of her feet as she walked in Regents Park. Her first walk in the UK, just to stretch her legs. I felt both guilty and angry. Why hadn't I thought about it? Did I not know that everyone in London would be at the park, sunbathing on a sunny August Saturday? I've been visiting London several times a year since 1995, I should've known better. Why did I expose her to all this, right after her arrival? It was too late to turn back now. Every bit of the park was occupied by nearly naked rolling bodies, and turning back would have been equally as challenging as walking on. Everyone had to endure it in silence, there was no other option. Mother had almost completely blocked her view with her chador. I asked my daughter to hold her hand so she didn't trip. It was by all accounts one of the most painful walks I remember.

***

Gulmir is stuck to a large frame in an x shape. Two thick panes pressed against each other, holding him in between. His uncovered back is immediately in front of me. His face is also towards me. I don't even feel the strangeness of the situation, as if I've always known people whose heads are turned completely around. He is breathing weakly. His eyes move gently, perhaps asking me to examine his back. At first, it looks like the skin of a zebra, with dark parallel lines running from the left side of his back to the right. The lines are a dark reddish brown, drawn over his skin. They are thick and swollen, pushing outward and, in some places, transparent too. I can see pus boiling in inexplicable colors, ready to burst. I have forgotten who did this to him, but somewhere in the back of my mind their shadowy images linger, just out of reach. And, anyway, there is no point in asking who did this to Gulmir. He is pasted between thick panes and doesn't seem to have the energy to talk. My attention turns back to the swollen lines on his back. I hold my thumb out to examine their thickness. There I discover that they are not as straight as they initially looked. In places they zigzag and appear to be twice as large as my thumb. I get closer to examine one of the lines more closely. My thumb goes through the glass and into flesh. The thick line bursts out into a stream of pus...

***

Having tea afterwards was awkward. All in silence, not a word uttered. No one commented on the tea, which usually leads to chitchat, at least in my family. It was usually enough for someone to say the tea was a bit too strong to open up a long conversation, and that is perhaps why Afghans are so addicted to tea. But tea after this walk was different. Everyone knew she was not in a good mood. And, when she was in that mood you didn't need her voice to work it out. The air in the room would weigh heavier, her silence louder than any words. She needed plenty of time to recover from the shock, I thought. Till then, everyone around her was affected. The air in the room was hard to breathe.

***

Gulmir is in his glass frame. Weak. Dying. I feel I am the only visitor he has. No one else from the family seems to be around. I trace his face, his lips, his eyes. There is no sign of his wicked smile. I try to remind him of it. I say, perhaps more in my mind than to him, how his smile told people he was about to say something really, really wicked and funny. He tries. I can see it in his eyes. I can see he is trying, but, of course, he doesn't have the energy to give me that smile. But there is something naughty on his mind. I know there is, but he can't utter it. I want to make him talk. But how? I find a lever on the frame. It will move the glass up and down. I know it will, so I try it. The glass moves and causes Gulmir immense pain. I know this pain is bound to make him speak. It will force him to say something. I move it again, and he makes a desperate move. The glass shatters. He stays in the frame. His head goes limp on his shoulder. He is motionless.

***

I went out to the veranda to get some fresh air. I started to wonder how alien everything must look to her. I thought about my own first day in the UK, a wet October day in 1995. Bayswater was a crowded scene of raincoats and umbrellas. Some umbrellas collided with each other, some even got stuck to halt their bearers for a moment or two. But the rest sailed through the air smoothly. My thoughts went to a woman on the pavement who kept screaming at passersby. Desperate. God knows what she was saying, still I stood at a distance, not understanding a word. I concluded I could be of no help to her, shocked at the indifference of all those people who rushed past without even looking her way. As if she were a ghost only I could see. Everyone else rushed to the tube station, traveling through mice-tunnels to other parts of the city.

The shock of that incident and the image of that woman on the pavement have stayed with me. I walked to that exact spot several times afterwards, searched other parts of Bayswater, hoping to see her again. But there was no sign of her. It was as if she'd been a transit passenger, leaving that day for her final destination.

For me, some of the communist propaganda about the heartlessness of capitalism was confirmed by that incident. Back home, in war-ravaged Kabul, even those nasty Jihadis who were tearing anyone and everyone apart for no reason, would have stopped to ask that woman what she was yelling about. Back home, nobody would go past the dead body of a total stranger without giving it some sort of burial, let alone pass by a living woman yelling so desperately. It was as if someone had deliberately staged this small show for me, to scare me off London. It gave me a new image of wealth and wealthy societies. I told my British colleagues at work about it, hoping one of them would give me a convincing explanation. But none did. Maybe they had seen a lot of this themselves.

This incident never sat right with me. The more I have thought about that woman over these years, the more mysterious she has become.

***

I sat beside the psychotherapist. She moved her chair to sit opposite me. I was sure that was because she wanted to examine even the slightest movements on my face. She kept looking me in the eye. "Tell me anything you want," she declared. I searched the archive of my mind. Work-related files were piled up, so I told her about them. "Tell me about the ones that cause trouble." A lot of them cause trouble, so I ran over a few of them. The session was over. She asked if I felt better. I nodded politely, but underneath I felt I hadn't said anything. Precious time wasted.

***

It was during my second visit to the UK when a stroll took me to Hyde Park, where I saw men and women sunbathing. It had shocked me too, but the shock had had nothing to do with faith or culture. It was people's sense of security that shocked me. All those men and women felt perfectly safe to strip and let their skin absorb the benefits of the sunshine. The whole scene stood in stark contrast with what was going on in Kabul in those days: the opposite extreme. Civil war had destroyed any sense of security. Venturing out posed a life-threatening risk, yet staying home was equally as risky. Blind rockets, as people in Kabul called them, could find you anywhere. It was just a question of time. If it was your turn, the rocket or the bullet that had your name on it would reach you. Rockets and bullets were the means by which God's wrath poured on Afghanistan and its people. But there were no signs of God's anger when I walked through Hyde Park that day.

It made me crave for the same sense of security for people in my own country. But this last time, noticing my mother's reaction made my heart feel heavy, buried by the weight of a mountain. It had shaken me to the core. The whole future looked in jeopardy. I wasn't sure whether my plans—to enroll the children in schools, rent a house for the family, teach my wife to do the weekly shopping using a bankcard, etc.—would ever crystallize.

***

I can't remember if it was the third or fourth session when she finally asked me to tell her about my nightmares. Finally! A new hope grew in my heart. I felt close to getting my life back. I picked the one in which Gulmir appeared. I called him

X to the psychotherapist, partly because he was stuck in that shape, partly because his real name might cause more misery to the family. But mainly because uttering his name forms a solid lump in my throat, which renders me useless. I don't know why I chose Gulmir, especially given that I had plenty of other horrifying cases I could talk about. I didn't call Gulmir's appearances nightmares. I called them dreams. Maybe I chose him because I felt guilty for causing more pain to him in those dreams. Or, maybe because his reappearance coincided with my sessions with the therapist. I told her how close I was to him and what he meant, and didn't mean, to me. Our time was up. I felt heavy. My chest felt packed.

***

I remembered showing Mother the ruins of Baghgai, the little village in which she was born, around April 2003. We had come to Kabul for her own mother's funeral. This was the first time she had returned since we had fled the civil war in 1994 and settled in Peshawar, where I had found a job with a British organization working with Afghans. She had been close to her mother, and the news of her death was a bomb that shattered her to pieces. I was worried she might suffer a stroke or a heart attack. In her late mother's house, grief had spread deep and wide, leaving no room for her to feel alive. To distract her I offered to take her and her only sister to their birthplace. My aunt was excited and got into the vehicle quickly. It was a long drive, most of it off-road in mountainous terrain, but I was glad to do it.

We arrived at the new village at the lower part of the valley, from where the ruins of the old village were easily visible. I drove up there and we started exploring. Mother leaned on the large old tree which stood right at the center of the ruined village, a witness and reminder of its past. Her eyes were fixed on the sky as if the tree had some magical power to awaken forgotten memories, though I knew that wasn't the case. She was only three when her family abandoned Baghgai and moved closer to the city of Kabul. Whatever I had heard about this village came from her late mother and stepfather. I looked at my mother again, so attached to the tree, and thought about her playing around this very tree as a toddler. I knew, though, that she was thinking about only one thing, her mother. She was still leaning on the tree when a small group of villagers declared their arrival in chorus. "Assalamualaikum!" After introductions were made, an elderly man introduced himself as her cousin. Instantly they all sat on their chadors next to the tree on a raised stone platform. One of them started reciting verses from Al-Baqarah and ended it with "Lo! we are Allah's and lo! Unto Him we are returning." They all offered heartfelt condolences to her, and her newly-found cousin referred to her late mother as 'Babo Jaane' which, to me, confirmed the truthfulness of his claim to be her cousin. No outsider would know or dare utter a woman's name (even a dead woman's name) back to you in Pashtoon culture.

I was lost. I had tried to distract her, to take her well away from grief, but grief had traveled to her birthplace faster than we had. And grief had greeted us like a gracious host. Her newly found cousin, Sher Alam, turned out to be a pleasant, sensitive man, who took her around the ruin, explaining which part belonged to whom. He showed her a tiny little room in which she must have been born. This was the first time she showed some interest. She sat by the door and examined the room, but I doubt if it reminded her of anything.

The ruins were situated at an elevated part of a very high mountain. You could see the entire expanse of the valley before you. But, at the same time, it captured the meaning of isolation in full. It could have been a perfect spot for Buddhist meditation had we, good Muslims, not made it so bloody difficult for the Buddhists to live there. I looked at her and wondered how she would react if I told her how much those ruins resembled a Buddhist monastery rather than a village left behind by her Muslim parents.

***

I cursed myself, and my own stupidity. How could I have subjected an elderly woman originating from such a hidden corner of the world with strict purdah to the near-nudity of London's Regents Park? How did I fail to predict the outrage it would cause? The air in the veranda still felt heavy. I tried to be casual, asking if everybody had tea. No response. Silence was still in control of the situation, as my wife quietly cleared the cups in the kitchen of our temporary apartment. I thought about us 36 hours earlier, back in Pakistan, with everyone making their last arrangements for the journey. My heart beat against my chest as I remembered what we had given up there. It was all too late. The house had been returned to the owner, and what we couldn't bring to London had been loaded on a truck and sent to Kabul. There was nothing to return to in Pakistan.

***

The local Taliban checkpoint was running low on resources. They were after another prey. They targeted Gulmir who, in their view, came from another rich family in the village. Two Taliban soldiers knocked. He answered. They had a report, so they claimed, that Gulmir was in possession of weapons. Several Kalashnikovs, they claimed. Gulmir pleaded with them that he hadn't held one in his life. He offered his entire house for a thorough Taliban search. But they insisted he put on his sandals and accompany them. His family came out, and a crowd of family members pleaded noisily with the Taliban soldiers to let go of Gulmir. They made quite an entertaining scene for onlooking villagers. Gulmir was embarrassed, wishing he were dead so he wouldn't have to see the women in his family pleading with strangers, especially the lice-covered Taliban strangers (as his family liked to refer to the thugs). But no amount of pleading made the Taliban soldiers budge. Gulmir was quickly dragged away, leaving his entire household in a state of shock.

***

I used my leave from work to look for schools. I was worried most in our area would be already full, with places allocated back in June and July. With the help of a friend we found placement at a nearby primary school, but the secondary schools proved harder. Still, a kilometer or so away one headteacher agreed to interview my children. I took both of them there and urged them to do their best to secure a place. The interviews were short. The headteacher was reassured they wouldn't cause trouble and offered them spaces. Schooling was sorted.

My holiday came to an end. I worked at the London headquarters for a week, but hesitated to tell colleagues that we finally had an address in the city. There was no certainty yet. No way to predict what Mother would decide to do next.

***

Gulmir's house was searched the following day while he was kept at the checkpoint. No weapon was found, yet a penalty was imposed anyway. The family used their savings and borrowed more from relatives living in Pakistan to make up the sum. They paid the penalty, still he was not released. Local elders intervened. The Taliban finally let Gulmir's family take his half-dead body on a stretcher.

He was in poor shape, beaten by several Taliban who took turns hitting him with a heavy metal rod. His back looked like the recently plowed field outside his house. In some places, the skin had broken, letting the pus flow. He couldn't lie on his back, so he lay on his belly in the corner of his room, I don't exactly remember for how long. Until he breathed his last breath.

***

I felt the need to prepare my wife and children for all eventualities. My wife was reasonably happy to follow me anywhere but the children had already made friends in the local park. They had been to cinemas and concerts and, as one can imagine, were not so easy to convince. For them there was no comparison between the restrictions of Peshawar and the liberties of London. I remember several conversations turning into inconclusive arguments, and I was stuck in between. They were children, and didn't understand familial responsibilities. They had that kind of freedom to only think about themselves.

***

The therapist assured me that my experiences were complex when I protested that nothing had changed. She said she wasn't surprised that the nightmares hadn't gone away and urged me to continue to capture them in writing, drawing, or any other form with the aim of grabbing control of them. But no amount of expression in various formats gave me back my peaceful sleep. The human mind, challenged by complex experiences, reacts in a manner not easy to understand. This was my final takeaway. Horror had taken up residence and rose every time my eyes closed. That was my reality. There was no point in trying to push it out. What I failed to understand was why a simple move to London, which had been made in consultation with everyone, including my mother, became so complex.

***

On the first day I returned from work, my daughter, looking worried, took me quietly to the veranda to tell me "something important about grandmother". My daughter had been taking a nap when Mother had gone in and stood by the window, staring at the world going by. The opening of the window must have woken my daughter, who then heard her grandmother saying, "Oh God, I wish my hand could touch the sky to see if it is also made of stone."

I felt defeated.

A day or so later when I returned, my mother had taken a walk around the streets and had overheard people in a shop speaking Dari. She had gone in and discovered the shopkeeper to be an Afghan. She had bought some fruits and vegetables from him. She was clearly making the effort to integrate and make it work for everyone, and I felt a little reassured. So, I declared that I would soon be preparing to return to my work in Kabul. She fixed her eyes on me.

"When are you leaving?" she asked pointedly.

I looked at her and told her the date. Her eyes welled up, tears rolled down her wrinkled cheeks.

"Please take me with you," she pleaded.

I wanted to remind her that there was nothing left there for us to go back to, that it was her advice in the first place to make London our new home for the sake of the children's education, that taking her back on her own could rip the family apart and shatter all our dreams... But instead, I fixed my eyes on the crack appearing in the worn-out laminated floor of the apartment. It looked tired and in need of attention. Mold was building up at the corner of the ceiling. I tightened my lips and left the room, holding back a heavy sigh.

MAIN HOON JUNAID

Based on her research, Samia Ahmed reconstructs the true story of a boy's violent death in India as a tribute to all those who have suffered from hate crimes against minorities.

SAMIA AHMED

SAMIA AHMED grew up in India and now lives in the US, where she is studying the art of writing at Old Dominion University. She has a Masters in journalism, and her work has been published in *Coffin Bell Journal* and *Indus Woman Writing*. Currently inspired by dark literature, she hopes to bring gothic back in style. She believes in breaking stereotypes and continues to practice this while petting pretty black cats and sipping chai. @she_banshee on Instagram.

What do we know about human nature, about invaders and rulers? A foreigner, on a horse, with cavalry behind him, armed and ready to kill. For some, this image may be of a white man. For others, this could be a brown man with a beard. And for some others, it could be a man in shrouds, chanting prayers in a foreign tongue, asking people to follow him. But who gets to write this narrative? Who gets to say who invaded whom? From the natives in the West to the Arab tribes in the Middle East and the Indians in the East, what do we have in common? The challenge of otherness and the majority-minority divide.

In India, for example, hate crimes against religious minorities have been on the rise, mirroring the global phenomenon. In 2018, Amnesty International documented 218 incidents against people from marginalized communities, relying on reports in mainstream English and Hindi media. The true extent of hate crimes is unknown because, with some exceptions, the law does not recognize hate crimes as specific offenses in India. Most of these crimes are stimulated by religious provocation, hyper-nationalism and saffronism, which is Hindutva propaganda that claims India to be the land of Hindus. This has led to intolerance, a nationwide ban on beef and a looming threat from the majority. In August 2019, BBC reported the final publication of the National Register of Citizens list, which effectively strips about 1.9 million people in the northeastern state of Assam of their citizenship. The minority population in the area was declared "foreign" even though they were born in India.

Because I am a religious minority in my country, I have often been branded foreign. Like a child outside a candy shop, I have always stood on the other side—what felt like the wrong side—fighting between "us" and "them." I never accepted that my identity was different from others around me, not even when I was bullied as a teenager, not even when my roommate's prejudices were gaslighting me. I hoped that her animosity for me came from anything but my religion, but my hopes were trounced when I confronted her with this. She validated my darkest fear.

Junaid's story started off much the same. He was a teenage boy who was caught in the flames of intolerance as people refused to look beyond his religion. This story is reconstructed from my research, as is most of the dialogue, which is based on the social media commentary that arose after the actual event.

Junaid was a Muslim, and this is his story. I am a Muslim. This is my story, too.

***

Junaid was 10 when he first saw the billboard being put up on the side of the road. He was not old enough to go to the mosque that day, so his mother Rasheeda took him to buy chicken from Fareed Uncle's meat shop. He craned his small neck as high as he could to look up at the orange billboard that invited young boys to join the political group and further the cause of religion through hard work. His eyes then fixated on a cow, standing in the middle of the road chewing a green plastic bag. A car was trying to go past her, and the driver was honking loudly. The cow did not move. Rasheeda picked her son up to offer him a better view of the animal. The car squeezed past her, and Rasheeda walked over. Junaid petted the animal lovingly, who mooed in response, its tail swatting the flies on its back. When Rasheeda was certain that Junaid was satisfied, she took his hand and they began their journey back home.

The boy moved his little legs as fast as he could amongst the narrow galis of Meerut. His home, which was in a predominantly Muslim locality, was not far from the shop, nestled between several brick homes and Ek Minara Masjid, where his father and brother went for Friday namaz. Junaid's two-story house was painted blue and white, and unlike the landscape of the place which was littered with trash from the surrounding houses, narrow roads and overflowing sewage line, the roof of his house was magical—especially during the evening, when the whole family sat together drinking chai, looking out over the canvas of crimson and orange sunset. The turquoise minaret of the masjid stood in stark contrast, soothing the eyes of the residents as the echo of magrib azaan doused their ears with the call of God.

It was Juma, an exciting day for Junaid. His Abba had a gift for him when he returned from the mosque: Junaid's first skullcap, soft and white, crocheted with intricate flowers. Junaid wore it at lunch as Rasheeda fed him handfuls of long grain biryani soaked in a maroon curry spice mix. As he chewed, Junaid tasted the chicken he did not like.

"Today when we went out we saw their billboard in our area. I'm not sure if we should stay here," said Rasheeda, putting a handful of food in Junaid's mouth.

"Where will we go Rasheeda?" asked Mansoor. "You want me to leave my ancestral home for a billboard? This is my land."

"I don't know, Mansoor, I just have a feeling that we aren't safe here. Mureed is almost 18, and you know I worry about Junaid all the time. If something were to happen to them..."

"Rasheeda jaan, you worry too much. We have been through this before, we live amongst our people. People around here know us, this is our home. If something were to happen we would stick together and get through this. Now let me eat in peace."

"Junaid, take off that topi, we are eating!" Rasheeda replaced her worry with anger, and redirected it towards Junaid.

"But Ammi, I like wearing it."

"You can wear it all you want when you are in the mosque praying. I don't want to hear another word." Rasheeda stuffed another handful of biryani in Junaid's mouth to shut him up.

***

Junaid never really paid attention to what his mother said, even when he grew old enough to go to the mosque.

"Now listen to me Junaid, you come straight home after namaz. If I catch you playing cricket again with those Hindus, I will take your bat away." She repeated this daily, but the mind of a 16-year-old boy is a strange place where mother's words seldom visit. So Junaid would stay back to play cricket on the field behind the masjid. What ate his mother up was the fact that the ground they played on was the property of the Shiv Mandir Hindu temple.

"They are just kids, nobody will do anything to them," Junaid's father would say to her when she expressed concern about their son's safety. Then one day, after about two and a half hours of waiting, Rasheeda went out to look for him. She reached the masjid and found it deserted. A loud commotion caught her attention, and when she went to look for the source she saw her son. Junaid was kneeling on all fours on the ground, his brown face covered in dirt. Some of it was dry, and some wet from the blood seeping out of a dark spot on his forehead. His frail body was surrounded by a group of kids roughly his age looking down on him. One of the boys continued to pound Junaid in the stomach.

"Stop! Stop hitting him!" yelled Junaid's mother, rushing to his aid. Her booming voice made some of the kids run away. Rasheeda knelt down to where her son lay unconscious, then looked up, but she couldn't make out the face of the bigger boy. She squinted, shielding her eyes from the sun. The boy had vanished, his motorcycle leaving a trail of dust that made Rasheeda cough.

Junaid was given first aid in the emergency room of the hospital. He lay with his back towards his mom. The movement of the air conditioner's fan played with his hair. He turned around and looked at his mother in confusion as she bombarded him with question after question. "What happened? Who were those boys?" But Junaid's vision was fixated on the medical instruction manual behind his mother's figure. In case of emergency call 108 for ambulance, it read in red block letters. Above it was a child and a doctor figure attending to his wounds. Junaid stared intently at the poster before falling back to sleep.

Junaid's father helped him remember what had happened when he woke up. He recounted that he had been playing cricket when an argument had broken out about who would bat next. The kid he got into an argument with had started threatening to call his brother. Junaid declared he wasn't afraid of anyone, but had later regretted saying that. The boys who came next, on their heavy motorcycles, used Junaid's own bat to hit him in the head. They were kids of kingpin politicians, and called him names like Muslim pig. "Don't you dare come on our land again," one had said, breaking Junaid's precious bat in two. Junaid fell back to sleep, promising his father that he would listen to his mother from then on.

Rasheeda's lips moved incessantly, chanting prayers for Junaid's health. No audible words came out of her mouth, and her body swayed back and forth. She was sitting cross-legged on a plastic chair in the hospital waiting room, and when her husband came and sat next to her she said, "Send him to Delhi, to his brother. It is a bigger city. He will be safe there. He can come back when the situation here gets better." Mansoor nodded in agreement.

***

Big cities don veils of progress and liberal ideas. High-paced city streets and well-educated families practice living room politics in conversation. But prejudice fills their eyes when they look at us. When they look at me and my kind.

In my high school senior year, I recall raging hormones and a focus on social media. India was in the cricket World Cup finals, and everyone was on the edge of their seats because our final match was going to be against Pakistan, our long-term cricket rival and national enemy. What made this situation particularly contentious was the fact that Pakistan is an Islamic nation. During the match, if you expressed any kind of happiness with anything that Pakistan did, you were branded anti-national and sometimes told to go "back" to Pakistan. Cricket is a religion in India. Cricketers are gods. Pakistan is an enemy. It's all very black and white.

"Shahid Afridi is such a good cricketer," I said one day in my physical education class. We were openly discussing our opinions about the upcoming match, and I assumed I could too. Amidst the lull that followed a few heads turned towards me. Most refused to indulge me, but one, a Punjabi girl, glared at me from across the room. "Of course, you would say that."

"Excuse me?" I said, knowing what she meant but refusing to understand.

Our teacher interrupted then, knowing better than to indulge the class in a never-ending conversation. After class the same girl pushed me as she walked past. But that was not the end of it, and the next day I was tagged in a Facebook post.

The post read: *India will win the World Cup, the cup is ours this time, bye bye Pakistan*. It was followed by a few curse words, and mentioned my name, my infidelity. The post talked about the fact that I had an opinion, and about the questionable nature of my existence in a world ruled by the opinions of the majority. My voice, my opinion was wrong. Like an itch on your back, you know it's there, and you can't do anything about it. I was that itch. We were all itches.

The hatred in that Facebook post filtered into our class. Most of my Muslim classmates started attacking me, a defense mechanism they'd been taught as children. Stop associating with what is undesirable. And so I had classmates speaking against me. Of course I had friends who still stood by me, like my best friend Zenab, who one day, with all her rage, got into an argument with one of the Punjabi girls. What was said that day still echoes every time I feel cornered.

"You never hear her say good things about Indian cricket players," the Punjabi girl said, moving in a little closer. I was standing behind Zenab and could hear my father's voice in my head: *They hate us and you can't do anything about it, it is what they are taught.*

"You are all like that, *jis thaali main khaate ho ussi main ched karte ho*, you bite the hand that feeds you," the Punjabi girl continued. To her I was the person who had killed her ancestors. I was defined by the crimes of the past. I was an invader.

I held onto Zenab's arm to stop her from doing something she would later regret. But why did I stop her? Was I afraid the other girl was right? Are we really infidels in our hearts? Is it possible to live in a country where time and again I am reminded that I do not belong? Mostly I wonder where this hatred comes from.

***

Junaid scratched his back as he sat down on his train seat. It was a particularly hot day and so he had decided to wear a white cotton kurta and his patent skullcap to protect him from the heat. Before leaving, his mother had insisted he not wear it. "Remember what happened to Abdul when he was seen wearing a topi? You don't need it for the train journey. You can get one from your brother when you reach Delhi." Junaid had snuck one anyway, an old one, turned off-white from washing, with a few stray threads coming out of it. He had boarded the train on time. The train had picked up its slow pace, but not enough to leave behind the peculiar sting of urine that always surrounded Indian railways.

The compartment was filling fast. Junaid sat across from a burly man who reminded him of the man on election billboards outside his house. Wide mustache and a long line of tilak dividing his forehead, painted in saffron, hands joined together. The man clung to his briefcase, his knuckles whitening where they curved on the edge. He stared at Junaid. Then at his skullcap.

"Is there something on my head?" Junaid asked him, to spite him in gest.

The man didn't respond, and looked away. Junaid got up and started adjusting his own suitcase, a blue duffle bag, stuffed between a red and a black suitcase. When he turned to sit down again, another man had taken his place. This one was middle-aged and skinny. Sweat had darkened the underarms of his blue shirt and he sat looking outside the window, pretending he had done nothing. Junaid shrugged and sat next to the burly man. The train had picked up speed and Junaid rocked back and forth as the train whooshed passed green fields and small brick houses scattered amongst the canopy of colors.

Slow like the summer heat in mid-May, drowsiness overcame Junaid. The conversation around him blurred. His thoughts danced between scrumptious street food in Delhi and Najma's first kiss that tasted like gulab jamun and rus malai. The train had come to a halt, and Junaid could hear the vendors outside, his stomach growling inside. He got down from the train and bought some snacks, which he devoured before boarding again. The crumpled wrapper made of old newspapers was the only evidence of his meal.

"Ticket please," the agent's voice made people move around to look for their tickets. Junaid took his out, the ticket collector looked at it, noted something on his register, and gave it back to him. While looking at the burly man's ticket, the collector said, "This is not your seat."

The burly man got up. "What nonsense, this is my seat. I paid for it!"

"That's not what it says on here. This seat belongs to Abbasi Hussain who will board the train at the next station. I want you off the train before then." With that, he left.

The compartment was quiet for some time after that. Junaid played with the leftover newspaper wrapper in his hands. The burly man glared at him again, but this time he also got up from his seat and snatched the wrapper from Junaid.

"Hey!" exclaimed Junaid.

"Muslim pigs, taking over everything we have. You breed like mosquitoes. You should be shot on sight," the burly man said. He pulled Junaid up by the collar of his shirt and shoved the wrapper in his face. Hurling abuses, he let Junaid go. And then he punched him. "This is for abusing our God." The newspaper wrapper in his hand had a picture of Lord Ram.

"You swine, you eat our cow. Your kind kills them and throws them inside our mandirs," he said, gearing up for another punch. Junaid's lips were bleeding and he was struggling to say something. But, before he could get punched again, he got up from his seat and tried to escape. One of the men in the compartment held onto Junaid's hand, not letting him go. Junaid looked at the man, but the man looked away, still holding him tightly.

Junaid's vision blurred.

The noise caught the attention of other passengers who began to flood the compartment. They stood as silent spectators. Nobody intervened. The burly man got hold of Junaid's kurta, threw his body on the floor, and started kicking him. Junaid was helpless. He stared into the vacant eyes of strangers. The women looked at him with sympathy, the men were amused. The children, lost.

The burly man hit Junaid until his body went limp and he stopped struggling. “Is he dead?” he asked nobody in particular. One of the men asked what was to be done to the body. The burly man said there was nothing to be done, bodies of terrorists don’t deserve proper burials.

The train came to a halt at Ghaziabad Junction. Khaki-clad men entered the train along with the ticket collector. The compartment was deserted except for Junaid’s lifeless body. People whispered amongst themselves about what had happened. “Speak up!” said the police constable, but nobody said anything.

Junaid was given a proper burial in the kabristan behind Ek Minara Masjid, next to his grandparents’ grave. His perpetrators were caught and then released several months later due to lack of evidence.

Rasheeda sobbed uncontrollably when she was presented the body of her son. She clung onto his topi, which had dried blood on it. She cried until her body refused to make any more tears, then she went numb. The only sound she made was the name of God, which she repeated while praying for Junaid’s soul.

***

I remember my father sitting in our black and white living room, turning pages of the day’s *Times of India*. He was shaking his head as he took a sip of chai. “Another one,” he said, turning to the next page. I looked up from my own textbook. “They killed another one.”

“Oh my god, what happened now?” I asked, moving to sit next to him, trying to read what he was reading.

"These people. This time a 16-year-old..."

My mother came and stood next to him. "What happened?" she asked him. We clustered around my father, peering into the newspaper. My father had already turned to the sports section where a huge poster of Zaheer Khan stared at him. He had bowled a hat-trick last night. Now his figure was covering half of the sports section.

"This kid from Meerut. Was lynched by the public. They say it started as an argument about seats, and then they accused him of eating beef and killed him. He was just 16," said my father.

That was the first time I had heard about Junaid. A year later, I would think back to Junaid and realize how our identities bind us. To the people who killed him, Junaid wasn't a 16-year-old boy. He was a symbol of something foreign, something unknown. He reminded them of a time, 300 years ago. Of old kings whose names you only hear in history books. Persians, Turks, Mughals, they all had two things in common: they were Muslims, and they were invaders. I once had an argument with a classmate about the origins of Bhopal, my hometown. I was talking about the famous Begums of Bhopal, who had done a lot for the development of the city during their time. He argued that Bhopal was ruled by Hindus and there were no records because the invaders had burned everything. In his mind, the Begums were invaders and any effort to defend them would have been fruitless. So, I asked him, "Am I an invader too?" That's when I realized the question wasn't for him, *it was actually for me.*

I simply looked at my classmate in the same way I had looked at my roommate, in the same way I had looked at that

Punjabi girl years ago, in the same way Junaid must have looked at the burly man on the train.

SWIMMING WITH ORHAN PAMUK

On a visit to the Princes' Islands near Istanbul, translator Erdağ Göknar examines the duality of his Turkish-American identity and his close connection with the famous author, Orhan Pamuk.

ERDAĞ GÖKNAR

ERDAĞ GÖKNAR is an award-winning translator and Associate Professor at Duke University. His research focuses on intersections of literature and politics in Turkey, specifically on late Ottoman legacies in contemporary Turkish culture. His books include *Orhan Pamuk, Secularism and Blasphemy: The Politics of the Turkish Novel* (2013), and *Mediterranean Passages: Readings from Dido to Derrida* (2008). He's translated *A Mind at Peace*, by Ahmet Hamdi Tanpınar (2011), *My Name is Red*, by Orhan Pamuk (2010; 2001), and *Earth and Ashes*, by Atiq Rahimi (2002). His most recent publications are a collection of poetry, *Nomadologies: Poems* (2017) and the co-edited volume *Conversations with Orhan Pamuk* (2024).

This wasn't the first time I'd found myself in the Sea of Marmara, swimming with Orhan Pamuk. The novelist spends each summer writing on Büyük Ada, one of the Princes' Islands, a small archipelago near Istanbul that has been a haven for writers and exiles since the late Ottoman era. In the 1930s, Leon Trotsky completed his *History of the Russian Revolution* here, and there's a museum dedicated to Sait Faik, the famous flâneur and Turkish short story writer, on a neighboring island, Burgazada.

After an hour or so on the open deck of the ferry against the penetrating blues of sea and sky, I'm transported out of the city and seemingly out of time. There are no cars on the islands, only horse-drawn carriages. The combination of the heat, the horses, the smell of manure, and the wooden spoke-wheeled, sprung carriages evokes the 19th-century setting of a Chekhov story. Here, Pamuk returns to the intensive daily ritual of being a novelist, to "writing, the sole consolation" as Galip, the protagonist of *The Black Book*, declares in the wake of a devastating military coup.

My visits give me a sense of ritual and pilgrimage. On the way to Pamuk's house that day, I step up onto a phaeton with a pair of seats facing each other and sit so I can see the driver, whip in hand, and the backs of the two horses. A slight conductor's stroke of the whip and the horses begin to move. From under the tasseled edges of the carriage canopy, a theater of market activity unfolds: locals in daub-colored clothes and tourists in primary colors flow over the sidewalks; greengrocers hawk fruits and vegetables; fishmongers display recent catches of bluefish and seabass, including lines of salted mackerel hanging to dry; a woman offers boiled corn from a three-wheeled cart; and an old man sells the island's famous pine mastic ice cream. The driver barks instructions to his horses, and as we move out of town, the bustle is replaced by carpenter shops, used furniture stores, boutique hotels and a scattering of stray cats. The rhythm of the horses' gait jostles my thoughts. The shadow of a bike leans against a stuccoed garden wall.

The phaeton driver, unkempt with enormous hands, glances at me, giving me a glimpse into another world. Later, Pamuk informs me that the drivers are all Kurdish. He mentions that they like him because "he stood up for them" in comments he'd made in the press about the state's mistreatment of its minority population. For writers, the risks of speaking out against the state have always been great. Just signing petitions can lead to jail terms. Pamuk's fiction and public commentary have raised the ire of nationalists and conservatives, the groups that continue to rule in Turkey, where authoritarianism has eclipsed democracy. He once explained, "You can take your pick of fascisms in Turkey: leftist, nationalist or Islamist!"

Politics and culture are intertwined in Turkey. At the time of my visit, the one-year anniversary of the 2016 failed coup attempt against President Erdoğan and the ruling AK Party was approaching. The circumstances of the "coup" raised an issue Pamuk frequently grapples with in his novels: the challenge of writing through periods of political upheaval. The scenes of that fateful night are rebroadcast regularly: fighter jets screeching overhead and crowds milling around tanks. In the background, the sela, or a variation of the Muslim call to prayer, is recited repeatedly from mosques. The swarming crowds, with fists in the air, chant, "Ya Allah, bismillah, Allahüekber!", "O God! In the name of God! God reigns supreme!" Automatic gunfire can be heard in the background.

The impression is apocalyptic, signifying permanent social and political change—revolutionary change.

Now, the vicissitudes of Turkish politics seem far away as squawking seagulls wheel overhead. To the clomp of eight hooves, the phaeton proceeds along narrowing paved roads. The path winds and climbs up past large houses and views of the sea through pine and terebinth trees. The architecture preserves the history of upper-class Greeks and the legacy of an intercommunal Istanbul life. The flora, the birds, the sea, and the legacies of cosmopolitan tolerance draw writers here. There is a scene in Pamuk's novel, *The White Castle*, in which the two characters' knowledge of each other enables them to seemingly switch places. The world of the other is seductive and liberating, he seems to argue; nevertheless, the self is sacred. What would it mean to sustain both perspectives, both "he" and "I" in one translational consciousness?

Being Turkish-American with extended family in Istanbul, I visited and lived in Turkey in various roles, such as returning to the homeland as a tourist, as a Fulbright scholar, as a graduate student and faculty member conducting research, as a translator and writer. Despite being a scholar of Turkish studies and a literary translator, I've nevertheless nurtured something of an ambivalent relationship to Turkey. Immigrants, like my parents, were in a sense obliged to become translators and, so it seemed, were their children. In my youth, I felt my Turkish heritage prevented me from fully belonging to my surroundings. I felt a debilitating double consciousness caused by Turkish-Americanness. It was like an affliction. There was a disapproving, somewhat pious Turk in my mind, dismissive of the popular excesses of American life. (I associated him with my grandfather, the chemist and Koran translator.) He faced a white Midwesterner, reminiscent of my public school teachers, who was suspicious of the otherness and Islam of Turkey. The split in my being was unreconciled. Among other things, I suffered aspects of distress described by postcolonial thinkers: marginalization and alienation, mimicry and hybridity, and being "white but not quite." It was challenging to find my identity between Turkishness and life in America.

At first, I just listened to the conversations, arguments and threats between the two apparitions in my mind like a child quietly witnessing his parents fighting. Then I began to intervene. I wanted to explain one half of myself to the other in an idiom that was legible. I began to explore the duality of being a Turk growing up in suburban Detroit through writing. Not surprisingly, one of the more natural approaches for me to express my split consciousness was through acts of translation between the two halves of my world. My parents socialized exclusively with brain-drain Turkish immigrants who were either engineers or doctors. As children, we existed in a state of in-betweenness. Sometimes we'd assume American names as a kind of feigned belonging; other times, we'd speak Turkish as a secret language. Though it wasn't quite intentional, managing both sides of myself forced me to develop strategies of mental and emotional accommodation, and internal negotiation. Not only was I mediating this duality through what academics refer to as cultural translation, I was creating a hyphenated self and developing what might be called "translational consciousness," the ability to think and act from multiple sites of cultural belonging. As for Turkey, I both resented it and felt that it held the potential for discovery and revelation.

On trips to Istanbul before college, and later for academic research, I asked my relatives detailed questions about my family. My mother's side of the family came from the Balkans, my father's side from the Caucasus and the Black Sea. My aunt gave me a Konica camera my uncle bought while serving in the Korean War in the 1950s. My cousin, the medal my great grandfather received in the Turkish War of Independence. I saw black and white pictures of relatives in Damascus and Central Asia that revealed a forgotten world. I began to learn Ottoman Turkish, which was written in a modified Arabic script. Each visit I engaged in the practice of cultural translation, the ongoing introduction and explanation of one part of my divided self to the other. By dint of the fact that I was coming to Turkey from America, people were interested and wanted to talk. I was held in high regard, in a way that often made me feel guilty and uncomfortable. Other times I was cast as an outsider, not quite Turkish or Muslim enough. Shuttling between sites, often I could be neither self nor other.

At times this consuming project of subject-formation collapsed, and I would find myself self-destructively negating aspects of myself. When I was a graduate student studying Turkish literature, culture and politics, it was translation that brought me and Pamuk together. He was looking for a translator; I was looking for a way to apply my graduate training in languages, texts and cultural studies. In his book-lined Cihangir studio that overlooks the Bosphorus and the old city, our first conversations about literature and Turkish popular culture were transformative. We seemed to understand the various subtle contradictions of our lives and could make each other laugh. For all of his fame, even then, he could be vulnerable. At other moments great urgency would kick in, and he'd become managerial and insistent. The phone would ring and he'd begin directing and delegating like a CEO.

The characters in Pamuk's novels are also divided, whether it's the historian who becomes a fiction writer, the Christian slave who becomes a Muslim master, the lawyer who assumes the identity of a newspaper columnist, or the Marxist who becomes an Islamic terrorist. The duality is reflected in form as well: Islamic miniatures become the basis for postmodern texts, or the "memory" of traditional objects helps constitute a modern, global novel. My intellectual engagement with Pamuk's fiction proved revelatory because one of the dominant tropes in his work is the particularly Turkish perplexity of the split between local Turkish life and European modernity; specifically, between Islam and secularism, capitalism and socialism, or tradition and modernity. The protagonist Ka in Pamuk's novel *Snow*, alienated from the bourgeois circles of Istanbul yet yearning to return from his German exile and belong to a radically changed Turkey, suffers rejection for daring to cross ideological, class and political boundaries. The dualities Pamuk explored weren't quite the same as mine, but they overlapped enough to provide personal and political insight.

His work quickly became central to my own understanding of history and cultural translation. Productive and healing, processes of cultural translation involved a redemption of sorts: exposing the condition of my divided self to the outside, to friends, colleagues and readers could turn what in my youth felt like a debility into a source of transformation. Meanwhile, my practices of translation became ritualistic and quasi-religious. When I walked through the old city, talking with the various sundry people of the street always up for a conversation, an unspecified melancholy would descend upon me. I was not of their world but had profound empathy for their lives.

Under the gaze of a dutiful bed and breakfast proprietor the phaeton stops and I step down. It's quieter here, away from the crowds of day-trippers and tourists. I reach through a metal fence and pull on a wire which unlocks the gate. I enter an overgrown garden with concrete steps that descend steeply. The apartment Pamuk rents is the bottom floor of a two-story house with unobstructed views of the sea and Sedef Island. The building has been recently whitewashed with lime. The wood door is locked. I knock once, twice, and hear something indeterminate from the inside before it opens. Pamuk's girlfriend appears and we greet each other happily. Behind her, he strides in from the wide, open balcony, a dark, moving shadow against the bright summer light. Seeing him always brings a smile to my face because our rapport is often needling and humorous. We exchange a traditional Turkish greeting by touching cheeks. The connection between us is in turns fraternal and filial.

I step out onto the veranda, where Pamuk writes on a small wooden desk. As is his custom, it is covered with a green card-table cloth. He writes longhand in a spiral notebook of graph paper—another ritual. There are about ten books there, a classic green banker's lamp, which gives the odd impression that he's busy with some accounting, and eight or ten pens and pencils. The balcony extends the length of the building and looks out on a picture postcard view: trees frame a swathe of blue sea, with a small island in the background whose central pine-covered hill rises suddenly and falls gradually. A moored sailboat floats in the foreground.

Beside the desk, there is a wicker settee with white cushions and another bare wooden table. We talk animatedly about the day, recent events and news of mutual acquaintances. Then, within a few minutes, he says that he wants to share what he's written. He strives for two pages of writing each day, but today, he's only managed one and a half. "I had an interview," he says. This reminded me of the many other times, sometimes for work, sometimes for friendship, that I'd been around this writing desk with its green tablecloth, the workbench of Turkey's first Nobel Prize.

The almost obsessive nature of Pamuk's workday reminds me of my immigrant father. Pamuk works ten hours a day, including sometimes on weekends. My father didn't retire until he was 79, and even then, continued to do an occasional temporary psychiatric assignment. While, in both cases, this drew my admiration, it also filled me oddly with sadness for a life not lived, but labored. As an academic, I knew intensive focus could be a source of intellectual pleasure, but I was also eager to escape into distraction and creativity that wasn't part of a plan to prove myself.

I developed the notion of cultural translation in academic scholarship after the success of *My Name is Red*, which won the Dublin IMPAC Literary Award. In a book of literary analysis, *Orhan Pamuk, Secularism and Blasphemy*, I worked to provide cultural and political contexts for the understanding of Pamuk's fiction, which despite its importance could be dense and complicated. At this point, Pamuk became something more than a novelist for me. He represented an "other" who also doubled for an unilluminated part of myself. Interpreting his work also meant examining my own Turkish-American life. Pamuk's fiction demonstrated how to turn paradox and contradiction into ways of being. In novels like *The White Castle*, *Snow* and *A Strangeness in My Mind*, characters torn between two worlds are permitted to live through a plot that opens opportunity spaces for them. I aspired to locate or create such spaces.

Pamuk's custom of reading his writing aloud at the end of every day is a ritual reserved for a companion or a friend, and today his girlfriend and I oblige, sitting around the green desk. Nervously, he begins a long preamble that describes his next novel, *The Nights of the Plague,* and the section he is about to read. He stops, slightly flustered, and says, "No, let's go swimming." We insist, and he continues the preamble, explaining that he's thought about this historical novel for over 30 years. "I don't want to bore you." He reads in Turkish from his standard writing notebook: top-spiral, checkered and covered with blue and black ink. The novel, which addresses the roots of authoritarianism, is set in the late Ottoman era of Sultan Abdülhamid II, around 1900. The scene is one of quarantine during wartime, with echoes of migration and refugees, of state-formation and themes of "the camp." It's clearly an allegory for the present, with satirical flourishes. The people described in the novel are Mingrelians, a nation of the Caucasus that he first refers to in *My Name is Red*. As a historical novel that explores the cultural schizophrenia between Turkey and Europe through Islamic art, it addresses classic Pamuk themes. Hearing him read in Turkish is always inspiring; his dedication to his craft is astonishing. And although set in the late Ottoman era, I sense from this novel's political themes that it will be a significant allegory for and commentary on our current geopolitical circumstances.

Standing, Pamuk shows me pages from another project on another table, a collection of photographs that the publisher Steidl will be publishing. They are two-by-three feet large exhibition format images he took of Istanbul from the balcony of his writing studio while writing his novel, *A Strangeness in My Mind*. The photographs are most often in a series of two to eight, variously depicting, for example, the snow-covered dome of the 16th-century Cihangir mosque; triangles of phantasmal light over the historic Topkapi Palace; patches of white light near the Princes' Islands; the impressionistic disappearance into haze of the Hagia Sophia and the Blue Mosque, or conversely, their combined ten minarets marking an Ottoman legacy; and the scales of light on the ripples of the surface of the straits. Subtle shifts of light, often breaking through clouds in epiphany and revelation, are captured here. Some photographs show the island where we presently are.

In this way, I get a snapshot of his current life and work and file it away in my mind. As I listen to him talk, these are the things that take my notice: the place is sparsely decorated and brings to mind a bygone era of 1970s Istanbul; despite the traffic of visitors from the outside every day or so, it is lonely here. Pamuk doesn't write novels from a room of one's own, but from an island in the sea, and the sea provides the distance from society that he needs to write.

After the reading, Pamuk and I go for a swim. The path leads past wild fig trees, with a distinctive sweet acrid smell, and shrubs, some with fruit. We each eat a plum. Seagulls laugh and mewl, at times like babies. The path winds past old cement building foundations, what looks to be an abandoned property, that leads to a dilapidated dock. The water is dark blue-green, naphtha, not quite inviting. Pamuk walks down a rusty metal ladder and dives in silently. I follow him. The cold water of the Sea of Marmara is slightly viscous. It is the smallest sea in the world and connects to the Black Sea via the Bosphorus and the Aegean via the Dardanelles. This ritual swim is the silent, regenerative heart of Pamuk's long day of writing and contemplation. Occasionally, a jellyfish or strands of seaweed float past. Boats are moored here, but there are no other people at this time of day. Pamuk swims out about 75 yards, at times using an odd backstroke where he throws both arms behind him, his hands cupped together. I follow him as he moves in and out of the blue-green water, diving down. Under the surface, between continents, I have intimations of a vast apparatus of translation reconstituting my soul.

THE ART OF DRAWING A SHEPHERDESS

From her home in Oman, Summi Siddiqui shares a candid encounter with the subject of her painting, and learns that the only way to capture the true essence of the portrait is not through observation, but by standing side by side with her.

SUMMI SIDDIQUI

SUMMI SIDDIQUI is a teacher, artist, writer, traveling storyteller, performer, motivational speaker and poet, connecting cultures beyond borders. Her work is inspired by her family of poets, writers, artists, as well as her education in England, India, France, Italy and Canada. It comes naturally to her to connect cultures with her pen, paintbrush and voice. She has had solo exhibits of her artwork and organized workshops in British Council Centers in India, Sudan, Saudi Arabia, Libya, UAE, Oman and Canada. Her story *Second Coming* appears in *Canadian Migration Fiction*. Summi lives in Toronto with her husband, two daughters and sphinx cats.

There is a hill in Oman where I once met a wanderer.

She came into my life when the art association in the capital of Oman, Muscat, asked its members to contribute work for a charity exhibition. The romantic notion of someone roaming aimlessly in the wilderness, searching for something unknown, had always intrigued me and hence I decided to paint a portrait of a wanderer.

For inspiration, I drove around in my air-conditioned car looking for the right model in the mist of the mirages the summer heat created. Back home, I arranged my paints, assorted brushes and drawing tools on my little balcony. And then one day, I saw her climbing the hill opposite my house with her flock of sheep following her.

I had often noticed this shepherdess tending to her sheep and goats, sitting under the single tree, while they grazed around her. Perfect! She would be my wanderer. Quickly I started to sketch. The woman was easy to draw. She wore a long-sleeved light blue dress, gathered at her waist and flowing down to her calves. Her legs were wrapped in loose brown pants clutched at her ankles. On her head, she wore a large brown scarf, which draped her like a cloud and bellowed behind her in the breeze.

Sipping my orange juice, I spent the morning making a few sketches till the woman got up, stretched, paused and started to walk away with the sheep lazily stumbling behind her. Who was this woman? I thought, biting into a ripe pear. From where had she come, and where was she going? What did she ponder about while sitting all alone on that hill? Was she remembering those times when she was very young, those paths she avoided, those songs half sung, or were all her sacred dreams lying there in the sun?

In the following weeks, I sketched more images of her in different positions and at different times of day to catch the light and shadows. My husband and the art group could not see the wanderer in my shepherdess. Since I was not satisfied, my two teenage daughters suggested I get a closer look at my model.

The next day I decided to follow their advice and climbed up the hill with my art material. I greeted her with, "As-salāmu ʿalaykum." She answered, "Wa ʿalaykumu s-salām." I told her why I had come and she gave me permission to draw her. My hands began to move and so did my thoughts. I saw that her wrinkled face, dry hands and dusty feet could do with a good scrub and strong moisturizer. She must have been around 70 years old. How could she walk around in bare feet? How did she sit in this heat the whole day without doing anything? Without books or some sort of activity, how did she pass her time? My eyes kept bridging the distance between us. Could she read the rich Arab literature or write poetry?

There was no breeze. I missed the comfort of my soft leather couches and cool air-conditioned studio, so I decided to leave. Before packing my stuff I showed her the sketch and she laughed. It was a warm honest laugh.

"This looks nothing like me," she pointed out.

"Of course it does," I retorted.

"You don't know what you want," she noted, still looking at the picture.

"What do you know of art or how paintings are done?" I snapped back. She said nothing and I immediately apologized. The due date to submit the painting was fast approaching and I was panicking.

"I know exactly what I want. It's a wanderer that I'm looking for."

"So that is how I appear to you," she smiled. "Do you know that I was aware of you looking at me from your home but I did not know the reason for it?"

"Really, from that distance?"

"When someone sits alone, they develop the eyes of an eagle and the nose of a hyena," the woman explained. "I also know that you are not happy with this drawing. Draw what you see, not what you want to see. You want a wanderer. Why then are you drawing me?"

"Well! How do I find a wanderer?" I inquired.

"Come back tomorrow and we will find a way," she answered. I repeated my steps the next day, sketchbook and paints in my backpack. Yusuf, my young gardener, agreed to accompany me with egg sandwiches, orange juice, small yogurt cups and fruits for the flock. The shepherdess brought dates, milk and words of wisdom that were outside the realm of my books.

"I used to accompany my father up this very hill as a child," she said, helping me set up my art tools on a flat stone under the tree. "He taught me to help little lambs walk, to milk goats, search for grass patches and sit still with nature. My mother taught me to cook, weave cloth and pray."

She had a thoughtful far-away look, as if she was trying to trap a memory with her eyes. I hurried to capture it. "After my husband died, I started taking the neighborhood goats for grazing. It's a man's job but comes natural to me. We should follow where our nature takes us." The drop in her voice made me pause. She was looking straight at me. "That is our true path." At that very moment Yusuf called us to eat. He had laid out the food on a large cloth.

After we shared our meals, the shepherdess picked up an earthen pot and poured water into a large mud container. The sheep gathered around her and I quickly picked up my sketchbook.

"You are not happy," she said, placing a goat closer to the bowl. "That is the reason you struggle so much, and you frown a lot too." Bending down she picked up a spider from the ground and placed it on the branch near its web.

I sighed. "Unlike you I'm not a native of Oman. Eighteen years ago, I left the land of my birth to join my husband in this country as a young bride. Our two daughters were born here, and we have been blessed to have lived among such kind, gentle, helpful people. This is home to us. But now there is talk of us moving to Canada, a country far away."

"That is good, is it not?" she questioned.

"It is good for my girls' future, I know, but a part of me doesn't want to go. It is not easy setting up a home all over again. Our family and friends are here. This is our life."

The silence that followed was only interrupted by Yusuf reminding me that we should be going.

Days that followed were no different from before: shopping, socializing, parent-teacher meetings, book clubs, the gym. But something had started to change. I had begun to feel as incomplete as my unfinished painting lying on the balcony. But a commitment is a commitment and the date for the exhibition was drawing near. It forced me to climb the hill again. I had entered my piece as *The Wanderer* and could not turn in a painting of a shepherdess.

"What do I look for?" I asked her. "There are pictures I could get inspiration from, but I want to paint a real live wanderer."

"Anyone can be a wanderer," she whispered. "People with pens or those that have never read. People sitting in large cars or those on dusty benches by the roadside. People who laugh loudly and those whose eyes do not shed tears."

We were sitting on the bare ground and eating. A lamb had come and nestled by her side. "Look for someone who journeys within, walking on hidden paths. Someone who has a quest, a thirst for the wonders and meaning of life. Who searches. Who travels far, even when standing very still."

Strangely, I started looking forward to going up the hill to just sit and talk to her. I even stopped taking my art bag with me. She would look into the distance and tell me about the mysteries of the sky, the seas and the land on which creatures crawled, flew and ran. About laughter, tears, secrets and dreams. About human struggles.

Slowly I began to see her as if for the first time. I saw her wrinkles speak, and hands give solace to the sheep. Her bare feet tread gently on the ground as if it were sacred, eyes as calm as a pause between two breaths, a face that seemed touched by moonlight. I realized that the vastness of her days could not be imprisoned in pages of my journal.

"I think I now know how to draw you," I said in wonder one day. The old woman smiled. She came close to me and, taking my hands gently, she whispered, "We are all wanderers. Forever moving from place to place like birds, clouds, waves and air. All nature moves, it is natural. I was told stories of the great Omani sailor Sinbad and Ahmad ibn Majid, the lion of the sea. Don't be afraid to travel. Go where life takes you. This is Allah's earth. Wherever you are, you are home." I found my vision blurring.

Letting go of my hand, she bent down and picked up a fist full of dry mud, poured it on the back of her other hand and looked at the sun. The temperature of the sand and direction of the sun was a common method of assessing time here. "Come," she said. "Let's pray."

The sun was hot, the air tolerable in the shade of the tree. The sounds of sheep and goats walking, bleating, the distant honking of cars, the sky forever stretching overhead and the anchoring earth beneath our feet connected us as we stood shoulder to shoulder with our heads bowed. Just then the call for prayer sounded from the nearby mosque.

Eventually, my painting did make it to the exhibition and was one of the first ones sold. However, I kept going up the hill to walk barefoot among the goats, to feel the heat on my back, to sit still on the rock doing nothing. And, of course, to pray with her.

We ended up moving to Toronto and settling down. Both my daughters reached their goals of becoming a doctor and a lawyer. My husband ran his own business and traveled a lot.

As for me, I realized that I never did leave Muscat, even after 30 years. I find it coming up in my conversations, teachings, writing, storytelling, poems. Even today when I sketch, I remember painting in tents on full moon nights, in the desert under traditional Omani lamps that would throw shadows all over the place. My mother once told me that shadows were a blessing from Allah, since our eyes would not be able to see if everything was pitch black or stark white.

Very often I catch myself silently observing people around me and wondering if they were walking on paths I could not see, or traveling far even when standing very still.

And then I think of her.

BEFORE THE BOMBS

What does nostalgia look like? Through a series of memories portrayed in pit stops like polaroids, Amira Pierce shares her experience of being Lebanese-American and her relationship with Lebanon and its civil war.

AMIRA PIERCE

AMIRA PIERCE got her MFA in fiction at Virginia Commonwealth University in 2011, and has won prizes from *Cream City Review* and *Colorado Review* for her short fiction. She teaches in the Expository Writing Program at New York University, where she specializes in working with international students. She was born in Beirut during the Lebanese Civil War, and lives in Bushwick, Brooklyn, with her husband, Lee, and their dog, Sharpie. amirawpierce.com

Mama has told me again and again that she had a craving for lemons towards the end of her pregnancy with me, and that she ate many of them fresh off the trees in her father's orchard, an expanse of citrus and stone-fruit trees, of tangled grape vines, at the edge of the village in Southern Lebanon where she grew up.

She was 25 years old and induced into labor in anticipation of the hospital closing due to impending skirmishes in the area. We left Lebanon after a few weeks, but all my life, I've gone back.

What is widely known as the Lebanese Civil War ended when I was 11 years old. I've asked Mama who it was that was fighting when I was born. Was it Christians versus Muslims? Muslims versus Muslims? Or was it the Israelis, the Jews? The Americans? The UN? Again and again, she's said she doesn't remember.

How to choose what to remember and what to forget? I remember stretching up on tip-toes to smell the blossoms in the jasmine tree by the front gate; I remember wincing, from the back of the car, as the men stopped us, leaned in, then waved us on, those men with their various uniforms and small shacks by the side of the road, semi-automatic weapons easy, shoulder-slung, glinting in the sun; remember watching, from the balcony each evening, the sun fall slowly into the sea while a haphazard chorus of prayer calls echoed off the sherbet colored sky; pacing the empty rooms as I memorized the smiles trapped under glass, the faded old photographs of family scattered over the world, hanging from my teta's walls. Mostly, I've thought my memories, especially of Lebanon, are like a film strip of recurring images—but I wonder if a more useful way to think of them might be as a headful of polaroids, as reality creating some semblance of itself, one tiny window at a time.

My younger sister Lara was born in Lebanon too. This was two and a half years later, and the hospital where I had been nudged towards birth was closed for the long term, so she was born in the south. I was close by, at home with my grandmother, and the story goes that during that time she potty-trained me, but I can't say if I remember that.

Much more clearly I can see Lara's 25th birthday, when I got her a pink baby-tee, the first gift I ever bought anyone off the Internet. It had the line "Everyone Loves a Lebanese Girl" printed across the chest, over a heart symbol and a Lebanese cedar. This was in the era of baby-tees being worn by adult women, and the shirt fit just right. Lara loved it and wore it whenever she could; my sister has always been the busty one, the brash one, the heart-on-her-sleeve (or chest) one.

Some time after that, a video appeared on YouTube of her being interviewed in front of a CVS in the DC suburb where my parents live and she lived then too. The clip begins as her interviewer—a kid with floppy hair falling out of his baseball cap—catches up to her. She looks like any woman, with her long dark hair, her short skirt. Then, somehow, he gets her to turn around and the camera comes in close, and I see it's my sister in that pink tee-shirt. Does the kid grab her by the arm? Or only call to her? A mic gets shoved in her face. "Hey, hey! Lesbian? Are you a lesbian?" he wants to know, eager for her answer.

Lara looks confused. "Lebanese?" she says. "Do you know Lebanon?"

"What?" The boy looks back, grinning at the camera, at the person filming—another boy, most likely—who has no idea either, both of them hoping to have met a lesbian wearing a shirt that claims everyone loves lesbians.

"It's a small country north of Israel?" Lara asks as she explains, like it's still possible for him to understand.

"I thought her shirt said *lesbian*," he says, chuckling, as is the young man standing next to my sister, a tall, dark-haired out-of-focus stranger, my cousin Kamal it turned out, who was fresh-off-the-boat back then.

The camera shakes and the video cuts out.

Before either I or my sister were born, Beirut was known as "The Paris of the Middle East." Have you heard that one before? When I tell people I was born there, they still dredge it up. "Beirut! Like Paris!"

But how can a place really still be a Paris after all that war? I've always wanted to ask them this but have never quite found the words. *And even if it's not a Paris, is it still worthy of our love?*

"Oh, yes, it's like Paris. Lebanon is so beautiful, you've got the sea right there and the mountains right there." This, from the guy in the shoe store in Georgetown who fit me for the steel-toed Doc Martens I got one summer in high school. He told me he'd been to Beirut once, before he'd ever moved to the States. And, if I remember right, he was from some country in the former USSR to which he could never return. My friends called the boots shit-kickers; the three of us each got a pair. I've never been much of a shit-kicker, but I did feel like a soldier when I wore them. I felt bad-ass. "Too bad about the war," the guy said, then went on to tell me about his own wars.

After I paid and before I left, he told me that "the women in Lebanon are the most beautiful in the Middle East." This line I've heard again and again from people, mostly men, who aren't from Lebanon. Sometimes they go so far as to say we are "the most beautiful women in the world." I say "we" but really I never quite believe they mean me, since I'm half-Anglo, half-white, half-American, half-something else, and, besides, I was born before the bombs—and I got to leave, and also to go back, again and again. No matter where we were living, we went to Lebanon every summer during my childhood. And as an adult, I've returned sometimes with my family and sometimes on my own, staying one month, two months, three months at a time.

My college roommate in New York was like me, new to the city and hoping for a fresh start, her head crammed with images from too many other places: a birth place, a mother's place, a father's place, other places. Like me, she was someone who told different versions of the same stories over and over. In one of those stories, she described her own birth as a sudden consciousness of moving from liquid darkness into the cruelty of air and dirt and light. The shock of a hand slapping her bottom. She said the doctor's voice was the first her naked ears had ever heard, and it had turned her off to all doctors since.

Sometimes I believed her and sometimes I didn't. I think I was envious of her confidence, as my own birth story has remained just out of reach. I can say that I was born before the bombs, but I can't say I remember being born, or what that felt like, and I wonder why I am attracted to the memory that's mine but also isn't, like a fly to overripe fruit.

Because there was a travel ban on Americans, Dad was not there when I was born. Still, Mama's younger brother Mohammad posed as my father and hung out with her in the hospital room past visiting hours.

I like imagining my uncle there, young, with a thick mustache and his swirling-war thoughts, reckoning with my baby self. This was just a couple years before his dad got wind of him being courted by a local militia and sent him to Wyoming to follow a cousin to university. These are more things I don't remember but can create, more things I have been told and then told others, again and again.

It's harder to imagine my father, knowing I was being born and all alone just across the Mediterranean Sea in Tunisia, where he had been posted to learn Arabic. And just then, he was in the process of packing his and Mama's stuff for their next move, to Jeddah, which would be my first home—after Lebanon, if I can even count Lebanon as home at all.

Dad must have been used to being in between worlds by then. He had grown up in a small town in Georgia—the state and not the country—where at the age of 16 his mother had gifted him a translation of the Quran. I suspect that she—who I've been told battled him to come to church with her each weekend—didn't choose the book entirely of her own volition. I wonder if she thought his interest in worlds beyond theirs was a harmless phase, a passing thing. I have the clothbound, yellowed copy on my bookshelf in Brooklyn now, and mostly have only read the inscription inside the front cover, in her shaky hand: "To Bill, from Mother, Christmas 1960." I wonder how she felt when, less than a decade later, he left home for Thailand, then later for the Netherlands, for Indonesia, then Syria.

We watched the YouTube clip of Lara being inquisitioned about her lesbianism for years, dredging it up to amuse each other and new acquaintances. It was our inside joke, available for the world to see, and her interviewer's innocent ignorance was something we could laugh at without reservation. But now, 10 years later, the link is broken, the video gone, and I can't help but feel a pang at the loss of that floppy-haired kid. YouTube is no longer a novelty where I search random videos, it is now constantly open on my computer. It has shown me everything from Fairouz and electro to Kanye and the last of the whirling dervishes, from mass riots in Ferguson to mass riots in Egypt, from talking heads and grand muftis to shami poets and American imams, from ex-soldiers recalling what it was like to operate killer-drones to teachers and philosophers and poets telling me how to stay in love, how to mourn lost love.

As the years reliably stretch themselves out, one after the other, Lebanon's War has gone from being something that we quietly returned to, to something that persists even though it is done.

For the first time, when I am 36, 37 or 38, it occurs to me to ask Mama how it felt to be alone in Lebanon with me, a tiny brand new human she'd created, a shitting and crying machine, without Daddy and amidst all that war. She shrugs, smiles. She wasn't alone but with her parents and her siblings, and war became and was and is the backdrop of our lives.

Mute and dry, I cry.

We are in the quiet cool of her suburban American kitchen, and she is chopping vegetables for dinner. I can't remember the exact collage that afternoon on the bulletin board that has hung for years near the doorway, but I'm sure they caught my sight as I looked away. She always pins them carefully in place, then shifts them around from time to time, her customary cacophony of polaroids, color photos, black and whites, of Lebanon and here and everywhere else, digital printouts and images of the smiling children of cousins and friends I rarely see anymore. (*How did they grow up so fast?* I wonder, each time I am here.)

And I ask her about what happened before I was born, about Damascus. A two-hour car journey from Beirut, it was the farthest she had ever been from home—her entire office transferred to the embassy there due to the War, just in its infancy then. She tells me that one of the first things she noticed about Dad was this jacket he always wore, with elbow patches, "as if he were a university professor." It was at a staff party that he finally made contact. "And I thought Americans were supposed to be confident and cool," she says, giggling.

Everything must have happened so fast. Within months, Mama and Dad took the rare journey to Ghazieh to meet her family, where he pronounced the shahada before marrying her. But there is no photo of that.

A few years later, in a long-ago land of photographs and fruit, I was born before bombs and between them, after and above them. I escaped them, I forgot them, and still, they are here, and they are mine. But they wouldn't be without Mama and Dad, without my grandmothers, without Lara, Mohammad, Kamal, or the boot man, the soldiers, the roommates, the friend who passed the compliment from Dad to Mama before finally, they danced. I need the people who took the photos and made the videos, the ones who read these words. The bombs are mine and now they are yours too, our hearts pumping to their rhythm from their first beats, born, as we were, out of nothing—

GLOSSARY

One traditional English punctuation rule is to italicize "foreign" words. I have broken that rule in the body of this book, and added a glossary instead. Why? Because the words in this glossary are not foreign to the writers of these stories and also not foreign to many of its readers. For example, italicizing "shalwar kameez" effectively alienates an entire group of readers for whom this item of clothing is as familiar as a pair of blue jeans. The same would be true of the many Arabic terms that are often used by English-speaking Muslims. At the same time, I want this book to feel accessible to readers everywhere, so I've added this glossary for those interested in learning words that might be new to them.

Please note that each definition is meant to clarify the meaning of the word within the context of the story in which it appears. It is by no means an etymological study of the word, which you may find across multiple languages in different spellings and in different contexts that do not appear in this book. The definitions have been reviewed by the contributors of the book. – M.K.R.

abaya	a long-sleeved, floor-length and traditionally black outer garment worn by some Muslim women
ahweh bayda	a caffeine-free drink made with orange blossom water and sometimes sweetened with sugar, sometimes served instead of coffee
Alhamdulillah	Arabic phrase meaning "praise be to Allah," sometimes translated as "thank God"

atr	Arabic word for perfume, or a specific Arabian oil or scent
azaan	also known as adhan or athan, it means "announcement" or "call to prayer," and is the Islamic call to worship, recited by the muezzin at prescribed times of the day
bakhoor	or bukhoor, refers to rocks of resin or wooden chips or blocks soaked in fragrant oils, and mixed with other natural ingredients to burn as incense
bambar	a traditional Sudanese stool with a seat made of rope
banca	a small dugout canoe fitted with outriggers and a bamboo roof, often used in the Pacific Ocean around the Philippines
bhaat	derived from the Sanskrit word bhakta, it means "boiled rice," and sometimes refers to food in general
bhabi	also spelled bhabhi, it is the Hindi and Urdu word for sister-in-law, specifically an elder brother's wife
biriyani	or biryani, biryani, birani, it is a fragrant one-pot dish of rice and a protein, with spices, herbs and more
Bismillah	in the name of Allah
bisous	kisses, in French
Bonjus	a juice drink brand in Lebanon popular among kids
campesino	Spanish word for a farmer or person who depends on and lives off the land
cha	tea, usually with lots of milk

chador	an outer garment that covers the head and upper body so that only the face can be seen, worn by some Muslim women
charpoy	a traditional four-footed bed, woven and portable
cunji	or congee, conjee, kanji, it is a type of rice porridge or gruel popular in many Asian countries
deen	Arabic word for faith and religion, especially the religious observances of a Muslim
desi	Indian term from Sanskrit for province or country, commonly used to refer to a person of South Asian birth or descent who lives abroad
dhaal	or daal, it is a dish made with dried legumes, often lentils
dhaavani	Tamil word for a half saree worn by teenagers
dhow	a traditional wooden sailboat historically used by merchants and fishermen
dishdash	also called a thawb or thobe, it is traditional dress worn by men in the Arabian Gulf
du'a	a prayer of supplication or request
dunya	Arabic word for world
dupatta	a shawl-like scarf traditionally worn by women over the shalwar (or salwar) kurta
egusi	a melon with fat- and protein-rich seeds similar to pumpkin seeds, which are dried, ground then used as a main ingredient in West African cuisine
Eid	Eid al-Fitr, a holiday marking the end of Ramadan, or Eid-ul-Adha, a holiday marked by a sacrifice, celebrated by Muslims worldwide

falooda	a cold drinkable dessert made with rose syrup, vermicelli, sweet basil seeds, milk, and often ice cream
fitnah	Arabic word meaning tribulation or test, with many subjective connotations, as "to seduce" or "lure away"
fitrah	Arabic term referring to the natural goodness and God-consciousness we are all born with
flâneur	French word for an urban dweller who wanders around and observes
fouta	a piece of thin-patterned cotton or linen fabric used in Yemen and many Mediterranean countries
gali	Hindi word for alley
gambia	also known as janbiya, it is a decorated dagger or blade most commonly worn on the waists of Yemeni men
gele	a head accessory of a traditional Nigerian outfit, worn by women on special occasions
gulab jamun	a sugar-syrup or honey-drenched, milk-solid-based sweet popular in India
habibti	popular Arabic word meaning "my love," used when addressing a woman; habibi for a man
Hajj	a pilgrimage to Makkah, Saudi Arabia, undertaken during the last month of the Islamic calendar, mandatory for Muslims at least once in their lifetime
haleem	a hearty meat, lentil and barley or wheat stew popular in the Middle East, Central and South Asia
haram	forbidden by Islamic law

harmattan	the dry season, often characterized by dry, dusty wind on the Atlantic coast of West Africa
iftah ya simsim	"open sesame" in Arabic; it is also the Arabic title of the television program Sesame Street
iftar	also known as fatoor, it is a religious observance of Ramadan when people gather, often in community, to break their fast together
iro ati buba	a traditional blouse and wrap attire worn by Yoruba natives in Nigeria
isha	a four rak'ah prayer, it is the last and fifth of Islam's five mandatory daily prayers
jaan	Hindi and Persian word meaning life, widely used as a term of endearment, as a way to express devotion, like my love, my darling
jalabiya	or jellabia, jellabiya, it is a traditional Arab garment worn by both men and women
jinn	or djinn, a supernatural spirit in Arabian and Islamic mythology, able to influence humans in evil or good
juma	or jumu'ah, the Friday or Congregational Prayer, an Islamic prayer held every Friday in place of the zuhr prayer
ka'ba	or Kaaba, the black cube-shaped building in the center of the Great Mosque of Mecca in Saudi Arabia
kabristan	Hindi word for cemetery
kadadeish	the Lebanese word for sandwiches pronounced in a Southern dialect
kafir	Arabic term meaning infidel or non-believer
kisra	a thin, fermented bread made from durra or wheat, popular in Sudan

kufiyah	or keffiyeh, a square of cloth, often embroidered, traditionally worn by Arab men as a headdress, either wound around the head or folded into a triangle and secured with an agal, or cord
kurta	also known as kameez, a loose collarless shirt or tunic worn in many regions of South Asia
Likha	a four-player card game similar to Hearts
Malayalee	a term for people from the Kerala state in India, derived from the Malayalam language
ma'moul	small brittle pastries stuffed with dates and served during holidays
magrib azaan	or maghrib azan, the call to maghrib prayer, which is the fourth of five obligatory daily prayers performed by practicing Muslims, prayed just after sunset
mamoni	a term of endearment
mandir	a Hindu temple
masjid	a mosque and Muslim place of worship
Ma Sha Allah	or MashaAllah, is an Arabic phrase used to express a feeling of awe or beauty regarding an event or person just mentioned
massar	or masar, a traditional head wrap worn by men in Oman
mehrab	the niche inside a mosque indicating the direction of Mecca, where the Imam leading prayer stands
mesh keda	in Egyptian Arabic, literally "not like that," often used to emphasize an idea, as one might say in English, "right?" or "isn't that right?"
mimbar	the pulpit used by the Imam to give sermons

muezzin	the person appointed to lead the call to prayer for every event of prayer and worship in the mosque
mufti	an Islamic jurist qualified to issue a fatwa, a religious ruling or opinion, on a point of Islamic law, or sharia
mulah	a simple vegetable stew in Sudan
mullah	a teacher or scholar of Islamic theology
namaz	also known as salah and salat, the term for the ritual act of prayer performed by Muslims
niqab	or niqaab, a veil for the face that leaves the eye area clear, worn by some Muslim women as an interpretation of hijab
noor	Arabic word for light or divine light
pappadam	a thin, crispy wafer-like snack made out of ground lentils, usually as an accompaniment to the main meal
paratha	a round flatbread popular in South Asia
PBUH	Peace Be Upon Him, solely used in reference to Prophet Muhammad
pide	baked Turkish flat bread
pirith mandappa	a sacred octagonal or hexagonal space built for chanting the discourses of the Buddha and his disciples
purdah	or pardah, parda, meaning curtain or screen, refers to the practice of strict privacy and observing modesty and cover by women inside and outside the home
qat	or khat, refers to the leaves of the Catha edulis shrub, used to make tea or chewed like tobacco, producing the effect of a euphoric stimulant

qurbani	a ritual animal sacrifice of a livestock animal during Eid-ul-Adha, or Baqr Eid
qurush	coins or cents
rakwa	a long-handled pot with a pouring lip, specifically used for making coffee
Ramadan	also known as Ramazan or Ramzan, the ninth month of the Islamic calendar, observed by Muslims around the world as a month for fasting, prayer, reflection and community
riyal	or rial, the monetary unit in Yemen, Saudi Arabia, Qatar, Oman and Iran
rus malai	or ras malai, rossomalai, a Bengali dessert like a rich cheesecake without a crust
sala	the ceramic-tiled living or sitting room found in most Middle Eastern houses, usually one long hallway where men congregate to smoke, chew tobacco, talk politics or make music
salaam alaykum	or as-salaam-alaikum, the Arabic greeting meaning "peace be unto you"
salah	also known as salat or namaz, an Arabic term for the ritual act of prayer performed by Muslims
samanu	a sweet paste made from germinated wheat and water
samovar	a metal container traditionally used to boil water, often decorative
seeniya	a round, metal tray used in most Sudanese homes and occasions to hold different plates or dishes
sela	a version of the call to prayer made outside of the five regular daily prayer times, sometimes for a funeral, or as a method for the government to encourage people to action

shahada	an Islamic creed declaring belief in the oneness of God and the acceptance of Muhammad as God's messenger
shalwar kameez	also known as salwar kurta, a woman's outfit composed of a long top and trouser-like bottoms or leggings
shami	a region on the eastern coast of the Mediterranean Sea usually including Israel, Jordan, Lebanon, Palestine and Syria
sharia	the holy laws of Islam that cover all parts of a Muslim's life
shutki	a pungent dried fish or shrimp
takbir	an Arabic word meaning Allahu Akbar (God is the Greatest), which can be used when raising hands to start the prayer and in other contexts
tante	French word for aunt, used in Lebanon as a title of respect for aunties, mothers-in-law or any elder woman
taqiyah	a short, round skullcap worn by Muslim men
taraweeh	or tarawih, are supererogatory prayers involving reading long portions of the Quran during Ramadan, or traditionally, the entire Quran
tariqa	a Sufi order or path, founded by a saint, usually with a lineage that can be traced back to the Prophet Muhammad
tashahud	or tashahhud, the declaration of faith, or shahada, read during the seated position in salah
tawaf	the act of walking in circles around the Ka'ba in counterclockwise motion, one of the Islamic rituals of pilgrimage

teta	Lebanese word for grandmother
tiffin	a boxed meal, often consisting of rice, curries, vegetables and meat
tilak	a mark generally made on the forehead, indicating a person's sect of Hinduism
tobah	or tawbah, taubah, repentance, or uttering repentance
tobe	or toub, toob, the national dress for Sudanese women, composed of a long cloth worn on top of a shirt and skirt or trousers, and covering the entire body
topi	Hindi word for hat
Umrah	the smaller Islamic pilgrimage to Mecca that can be taken any time of year, as opposed to the Hajj, undertaken during the last month of the Islamic calendar
wallahy	or wallahi, Arabic phrase for "I swear to Allah," used to insist or promise, as one might say "I swear to God"
wudu	ablutions or ritual wash performed before prayer
ya hurma	Arabic phrase indicating a woman's physical exposure forbidden outside the close circle of male family members: father, brother, husband and son
zaatar	a condiment made of ground thyme, oregano, marjoram, toasted sesame seeds, salt and sometimes sumac
zaatar manakeesh	round flatbread topped with an herb mix

CONTRIBUTING TRANSLATORS

CATHERINE COBHAM is a lecturer in Arabic language and literature and currently head of the department of Arabic and Persian at the University of St Andrews. She has translated the works of many Arab writers, including Naguib Mahfouz, Yusuf Idris, Mahmoud Darwish, Hanan al-Shaykh, Fuad al-Takarli and Ghayath Almadhoun. She has written a number of articles in academic journals and co-written with Fabio Caiani *The Iraqi Novel: Key Writers, Key Texts* (Edinburgh University Press, 2013). The more she translates fiction and poetry from Arabic to English, the more she is struck by the need to read English poetry and fiction.

SALAR ABDOH is the author of *Out of Mesopotamia* and a forthcoming novel, *A Nearby Country Called Love*. He is based in Tehran and New York and teaches in the MFA program at The City College of New York.

AMIKA ELFENDI, Syrian-born and Oslo-based, writes in Arabic, English and Norwegian. His work has appeared in *The Best Asian Short Stories* 2019, *New Reader Magazine*, *Sukoon*, and more. His first poetry manifest, *The Anunnaki Season: the Green Booklet*, was launched in 2023 together with Tamil transdisciplinary artist Ilavenil Vasuky Jayapalan. He also double-agents as DJ unnaki and filmmaker, and suffers from an itching obsession with Ramallahian rap, Clarice Lispector and Felis Concolor.

ACKNOWLEDGEMENTS

You're holding a very thick book in your hands with 42 excellent pieces of writing in it. I couldn't sacrifice even one writer to shorten it—I feel loyal to them all. This kind of personal storytelling takes sincerity, inspiration, courage, talent and more time than you can imagine. All my gratitude goes to them.

I have a team of sisters, most not by blood. Nancy Laforest has been my rock, my sounding board and my editor's editor since we started working together in 2007. Since the first edition of this book, Nancy jumped on board all pom-poms and no nonsense, total, unwavering support. I regularly profess my love to her, but I owe her the match of that praise in cold, hard cash. Camden Richards, who is actually my soul sister masquerading as my cousin, designed this second edition from cover to cover, mostly between midnight and 2 am, when she could fit it in. If that's not love, I don't know what is. Cynthia Pecking, who pitched in to proofread, has been my daily confidante on all things love, parenting and career since 2018. Without her, I'd feel a lot less whole. Thank you to Carina Giorgi, one of my oldest friends, whose passion and knowledge about the politics surrounding this book has helped me weed through my approach. Carina, I have (mis)placed you in the "sister" paragraph, not only because my love for you transcends gender, but because you belong among these non-family-family members that I hold most dear. And to Jessica Marie, whose open-door policy for all conversations on race provided me the safest of spaces to learn about (and learn how to talk about) my privilege. Of course there's my real sister, Sonya Richards, whose mere existence is a pillar to my strength, though she mostly encourages me to get on with my own damn book instead of keeping busy editing everyone else's.

My husband, Asanka de Mel, has challenged me to pursue this project from idea to reality, pressed me to fearlessly confront naysayers, and always reminded me to stop and celebrate the milestones. Baby, as much as I tease you for being a "dude," you are nothing of the macho stereotype you sometimes convey, and everything of a partner supporting his counterpart to take on the world alongside him. There's also Asanka's mother, Amma, another partner in parenting my two baby boys, who is to thank for the breathing room I needed to finish this book. Without her, this book would likely still just be a bullet point on the vision board.

To my parents. Thank you to Carol Richards, who has already signed up to be my mail center. Thank goodness! I'm not sure she knows what she's gotten herself into. And to Cheryl and Matt Horowitz who have always celebrated my endeavors. To my father, Jeff Richards, who passed in 2017, effectively missing out on this book, my wedding and the birth of my sons. I owe him my spirit, my sense of adventure and my understanding of the value of risk. I'm certain he would have been proud of this book. I can just imagine him at the local watering hole in heaven, paperback in hand, peddling his daughter's book to any willing stranger who pulled up a barstool.

I thank my most critical advisors, and my readers, those trusted friends and colleagues who took the time to give me unapologetically frank notes. Hisham Bustani was my north star from the start. Not only was Hisham one of my earliest contributors, but his readiness to dialogue and debate helped me shape the vision for this project. Our conversations expanded my US frame of reference into a global one, which was crucial. To Govind Dhar for our invigorating exchanges, and for helping me determine the kind of editor I want to be. Thank you to Nizrana Farook for her clear, informed perspective, and to Mary Winston Nicklin for reminding me to be bold. To Ameena Hussein, whose valuable conversations and brainstorming sessions helped me find certainty in the angle for this book, propelling me to stay the course.

I'm indebted to the talented Fabienne Francotte, who graciously donated the art for the cover of my first edition. To Larry Habbeger for his encouragement and confident responses to my unknowns. Thank you to Fleur Montanaro, Jonathan Wright, Margaret Obanks, Elizabeth Briggs and Marcia Lynx Qualey for helping me find great writers, and to Christine Bronstein whose knowledgeable feedback on my book proposal boosted my confidence. Thanks to Maggie Siddiqi and Rachel Laser for their openness to discuss the sensitive nature of this project. To Don George who gave me the freedom and space to write when I was first going freelance; without Don's support, I might still be doing a 60-hour work week in a Manhattan skyscraper, only dreaming of future books I wanted to make.

To Michel Moushabeck, Peter Clark, Tahir Shah and Adrienne Loftus Parkins for sharing their precious insights with me about publishing in this space. Thank you to Zareen Jaffrey for shining a fresh light on the value of this collection through American eyes after I'd been living out of the country for so long. Thanks to the Penguin RH SEA team for publishing the first edition of this book. The Penguin brand inspired confidence in many of the contributing writers. To the organizers of MFEST in London, whose fantastic platform for culture and ideas validated my belief that there was a home for this book among so many readers.

Special thanks to my agents, Jayapriya Vasudevan and Danielle Chiotti, whose enthusiasm for the book has kept me nourished through the ordinary chaos of this adventure.

MARGUERITE RICHARDS

COLOPHON

This book is set in Athelas and Neuron.
Printing and binding by Samayawardhana Printers
in Colombo, Sri Lanka.

EDITOR

Marguerite Richards is an American writer and book editor, focusing on memoir and diverse voices. She holds degrees in literature and translation, has taught in France and Chile, and fell in love with magazine publishing in New York. Her articles and essays have been published in various places, but she has found her calling with books. She lives in Colombo, Sri Lanka with her husband and two sons.
margueriterichards.com

BOOK DESIGNER

Camden M. Richards is an American designer and artist who engages others to connect in a deeper way with themselves and their community through her work. She holds degrees in English, art history, graphic design and book arts. In addition to creating work under her imprint Liminal Press + Bindery, she teaches book arts and printmaking, and works as a freelance designer for non profit and B corporation clients. She lives in Sonoma, California with her husband and three children.
liminal-press.com